My Wonderful
World of Elections

My Wonderful World of Elections

An Election Autobiography

CARL W. DUNDAS

authorHOUSE®

AuthorHouse™
1663 Liberty Drive
Bloomington, IN 47403
www.authorhouse.com
Phone: 1-800-839-8640

First published by AuthorHouse   08/25/2011

ISBN: 978-1-4567-9709-6 (sc)
ISBN: 978-1-4567-9724-9 (ebk)

Printed in the United States of America

Contents

Dedicated to my wife, Beverley.

Carl W. Dundas
Abuja, Nigeria, August 2011.

FOREWORD

The importance of elections in a democratic society is beyond question. The Universal Declaration of Human Rights provides that "the will of the people shall be the basis of the authority of government" and that that will is to be "expressed in periodic and genuine elections which shall be held by secret vote or by equivalent voting procedures." All four major international human rights instruments—The European Convention on Human Rights of 1950, The International Covenant on Civil and Political Rights of 1966, the American Convention on Human Rights of 1969, and the African Charter of Human and People's Rights of 1981—provide for the right of everyone to participate in the public affairs and the government of his country. It is now generally accepted that this right is achieved through free, fair and periodic elections held by a secret ballot on a basis of universal and equal suffrage. The right to participate in the public life of one's country by voting in free, fair and periodic elections is a right under customary international law.

To devote one's career, or a substantial part thereof, to devising systems that ensure free and fair elections is, therefore, to devote oneself to an activity that is the very foundation of democratic governance. Put in that context, the international community at large, and in particular, the many developing countries in which Carl Dundas has worked, owe him a great debt of gratitude.

The book entitled "My Wonderful World of Elections" offers us a view into the encyclopaedic knowledge of elections that he has acquired over the past thirty years.

Carl W. Dundas

In the last General Election in Jamaica in 2007, President Carter—former USA President who is widely admired for his work as an election observer in many countries—who had observed previous Jamaican elections, declined to come to Jamaica to observe the election on the basis that the electoral system had developed to such a degree that it was not necessary for him to attend. This vital improvement was due to many factors, not least being the reforms of the electoral system, including changes in the registration process, started by Mr. Dundas in 1979 in his first election role when he was appointed Director of Elections in Jamaica. After that auspicious beginning Mr. Dundas' globetrotting election management functions took him to many parts of the world. But I believe the assignment that he treasures most is his work as Election Advisor to the African Union. It was of course, an assignment of immense importance to a continent with fifty three countries, most of them newly independent and developing. To assess the relevance of Carl Dundas' work in Africa in setting the foundation for election practices that will inspire confidence, one need only look at the current crisis in the Ivory Coast, and the recent problems in Kenya and Zimbabwe. There is every reason to believe that the three years that he spent from 2007 in Addis Ababa, helping the African Union Commission to establish a Democracy and Electoral Assistance Unit, will be rewarded in the long run with more and more elections in Africa that meet the highest standards. That work was carried out as a consultant in the capacity of Chief of Party of the International Foundation for Electoral Systems (IFES) which was implementing a USAID funded electoral support programme to the African Union. But it is the many assignments he had while working at the Commonwealth Secretariat that constitute the main body of the contribution Mr. Dundas has made to the field of election management. Over a period of thirty years Mr. Dundas worked in numerous Commonwealth countries as observer, advisor, mediator, power broker in politically delicate situations, emissary to Prime Ministers and Presidents, and in a number of other capacities relating to elections. The book tells us in a frank, friendly and conversational style, and one that unmistakably reveals Mr. Dundas' enthusiasm for the subject, how he carried out those functions; at the same time it demonstrates a mastery of the subject that distinguishes him as a leading expert in election management.

The book is virtually a Manual of Best Practices in election management and will be valuable to students and practitioners in the field, and indeed, to anyone who cherishes the principle that "the will of the people shall be the basis of the authority of government".

Patrick Robinson
President, International Criminal Tribunal
For the Former Yugoslavia.

Introduction

Democratic elections have always fascinated me. The implications of a particular electoral system for fair and balanced election results sometimes elude stakeholders. The development and application of good electoral practices have not found favour with many new and emerging democracies. Election Day is part of a process and not an event as is perceived by some. The managers of this process have the responsibility to ensure that the process is conducted fairly and competently in accordance with the governing rules.

The institutions and their personnel who manage the electoral process need to be guided by certain principles such as fairness, non-partisanship, efficiency, integrity and competence. Democratic elections are competitive and concern power and the legitimizing of an in-coming government. In this environment, disputes are likely to arise and there should be reliable and impartial disputes-resolution mechanisms to offer expeditious solutions.

This work deals with my involvement with democratic elections over a period of more than thirty years in various capacities, including electoral reform, electoral management, electoral technical assistance and electoral consultancy. During this period, my electoral work took me to many countries of several regions of the world, including the Caribbean, South America, throughout the African Union and South Asia.[1]

The work commenced with tracing my first contact with electoral reform in Jamaica in 1979. I was thrown into the controversial area

---

[1]   See Schedule for list of countries worked in or visited (in some cases multiple visits) in connection with election activities.

by the Attorney-General's Office, after my return from a long stint as Legal Counsel to CARICOM, the regional integration movement. I was not entirely without interest in the electoral field, as I thought, perhaps rather naively, that I could assist in meeting the challenge of reforming the electoral process in Jamaica. As the technical adviser to a Joint Select Committee of both Houses of Parliament in Jamaica which was studying constitutional and electoral reform, I saw my role as essentially a technical one and being neutral as between the two main political parties. I paid much attention to the improvement of the electoral environment as well as to the content of the electoral reform. The reform did not succeed in delivering as sound an electoral process as was hoped for, but it did lay the foundation for improved election organization and conduct which, incrementally, took more than twenty years to win stakeholders' confidence to the electoral process.

Being the chief executive of an electoral process, even one with just approximately a million voters on the register, was a challenging task. The first test of the mettle of an electoral manager is to be comfortable with a non-partisan role with respect to the government and ruling party of the day, and with all other stakeholders. The second major hurdle is to ensure that all partisan and incompetent electoral staff are dismissed from the electoral outfit and new untainted and efficient staff be employed. Thirdly, there must be a comprehensive programme of training and development for electoral staff, particularly field staff who are usually temporary but who interface with stakeholders and who bear the bulk of the responsibility to apply the electoral rules and regulations in accordance with the electoral law. In new or emerging democracies the key to good electoral management is for the managers to ensure that elections are conducted in a transparent and non-partisan manner.

When I was Director of Elections in Jamaica in the late 1970s and early 1980s, election observers, domestic or international, were frowned upon, as the practice was seen by some as an impingement on newly achieved national sovereignty. Although requests were made by certain international entities to observe the 1980 national elections in Jamaica, they were met with a negative response, as the Electoral Advisory Committee and I, the Director of Elections, were not enthusiastic to receive election observers at that time. Upon joining the Commonwealth Secretariat in late 1980, I became a convert to the benefits of international election observation and was privileged to play a leading role in the development of the Commonwealth's election observation mechanism, as well as an electoral technical assistance facility.

I do believe strongly that while election observation is valuable to assess the quality and fairness of democratic elections, the emphasis should be on offering technical assistance in the form of support to electoral management bodies (EMBs) in order that these bodies may be better able to organize improved elections. My interest in elections began with being the technical legal adviser to the Joint Select Committee of both House of Parliament in Jamaica and I have not given up my embrace for the technical support to electoral institutions. More progress is likely to be made in good electoral practice through technical support to EMBs in a given period of time, than through electoral observation alone. This statement is not intended to downgrade the valuable tool of observation, but rather it is intended to highlight the need for observation to be followed up by technical support to implement recommendations made by observation missions. During my time with the Commonwealth Secretariat and later with Dundas and Associates, I offered technical assistance to some thirteen individual countries and the African Union.

For those electoral systems that require electoral boundaries to be drawn for electoral districts or constituencies, they provide opportunities for technicians to inject fairness and transparency into the electoral process. My interest in the delimitation of electoral districts or constituencies may be demonstrated in that I was twice appointed to chair the Electoral Boundary Commission of the Cayman Islands, in 2003 and 2010. The key to good electoral boundary making is fairness, transparency and participation of stakeholders. The outcome of a delimitation exercise should reflect an approximately equitable distribution of the electorate in each district or constituency

Registration of voters is one of the pivotal electoral processes of democratic elections. However, it is the one that is often most abused and perhaps the most difficult to get right even by EMBs in mature democracies. There are many characteristics that should be mentioned here about the register of voters. It may be created by a voluntary process, as in the great democracies of India, USA and the United Kingdom; or it may be created under a compulsory system of registration as in Australia and Belgium. The register may be compiled through periodic registration or through continuous or rolling registration. Compulsory registration apart, the most common complaint about voters' registers is that they seldom meet the ACC (accurate, complete and current) criterion. This perceived failure has frequently led to controversy and a general demotion of the register as a reliable electoral tool in the best practises armoury. One difficulty with the compilation of voters' register in a voluntary registration system is that qualified persons might not wish to register at the time of registration or at all where continuous registration is available. Thus the 'completeness' in the ACC criterion is rather more illusive than real. Notwithstanding that, the estimated percentage of eligible electorate achieved in some jurisdictions with the voluntary system may exceed 80% (Trinidad and Tobago) as against 93% or a bit higher in Australia which uses the compulsory system. I was instrumental in designing voter registration regimes in seven countries.

It is essential to have a sound voter education programme, extensive to cover geographical territory concerned, as well as all the inhabitants and their regional languages or dialects. Every voter should be thoroughly familiar with the voting procedure. The programme should be imparted by dedicated and trained personnel. Voter education programmes often extend to contents which belong to civic education and the matter of where to draw the line sometimes causes difficulties, as some jurisdictions have separate institutions to deal with civic education. Increasingly, the term voter education is proving to be too narrow a concept to deal with the range of stakeholders involved particularly candidates and party representatives. These categories of electoral functionaries should constitute a targeted category and the extended programme would more suitably labelled 'election education'.

I have recounted my several missions as special emissary of each of the three Secretary-Generals under whom I served in the Commonwealth Secretariat (chapter VIII). During the tenure of Secretary-General Ramphal, some colleagues felt that I was singled out for those special assignments because of my Caribbean connection, but that was not so, as my special assignments actually increased under Ramphal's successor, Chief Emeka Anyaoku and took place also during Anyaoku's successor, Mr. Don MacKinnon. It was mainly to do with my connection with electoral matters and governance, although in a few cases my Caribbean connection did play a role, as was with respect to the Grenada incident of 1983-4 and the search for a prominent Caribbean personality to head the Commonwealth's eminent persons group to report on apartheid South Africa.

My experience with planning missions (preceding the dispatch of Commonwealth's observation groups) and assessment missions (preceding the dispatch of technical assistance teams) extended to more than fifteen missions to some eleven countries. These missions were carried out not only under the auspices of the Commonwealth Secretariat, but also the United Nations Electoral Assistance Unit, European Commission, and several agencies of USAID. Assessment missions were designed to find out what the needs of an EMB were, since in many cases it was found that the requesting EMB did not appreciate the full range of its technical needs. Planning missions (called exploratory missions in the African Union) were designed to find out if the conditions existed, in the host State, which were conducive to the holding free and fair elections. Planning missions were often tasked with the responsibility of checking out the logistics (transport, hotels, equipment etc.) for the pending mission, if one was sent.

One of my more exciting projects was to assist the African Union (AU) to establish a facility called the Democracy and Electoral Assistance Unit (DEAU) in 2007. My involvement with the AU project came about as a result of contacts with the IFES (International Foundation for Electoral Systems) team in Liberia in 2004-06 when I was an election consultant to the European Commission in Liberia during the preparation for the 2005 elections. IFES approached me to find out if I would be interested in an assignment in Ethiopia to assist the African Union to set up a Democracy and Electoral Assistance Unit and I responded positively. It took a year to get the Unit up and running, beginning with three dedicated staff that operated within the Department of Political Affairs of the African Union Commission in Ethiopia. The project was funded by USAID and executed by IFES with me as the Chief of Party based at the AU Headquarters in Addis Ababa, Ethiopia. I assisted in the formulation of the terms of reference for the staff's recruitment and the development of appropriate work programme to get the Unit going. The broad mandate of the Unit was to organize AU election observation missions in a manner that would improve the credibility of AU observation mission reports. The Unit's mandate also included the improvement of the ability of national EMBs of Member States of the AU to organize democratic elections. The DEAU stood up in May 2008 and when the programme ended in September 2010, the DEAU was functioning competently. Its work and contribution have been discussed in chapter X within.

Several chapters, XI to XVI, deal with lighter matters such as my impressions of heads of governments and States met in electoral matters (XI); EMBs' capacity building (XII); my electoral publications (XIII); important election meetings attended (XIV); important election personalities whom I met (XV) and reflections on my contribution to the development of democratic elections (XVI).

This work would be incomplete without a chapter on my impressions of the contributions of women at all levels of the electoral process. There is no serious attempt here to make comparisons between the competence (particularly non-partisanship) of male and female electoral officers, although such an exercise should be attempted in good faith and a template be formulated for EMBs that would like to undertake such an experiment. As shown in chapter XVII, women are active participants in election organization and in capacity building programmes in many EMBs. Notwithstanding what is stated here, in many EMBs in the senior personnel category males typically out number women three or more to one. This trend is slowing but needs to disappear quickly. In the AU, it is noticeable that even in orientation workshops for observers, male attendees often far out number females. It cannot be said that the gender awareness, not to mention equality, is as yet firmly established at all levels in electoral institutions and in the process of election organization.

Electoral justice principles made it in a separate chapter (XVIII) because of my involvement in formulating and drafting principles of electoral justice. The concept of electoral justice needs to be developed and applied in such a manner that the identified principles can be used as a bench mark for evaluating healthy and robust democratic elections.

CHAPTER I

Technical Adviser on Electoral Reform—

role of electoral reform adviser;
electoral environment;
particular tasks at the time;
the stakeholders;
electoral credibility gap;
content of electoral reform—
main areas of dispute-registration of voters
Election Advisory Committee;
Director of Elections

Introduction

It was sometime in 1979 that I was assigned the role of Technical Adviser to the Joint Select Committee of both Houses of Parliament which was looking into constitutional and electoral reform in Jamaica. I held the substantive post of Assistant Attorney-General in the Attorney-General's Department. I had then recently relinquished the post of Legal Counsel at the CARICOM Secretariat in Guyana at the end of 1978.

The electoral environment in Jamaica had become unattractive and the perception that the electoral legislative scheme in place then was incapable of delivering free and fair elections without significant reforms. The Joint Select Committee therefore focussed on electoral reform and put constitutional reform on somewhat lower priority to be considered after electoral reform.

Electoral Environment

Like many new and emerging democracies at the time, the Jamaican electoral legislative scheme was unable to cope with weaknesses which were exposed in the management structure and in the organization and conduct of key election processes. The perception of vote rigging was strong among the supporters of the losing side in what was a long-standing two political party system. That notion of vote rigging was given credence by multiple registration by some voters and by general lack of transparency in preparation of the voters' list and polling process.

The electoral management body which was headed by a Chief Electoral Officer was thought to be under the influence of the government of the day and therefore was not considered to be impartial or even non-partisan. The staff of the Electoral Office, some of whom were co-opted from the civil service, likewise were believed to be corrupt, or incompetent, or often behaved in a partisan manner.

The national election campaign had become fiercely competitive to the point where particular campaigns in areas where one political party enjoyed strong support soon became no-go areas for the other party; thus was the beginning of the garrison phenomenon, which spread from about thirteen very confined areas situated mainly in the Kingston and St. Andrew in 1980 to other parts of the island subsequently.

Good practice in election organization and conduct was not taught routinely to staff and training and training materials were not handled in a professional manner. The conduct of election processes, including registration of voters and polling, was not routinely audited or evaluated in order to correct weaknesses identified at the last election.

The Nature of the Electoral Reform
The essence of the 1979 electoral reform in Jamaica involved a change in the management structure of elections and introducing, or tightening up of, safeguards against election fraud in voter registration and polling.

With respect to the election management structure, the old structure of chief electoral officer drawn from the Civil Service was swept away and replaced by a Director of Elections who was advised by an Advisory Committee of seven persons—four drawn from the two political parties and three independent persons, one of whom was appointed as chairperson. Key field staffs, such as returning officers, were asked to resign their position, although they could re-apply for the position and be subjected to interviews before re-appointment.

Numerous measures were put in place to mitigate or eliminate multiple registration, including photographing the qualified persons at the time of enumeration and finger printing. The screening of persons identified for the position of enumerator for the registration of voters by the political parties was provided for in the amended legislation. Similarly, election clerks and their assistants who would run polling stations were subject to screening with the help of the political parties.

In order to strengthen the security of election materials on polling day, two important measures were put in place, first each ballot paper was designed not only with secret features of water marks but the back of the ballot paper was designed with a diamond-shaped feature to prevent any perforation being seen of how a person voted. Secondly, ballot paper with a different colour was to be used to replace stolen ballot papers, so that ballot boxes that were stolen and returned to the system would not be counted.

The Technical Adviser's Task
The Joint Committee members were politicians. The Opposition (JLP) members were pressing for the tightest safeguards against multiple registrations of voters, and voting, perhaps in the belief that the ruling party (PNP) would benefit more from that form of vote rigging. The Technical Adviser's task was to ensure that a careful balance was maintained between safeguard against election fraud and good voter facilitation on polling day, as well as ensuring that undue impediments were not placed in the way of qualified persons who wanted to register. At times, the role of the technical adviser in essence was to convince one side or the other that their point of view would not improve the then existing situation.

It was also important that the new reformed provisions of the electoral law were capable of working smoothly. That was a concern of the technical adviser, for example, it was feared that by giving the political parties the right to participate in the screening of registration and polling officers, the procedure could become protracted, if the parties' representatives did not act in good faith in challenging prospective employees.

The Stakeholders

The primary stakeholders, particularly the ruling and opposition political parties, saw the need for reform of the electoral process. The focus of the Joint Select Committee was to identify and agree on an electoral reform package that would be acceptable to both sides and the country as a whole. There was considerable cooperation between the opposition and ruling party members of the Joint Committee. Both sides made timely submissions to the Committee and surprisingly consensus was reached in good time and the ruling party and the Government quickly enacted the reform package.

Electoral Credibility Gap

There was a large credibility gap between the pre-reformed election management and the general public. The reformed structure and safeguards were met with a measure of scepticism, because of the long-standing perception of rigging elections in Jamaica. There was hope that the new management structure would purge the electoral process through non-partisanship and better trained field staff. Some stakeholders felt that the new safeguards would go some way in reducing multiple registrations and voting in future elections. However, the true effect of the reform as a whole would not be tested until the election processes were carried out.

Content of Reform

The Director of Elections replaced the Chief Elections Officer as the head of the Electoral Office and the chief election executive. The distinguishing feature of the Director from the Chief Elections Officer was the fact that the Director was seen as independent of the government and any ministry there of. Although the Director was advised by the Electoral Advisory Committee, he could refuse to follow the Committee's advice provided that the refusal and the reasons there for were submitted to the Speaker of the House of Representatives. The reform fell short of creating a full commission which was in charge of electoral affairs because that would have required a constitutional amendment, but the stakeholders were not ready to go that route-it would take another almost twenty-seven years to establish a full electoral commission.

As pointed out above, the reform concerning the electoral processes focussed on safeguards in the voters' registration exercise against multiple registrations through improved identification methods. Those enhanced identification methods followed through to improved identification at the point of polling. The security of ballot papers was enhanced and measures were put in place to guard against ballot box stuffing by the introduction of the use of coloured ballot papers at stations where ballot box was stolen.

The Elections Advisory Committee

The Elections Advisory Committee (EAC) was a key element in the strengthening of the management structure. The EAC was largely responsible for policy issues with the concurrence of the Director, who was a non-voting member of the EAC. The reserve power of the Director to refuse to implement a decision of the EAC was seldom resorted to in practice, as, whenever the Director expressed concern over a decision of the EAC with reasons, the EAC would more often than not adjust its decision to accommodate the Director's concerns. The EAC did a good job, having lasted for some twenty-seven years during which the credibility of the electoral process steadily improved.

CHAPTER II

Chief Election Executive

first Director of Election;
implementing electoral reform;
purging electoral staff;
new staff recruitment;
 reform of registration of voters;
computerization of registration data
training of election officers
conduct of elections (1979)
two defaulters
election violence
change of Administration

Introduction

After advising the Joint Select Committee on electoral reform, I was appointed the first Director of Elections by the newly installed Elections Advisory Committees (EAC) and charged with the responsibility of implementing the reforms. The new provisions of the amended electoral legislative scheme had to be implemented with great care to ensure that the delicate balance between safeguards in electoral processes and delivery of good election services was maintained.

The Director's Tasks

The understanding of the EAC and the Director was that the proper implementation of the reform programme would take approximately eighteen months. However, a few months into the implementation programme (by February 1980), under pressure of the International Monetary Fund (IMF), Prime Minister Michael Manley indicated that he wished to call the elections so soon as the reformed programme was in place. That put considerable pressure on the new management structure to get the system up and running as fast as was practicable. Indeed, when that information got out that the Prime Minister had committed to calling election when the system was ready, representatives of certain civil society bodies went to see the Director to inquire whether some of the reforms, such as photographing of voters, one of the centrepieces of the safeguard measures, could be put aside. That suggestion was not entertained.

The first task of the Director, as the chief executive, was to dismiss most of the field officers, particularly returning officers and election clerks, and recruit new ones in their places. This task took several weeks. During the recruitment process, the parties kept a close watch on the process, although it did not amount to full screening in the same manner as recruiting registration and polling officers.

Review of Constituencies and Polling Divisions

It was a requirement under the electoral law to review constituency boundaries before the then pending general elections and customary to review the drawing of polling division boundaries. Both exercises were routine and uneventful and closely scrutinized by the main political parties. However, the constituencies' review threw up a surprise controversy. It came about because a couple of villages near the border between the administrative units (parishes) of Clarendon and Manchester, for many years were located in the parish of Manchester and the villagers voted in Manchester but the review of the boundary of the parishes placed them in Clarendon and the villagers and certain politicians were unhappy about it.

The Voters' Register

The main focus of the electoral reform was the improvement of the process of registration of qualified persons and safeguards against multiple registrations. The issue for the new electoral management was to ensure the smooth implementation of the new provisions. The recruitment of registration officers (enumerators) was done under the watchful eyes of the main political parties which had screening rights that allowed for challenges. The screening process worked relatively well.

The training manual for enumerators was brought up-to-date by the Director who, by virtue of his legal training, ensured that the safeguards were fully and accurately reflected in the manual. Each of the two main political parties had the right to observe the activities of each enumerator. The reform provisions set out a procedure to ensure that enumerators informed the parties' representatives of the time and place of the commencement of each day's enumeration. At the same time, the procedure allowed only limited time for lateness by any of the parties' representatives before each day's activity started. In some cases, the commitment of the parties' representatives, however, was limited and did not serve their respective parties' cause well as they merely turned up and signed on for the day's work before disappearing. The scrutiny by the parties was thus not as rigorous as was intended.

Improved training and greater vigilance exposed some of the old ways of rigging or attempting to rig the registration process, for example, many people were moved from their usual residence into new rental residence temporarily during registration period. This practice was designed to increase apparent support for one or other political party in marginal constituencies. This cheating was often exposed by discreetly talking to neighbours to discover whether or not apparently new persons in an area were living in that area for some time.

The registration field data processing was interesting as the country's general elections were awaiting the completion of the registration process. In order to move the process forward, the Electoral Office was helped with some ten diskette machines from Canada with the good offices of the United States Government. We had a self-taught computer expert whose creativity was very good. With his help, the Office was able to identify and eliminate multiple names on the preliminary voters' list.

The implementation of the reforms went relatively smoothly, but the pressure was always building up on Prime Minister Manley to set the date of the election. Towards the end of September 1980, Prime Minister Manley called me to ask my estimate for completion date of the preparation for the election. I said that early November 1980 about the 4th—the Prime Minister said that would coincide with the American presidential elections and so the 4th November should be ruled out. Then he asked what was needed to complete the process a few days earlier, and I indicated that a couple more printing machines to complete the printing of the final voters' list. He proposed that the Electoral Office should hire the additional printing machines and with that understanding, the election date was announced shortly afterwards for the end of October 1980.

A simple anecdote that occurred concerning the apparent loss of a batch of 109 voters' particulars on a list during the processing of registration data may illustrate the pitfall in trying to legislate for procedural details. During the formulation of the reform, it was decided that there should be a cut-off date for correction to the register even with respect to clerical errors. My Assistant Director (Administration) found the batch of 109 enumerated voters after the cut-off date, mislaid in the storage vault. He placed it in front me and was pretty much speechless. My investigation led me to conclude that it was an innocent human error. I immediately asked for an emergency meeting of the EAC and placed the batch of names on the list before the Committee and invite the Committee to carry out its own investigation. The reformed rules militated against any immediate remedy for the aggrieved persons who were disenfranchised, except the possibility of an election petition in the constituency concerned. In the competitive electoral environment of 1980, the ruling party which claimed that the error affected mainly its supporters was not amused and threatened legal action, if the error caused it to lose the election in that constituency.

The reform caused a stir amongst divorced women due to an oversight. The existing rules of registration required divorced women to register in their married name. The reform measures did not change the rules. Various women's groups which were affiliated to the ruling party bombarded the Minister under whose portfolio election fell and demanded a change in the law. Under political pressure, the Minister reluctantly made contact with me twice, but nothing could be done to change the rules at that stage.

The Election Campaign 1980

National elections in Jamaica had always been very competitive. During the lead up to the 1980 elections competitiveness assumed exaggerated proportions. It was evident that one reason was the fact that the criminal elements, particularly in the Kingston area took advantage of the political tension in the country. An example of the wanton acts of the criminal elements during the election campaign occurred one Friday evening weeks before polling day when just after saying good bye to the police guard at the Electoral Office after work, on reaching home about an hour's drive from the office, I received a phone call that the office guard was shot dead. It was not a political killing, as the policeman was chasing a man whom he saw robbing a woman on the street nearby and as he chased the robber the robber shot him dead. However, the combination of criminal violence and political violence by over-zealous partisans triggered unprecedented threats and violence against ordinary citizens killing between 800 and 1000 of them. The killings included murders by gun shootings, burning of houses, slayings by gangs supporting one or other of the two political parties, and creation of no-go areas (garrisons) by the supporters of both parties. Voting education was not sufficient to calm the political tension and the political leaders failed to calm their respective supporters. The situation got so much out of hand several days before polling that gangs on East Street one side of the down town Kingston were trading bullets with the other side (West Kingston) and the police authorities did nothing about it.

Training of Field Staff

In order to reflect the changes to the rules of practice, I prepared new manuals and instructions for returning officers, their assistants and other field staff and conducted training sessions throughout the island in the different parishes. The training was in part done on the cascade method. As was the case of registration officers (enumerators), some returning officers absorbed quicker than others and were better at imparting to their subordinate officers. Some of the officers made better trainers, perhaps because they were simply better listeners than others. Whatever the reasons, the subsequent performance of the officers on polling day showed wide variations qualitatively.

Polling Day
Polling day for the army and police forces took place about a week ahead of the general polling day for security reasons. It was then that I and the electoral management as a whole got our first taste of the old form vote rigging. The forces personnel were not subject to the use of the indelible voting ink and their returning officers were drawn from the army and police force respectively. In order to reduce the opportunity for multiple voting, ballot papers for the first time were sent only where army and police personnel were posted on polling day and not where they were posted at the time of registration. The instructions on the new procedure were given to each army and police returning officer, but perhaps sufficient voter education programmes amongst the police personnel did not take place.

Confusion erupted on the special polling day for the army and police personnel-indeed mainly amongst the police personnel as many of them sought to vote not only where they were posted during polling period but also where they were posted when registered. In other words, many sought to vote multiple times contrary to the election law. They complained that under the old system they could vote at either where they were registered or where they were posted on polling day. What the new procedure did was to curtail the number of ballot papers available at each army and police polling station and place their names on the voters' lists only where they were posted on polling day. Unwittingly or otherwise the opposition party (JLP) sided with the Police Federation and called for a rerun of the special polling day voting. The Director and the EAC readily concurred in the need for re-polling and a date was set for the purpose, as it was claimed that the majority of the forces' personnel was unable to vote on the special polling day.

Carl W. Dundas

In the meantime, the Electoral Office processed the returns from the first day's special voting and revealed the results of multiple voting by individual police personnel. Only a couple of multiple votes were found in the army votes. Some police personnel had voted up to seven times, some six times, others five times and so on. This was discovered before the re-polling day and I went public with the findings after discussing them with the EAC and informing the Police Federation. I also sent the list of names and the voting printouts to the Director of Public Prosecutions. There were many who ran for cover from the adverse publicity. On the re-polling day, only about 300 additional police personnel voters turned out.

Subsequent to that incident the army and police personnel were subjected to the use of the indelible ink and other safeguards that applied to the general voting public.

The violence that was experienced during the election campaign largely died away on Election Day. The day was eventful for other reasons. One of my most promising returning officers who was a college teacher of mathematics 'froze' on the night before Election Day and was incapable of dispatching the election materials in his constituency. In consultation with the Chairman of the EAC, I relieved him of his duties on the spot in his office and appointed an acting returning officer in his stead.

In Jamaica, it was said that the first two hours of a general election day were full of confusion. As if to corroborate this perception, I received word mid-morning on Election Day that there was no activity in one of the mid-island constituencies. I got the Jamaica Defence Force to fly down one of my field officers to find out what had happened. It was another case of a returning officer 'freezing'. It was a robust Anglican Priest who, like his mathematician counterpart in St. Andrew, did well in the interview for recruitment, discovered that he was not up to the task on Election Day. My field officer had to take over the reins in the constituency and oversaw the polling exercise. When, after the elections, I visited the Father and asked of him what happened on Election Day, he admitted that he literally 'froze' on election morning and could not carry out any of his election tasks. An Anglican Father, in his forties, accustomed to conducting weddings and funerals could not explain why 'election fright' took hold of him at such a critical moment.

While I never had cause to doubt the non-partisanship of either of the two polling day defaulters and believed both were men of integrity, I was alerted to the Mathematician's somewhat laid back approach towards the end of the preparatory period by his election clerk. However, when I called him in, he gave me his full assurance that the work was on course and that he was fine.

An Evaluation
The 1979 reforms were meant to usher in a new era of improved conduct of national elections. The majority of the stakeholders bought into the reforms, but a small hardcore sceptics and non-believers in free and fair elections remained committed to attempt to rig important preparatory processes, as well as polling itself. A very small amount of those might have succeeded resulting in irregularities.

However, a number of shortcomings on polling day were due to either inadequate training of election officers or weakness in the voter education programmes. There was at least one case of suspected partisan behaviour by a staff member that was brought to my attention and that individual was taken off his field inspection duties on polling day.

There were a few cases of ballot stuffing, but the use of coloured ballots papers in ballot boxes used to replace the stolen ballot boxes ensured that the stuffed ballots were not counted.

There were many instances where partisan supporters attempted to disrupt the election process after polling, and before the final count were completed. In one case, the building storing the ballot boxes after the preliminary count, but before the final count, was burned down and the results in that constituency were declared by using the figures from the preliminary count. In another instance, some of the ballot boxes were tampered with during storage before the final count by the returning officer, despite the fact that reinforced security of as many as nineteen security personnel being posted to guard the premises. It was clear that there was connivance by some security personnel in the security breach. This incident resulted in the winning candidate by over 300 votes on the preliminary count lost by about a similar margin on the final count by the returning officer. However, the final count was subsequently reversed on magisterial recount.

In many respects the 1980 general election was work in progress. The culture of fairness and non-partisanship in election organization had not yet taken root in Jamaica. The dominant two-party system was healthy but had become too competitive and led some misguided supporters to resort to unscrupulous measures in the hope of winning. For example in a particular constituency, the ruling party's candidate knew that he was unlikely to win and so election officers, including presiding officers, were threatened resulting in many not turning up to open their stations on polling day. The situation was saved from an election petition because the opposition candidate won by a 'landslide' in the constituency.

Looking back on the general elections of 1980, it was surprising to some who held the view that there was the possibility of the incumbent party and government influencing the conduct and outcome of the elections; not only did that not happen but at no time was there any attempt by any of the two major political parties to influence the managers of the electoral process. That there was such a relatively widespread perception at the time was true and that was the challenge that the Electoral Office had to overcome.

The 1980 general elections, wracked by unprecedented violence, nevertheless laid the foundation for confidence-building measures that would deliver genuine free and fair elections over a period of four or five subsequent general elections during which incremental improvements were achieved.

CHAPTER III

My World of Election Observation

Ten years of election observation
Selected observations missions of special interest . . .
Namibia 1989;
Malaysia 1990;
Zambia 1991;
Kenya 1992;
Guyana 1992/97;
Pakistan 1993;
South Africa 1994;
Mozambique 1994;
Malawi 1994;
Tanzania-Zanzibar 1995;
Bangladesh 1996;
Zanzibar 2000;
Trinidad & Tobago 2000.

International election observation has become a huge global activity today. The accompanying domestic election observation has also grown and usually far exceeds international observers in numbers in many national elections. It was not always so. For example, during the era of one-party regimes on the African continent election observation was not well known. Indeed international observers would not be welcomed to witness such elections and most international observers would not be interested in observing elections with little or no competition in a one-party regime.

Because election observation was associated with countries that were not known to hold competitive elections, the practice of welcoming observers was frowned upon in some countries. Indeed when I was Director of Elections in Jamaica, as mentioned above, I did not accept observers at the 1980 general elections. The endorsement of an election as free and fair by observers did not then seem vital for legitimacy of the incoming administration or for attracting foreign investments. Election observation was seen by some nationalists in emerging democracies as outside interference in the host country's internal affairs and in the view of some as an impingement on the country's sovereignty. It took Jamaica many years after 1980 to reconcile itself to the idea of grudgingly accepting international election observers, let alone enthusiastically extending invitations to such international groups.

Over the past thirty years, the democratic election environment has changed significantly. Democratic elections are today associated with good governance and widespread participation by stakeholders. Moreover, democratic elections are the popular means of creating reconciliation of warring sides in conflict situations and to restore lasting peace and security. Further, democratic elections have the ability to strengthen the legitimate credentials of incoming administrations and attract foreign private and bi-lateral assistance from the international community. These developments have raised the profile of democratic elections internationally and regionally and have increased the interest in the organization and conduct of these elections. Many host countries are now eager to invite and open the electoral process to observers, domestic and international.

The Commonwealth was one of the institutions that showed an interest in observing elections in selected circumstances, for example it was instrumental in organizing observation of the Guyana elections in 1964 (even before the Commonwealth Secretariat was set up), and in sending observers to the Gibraltar referendum in 1967, as well as Southern Rhodesia (Zimbabwe) elections (1980), and Uganda 1980.

Multiparty democratic elections became fashionable when, in the early 1990s, the cold war ended and erstwhile communist one-party regimes in the former Soviet Union States became liberated and introduced multiparty democracies. Before too long, in Africa, former military, or apartheid regimes followed suite and competitive democratic elections began to take root. The idea of assisting these new and emerging multiparty democracies caught the imagination of intergovernmental and non-governmental organisations alike, initially led by the United Nations. The business of helping countries to enter the democratic age soon became exciting and interested players popped up often keen to get involved in election observation. There was frequently a measure of distrust of those organising the transitional elections from military, one-party or apartheid regimes to multiparty democracy. Thus there were those in the Commonwealth who were fearful of any deal between those in the UN who were assisting the South Africans with the Namibian pre-independence elections in 1989 and regime in apartheid South Africa against the South West Africa Peoples' Organization (SWAPO) and so a Commonwealth pre-election mission was dispatched to monitor the preparation by the UN about six weeks before the election.

I was the technical adviser to that Commonwealth Pre-election Mission to Namibia in 1989. The goal of the Commonwealth was not to keep surveillance on the UN Mission, far from it, but rather to ensure that the election preparation was being done to the highest standards. The UN Mission was instrumental in facilitating some aspects of the Commonwealth Mission in so far as the UN Mission lent the Commonwealth Mission a small plane to travel across central, east and northern Namibia to meet stakeholders, including traditional leaders.

There was no doubt that the UN Mission to Namibia in 1989 was committed to the cause of free and fair elections. However, the UN Election Administrator, as distinct from the Head of Mission (Mr. Martti Ahtisaari), was poorly advised and was not on top of the election logistics management. There was confusion between the number of polling stations and polling booths that would be in place for the elections.

A memorable anecdote arose out of our visit to the border area of Namibia with Angola. Our UN plane made a stop just by the border outside the Angolan town where it was alleged that the Cuban fighters had defeated the South African Forces. The town was completely shot up with ruined buildings and a few of us from the Commonwealth Mission stepped over into Angola taking photographs. Momentarily we saw Angolan soldiers with guns with bayonets point down on us and signalling that no photographs should be taken. We froze. The border in that area was unmarked and we were not sure whether or not we were in fact across the border, but there was no time for argument. We went as directed back into Namibia unharmed!

Another memorable incident in Namibia was on a trip to the Kaprivi Strip where we went to visit a chief. When he learned that we were from a Commonwealth Election Observation Mission he pleaded what most of us believed was diplomatic illness and refused to see us. Then after a long wait he sent his emissary whom he dubbed his 'Prime Minister' to see us. The Prime Minister then went through his reception ceremony before talking to us. We gathered after the meeting that the chief was in the pay of the South African apartheid regime and that was why he did not wish to see us.

The Commonwealth's mission was a pre-election mission concerned with the preparation for polling, and aimed to satisfy itself that all the contestants, particularly SWAPO, was being treated fairly. There reports of intimidation and isolated sporadic incidents against the supporters of SWAPO, but on the whole the campaign was relatively peaceful.

Malaysia 1990

At the beginning of the last decade of the last Century, the Commonwealth made the promotion of democratic elections in Commonwealth countries a priority. Emphasis was placed on election observation, as well as on technical assistance to Member States. Malaysia volunteered to be the first Member State of the Commonwealth to submit to Commonwealth election observation at its 1990 general elections. This commendable gesture was made to usher in the newly formulated Commonwealth policy of promoting democratic elections as one of its priorities in the decade of the 1990s. There is no doubt that Malaysia's Prime Minister Mahathir was sincere in wishing to point the Commonwealth members in the direction of democratic election and away from one-party regimes which were still prevalent in many parts of the Commonwealth, particularly in Africa. The Chairman of the Commonwealth Observer Group (COG) was the Hon. Dudley Thompson Q.C. former M.P. and Minister of Defence in Jamaica, and I was leader of the Commonwealth Secretariat's Support Team to the COG.

The implementation of Malaysia's offer was a challenge for the electoral management body (the Electoral Commission) of Malaysia and for the Commonwealth observer mission. The first significant difference in approach to election observation by the majority of the Commonwealth representatives occurred with respect to whether or not an *Interim Statement* should be issued by the election observer mission. The Malaysian Foreign Ministry spokesperson raised the matter with the Commonwealth observer support team (of which I was the leader) but the policy of the Commonwealth was that observation missions were to issue an Interim Statement at the close of the voting and before the results of the elections were known. The Malaysian Foreign Office spokesperson pointed out that Malaysia had voted against that procedure when the matter was discussed at a meeting of Commonwealth Officials in London. The Malaysian position did not prevail, as the mandate of the observer mission, as given by the Secretary-General at the time, included the issuance of an Interim Statement.

The second contentious issue confronting the Electoral Commission and the Commonwealth observers was the state of the voters' register. There was a new head of the Electoral Commission who had just assumed office two weeks before the elections.[2] The new Chairman, Dato Harun Din, was affable and had a great commitment

---

[2] The electoral law in Malaysia at the time required that the Chairman of the Electoral Commission retires promptly on attaining the age of 65 years.

to transparency in election organization. He promptly confirmed what many stakeholders had told the observer mission that the voters' register was defective in that almost 400,000 names thereon had defects of some sort. The Chairman explained that it had come to light and his predecessor had publicly acknowledged the problem and set about rectifying it. However, due to the fact that the voters' register was compiled manually, only about 10, 000 names were processed between January and October 1990.[3]

The third difficulty was caused by the restrictions on freedom to campaign imposed by the Internal Security Act which was a measure that was enacted in 1969 to deal with ethnic conflict then and was still in force. That security measure prohibited open air political rallies and the use of loud speakers in the streets, among other things. Political rallies were held in enclosed premises. Some stakeholders felt that the Act was being used for political purposes and to the benefit of the ruling coalition parties. An accompanying complaint by opposition parties was that the ruling coalition secured the larger and more central meeting venues where rallies could be held.

The fourth difficulty for the Commonwealth election observer mission was the uneven access to the state-owned media by the opposition parties. Political advertisement was not encouraged on the publicly owned television stations, but government ministers were frequently given long exposures in their ministerial capacity which appeared to circumvent the campaign prohibition on the television to the advantage of the ruling coalition.

The observation mission was of mixed views. Some members felt that the elections, though relatively well-conducted, had some glaring flaws, such as the relatively large amount of discrepancies in the voters' register; the restrictions on campaigning; and the lack of fair access to the state-owned media, which rendered the elections neither free nor fair. Other members felt that the identified flaws

---

[3] However to put the situation in perspective 400,000 defective entries in a register of approximately 9 million was not unusual in a voluntary registration system.

did not rise to the level of rendering the elections not credible, or not valid.

The report of the Commonwealth observer mission did not wholeheartedly endorse the election as free and fair. Prime Minister Mahathir was no doubt disappointed that his voluntary submission to the Commonwealth's new election scrutiny machinery did not unreservedly endorse the quality of his country's election organization and conduct. He took many months to send his response to the mission's report to the Commonwealth Secretary-General and when he did so, he was critical of the report, particularly its finding concerning the role of the publicly owned media. The Prime Minister complained that the inability of the mission to read the local language newspapers led them to draw unbalanced conclusions.

Post Script
One of the lessons learned by the Commonwealth Secretariat was to be more circumspect in what a host government might assist an election observation mission with during the mission. The Malaysian Government had volunteered to put a fleet of Mercedes Benz cars to transport the Commonwealth observers on their missions on polling day and the offer way accepted. This approach was criticized by some local stakeholders publicly and by some observers privately. The criticisms were noted and the Secretariat immediately abandoned the approach of accepting similar gestures for observer missions from host governments subsequently.

Zambia 1991
The Zambian elections in 1991 were of international importance in so far as it was heralding in a new era of multiparty elections in Zambia and indeed in Africa. The incumbent President of Zambia, Kenneth Kaunda, had been in power for about twenty-seven years as head of a one-party regime. The Chairman of the Commonwealth observer group (COG) was the Hon. Telford Georges, a former Chief Justice of Tanzania and Zimbabwe, and I headed the Commonwealth Secretariat support team to the Commonwealth

election observation mission. On the whole the preparation and conduct was relatively peaceful.

There were however a few interesting developments leading up to the elections. There was a state of national emergency in place in the country which the President had promised to lift. The President dissolved Parliament before lifting the state of emergency and then was advised by his Attorney-General that the state of emergency could not be lifted while Parliament was dissolved. President Kaunda then assured observers and stakeholders that the state of emergency would not be enforced during the election campaign. The Commonwealth observer teams received credible reports that the security forces were erecting roadblocks (unauthorized though they might have been) after dark in the rural areas.

The Government, through the Ministry of Foreign Affairs and the Electoral Commission, invited international election observers, including from the Commonwealth, and then at the level of the General Secretary of the ruling party a bitter attack was launched on international observers generally. The essence of the General-Secretary's attack was that the international observers had a colonial attitude and were biased in favour of the opposition and that they wanted the ruling party to lose and were not really interested in free and fair elections. The Commonwealth observer mission was concerned about the impression that the attack of the General-Secretary might have had on the credibility of the Commonwealth observer mission, since it was prominently displayed in the national media. The Commonwealth mission leader, Mr. Justice Telford Georges, after consulting with some other observer groups, led the way in placing a response in the form of a statement to the General-Secretary in a couple national news papers, and by arranging a meeting with the General-Secretary to request him to withdraw his general attack on observers. The General-Secretary did withdraw his attack on observers—at least in so far as Commonwealth observers were concerned.

The Commonwealth Group of Observers paid a courtesy call on President Kaunda a few days before Election Day and was struck by the confidence of the President in winning the elections, despite the widely held view among stakeholders that his party would be defeated.

The incumbent ruling party and President did lose the election. It was the end of an era not only for Zambia where President Kaunda's long reign had come to an end, but it was the beginning of the end for one-party regimes in Africa. In relaying the early elections results to the then Commonwealth Secretary-General, Emeka Anyaoku, he repeated on the telephone, as if to himself, that it was truly an end of an era in Zambia.

Those were early days since the Commonwealth started to observe elections systematically. The Commonwealth had developed its own 'brand' of election observation methodology assisted by me and others in the Commonwealth Secretariat. The Commonwealth's approach was based on individual observers forming their own judgment on what they had seen as to whether or not the election was free and fair. The problem with that approach was how to reach a consensus when different members of the observer group formed different judgments. The modus operandi did require a fair amount of discussion and the notional assignment and balancing up of weight with respect to irregularities.

An early feature of the Commonwealth's approach to election observation was the issuance of an interim statement immediately after the close of the polls and before the counting of the votes had taken place. The purpose of this interim statement was to enhance the credibility of the mission, since that statement would point to irregularities occurring during polling before the election results were known. Some observer groups at that time did not issue interim statements and other groups were structured around a central office which received the data on polling from the field and interpret that data to extract the results. As mentioned above the Government authorities in Malaysia in 1990 were unhappy about the issuance of an interim statement by the Commonwealth Observer Group

Post Script

Justice Telford Georges and I had breakfast with former President Carter and Mrs Carter the morning after the elections. While the former President was happy with the peaceful nature of the elections, he was disappointed that his parallel tabulation (quick count) exercise did not work. It failed because the official election results came ahead of the quick count which no longer served its purpose. In any event, President Kaunda kept his word and there was no hitch or trouble with the transfer of power to Mr. Chiluba, the incoming President.

Kenya 1992

The Kenyan multiparty elections of 1992 had many interesting dimensions. The Kenyan experiment with a one-party regime lasted for just about one decade, but nevertheless many steps had to be taken to dismantle the one-party system. Besides amending the Constitution to allow for multiple political parties to exist and contest elections, amendment was required to the election laws to allow for good practices. Thus under the Commonwealth Secretariat technical assistance programme to Kenya, I assisted the Attorney-General's Department to draft suitable legal provisions to allow for international election observers. Further technical assistance was offered to the Electoral Commission in drafting a code of conduct for all election observers, domestic and international.

At the instance of the then Commonwealth Secretary-General and with the agreement of President Moi and the Electoral Commission, I was embedded in the offices of the Electoral Commission for several weeks offering technical assistance. I headed a small team of experts who were tasked to review the costing of the election and the proposed election budget to lend credibility to it in order to assure partners that the sums required were realistic. I subsequently headed another small team from the Commonwealth Secretariat to monitor the voter registration exercise.

The voters' registration exercise was poorly organized. The registration officers had little or no training. The registration forms and other documents were poorly designed and not standardized.

The entire process was manual. The field data was collected without any standardized format-some registration officers used exercise books in the field, others used single sheets of paper, while yet others used quire book format. The preliminary lists of voters at rural centres were prepared by way of outdated cyclostyled machines (office duplicator using a stencil). My monitoring team had a bit of fun tracing the cycle of selected names from the field entry to preliminary list. Many names were lost in the journey from field collection points to the preliminary list compilation centre in Nairobi.

Allowances had to be made for the fact that the 1992 elections were the first attempt at organizing multiparty elections in ten years. Yet there were more missteps at the policy-making and the operations levels. The then Chairman of the ECK was an erudite jurist who had to resign from the Appellate Court Bench due to the failure of business which he was involved with while on the Court of Appeal. Indeed, the business fell into bankruptcy. Justice Chesoni did not fully appreciate his role as Chairman of the ECK. He remained shy of the media and of the opposition parties.

As the Commonwealth Secretariat liaison officer with the ECK, twice I had to advise the Secretary-General of the Commonwealth to see President Moi. I accompanied the Secretary-General on both occasions. The first occasion was to impress on the President that it was important for the opposition and other stakeholders to see the ECK as a non-partisan body. The President took the Secretary-General's concern seriously and added some four additional Commissioners after consulting the opposition. The second occasion I relayed to the Secretary-General the fact that stakeholders-particularly the opposition and the media, were concerned that the lack of transparency was adversely affecting the election preparation and that it was time to see the President again. President Moi again was sympathetic and assured the Secretary-General that improvements would be made. After the second visit, there was significant opening up by the Chairman of the ECK to the media and with respect to contacts with the opposition parties.

Despite the behind the scenes pressure on the President and on the ECK, the supporters of the ruling party were not prepared to show tolerance to the opposition. There was widespread violence against opposition supporters. Numerous houses in the Rift Valley were burnt out. Hundreds of women and children fled their destroyed homes and were given refuge in several church premises in Nkuru. The Chairman of the Commonwealth Mission and I (as leader of the Support Team to the Mission) visited three of those church premises with several hundreds of displaced persons. We were told by persons in the areas that several tens of dead bodies were in the morgue unidentified, and that some were shot in the forest with poisoned arrows.

The ECK made a number of avoidable errors in the lead up to fixing the date for the 1992 elections. For example, many stakeholders felt that the ECK seriously compromised its neutrality when it acquiesced in the shortening of the period required for the parties' nomination of their candidates. The political parties were unaware that a notice had been carried in the gazette stating that the words "not less than 21 days" had been changed to "not more than 21 days" in section 13 of the National Assembly and Presidential Elections Act. The change in the Act was made by the Attorney-General purporting to act under a power vested in him by section 13 of the Revision of Laws Act, but in fact that power only enabled the Attorney-General to correct clerical or printing errors in editions of the Revised Laws. The change in the law was treated as a mere legal technicality and was not brought to the attention of the political parties. Acting on the change in the law, the ECK set the date for parties' nomination of candidates from 3 November 1992 to 9 November 1992, a period which fell far short of that previously available to parties. One of the opposition parties, FORD-Kenya, brought an action in court challenging the purported amendment to section 13 of the National Assembly and Presidential Elections Act as null and void. The Court found in favour of the opposition party and in so doing declared that there was no error in section 13 of the law to be rectified, and found that the notice had effected a substantial change, which had been sneaked in mischievously. The Judge held the Attorney General's purported amendment was a misuse, if not an abuse, of the powers conferred upon him by his office. The Court ordered the ECK to fix new dates for the primaries for candidates' nominations, as well as for nomination of presidential candidates and a new date for the elections which was for 29 December 1992.[4]

The registration of candidates (nomination) to contest the elections was a flawed process. The Commonwealth Observer Group (COG) received reports of complaint about this process from opposition parties, interested groups, and independent observers. The complaints pointed to forcible prevention of a substantial number of prospective candidates from filing their nomination papers. Formal complaints were made to the ECK and action filed in court. Nevertheless, the unlawful interference with prospective candidates resulted in sixteen candidates in the Rift Valley were declared duly elected unopposed on nomination day. All of these unopposed candidates belonged to the ruling party. Similar problems, though affecting smaller numbers of prospective candidates, occurred in the North Eastern Province. There were credible reports of nominated candidates being bribed to withdraw or defect to the ruling party.

The Chairman of the COG, Justice Telford Georges, and I, as leader of the Commonwealth Secretariat Support Team to the COG, both of us being lawyers, jointly conducted several interviews of aggrieved prospective candidates who had been abducted into the forest on nominations day and had their nomination papers destroyed

---

4   The Commonwealth Observer Group was very critical of the ECK on this matter, it states in its report that: *The fact that the Commission, headed by a former experienced Justice of Appeal, had accepted this obviously invalid exercise of amending power of the Attorney General as proper and had allowed the short period to be fixed, confirmed the opposition's suspicions that the Commission was acting in collaboration with the authorities. In their view, even though the law had been changed from "not less than 21" to not more than 21 days, the Commission could have allowed the maximum of 21 days and not fixed the unrealistically short period of seven days for organizing primaries—p.15 of the Report.*

before they were released about 10.00 p.m. or 11.00 p.m. in the evening.

Election Day was chaotic in Nairobi and its environs. There were long queues at polling stations, some of which did not have ballot box or ballot papers. Polling day was generally peaceful, but irregularities had spilled over from the flawed registration exercise. The counting of the votes and tabulation were relatively transparent and well conducted.

The COG had considerable difficulty concluding which side of the credibility line the election fell, that is to say, above or below that line. The polling and post-polling processes were balanced against the pre-polling processes and the verdict was given in favour of the former, that is, just above the credibility line. However, there were considerations other than pure electoral factors; for example, many of the forty members of the COG addressed the chaos which existed next door in Somalia and felt that if the Kenyan elections were declared to be not free and fair, the East African region would be further destabilized.

The COG did note that there were a number of serious irregularities in the organization of the elections. It pointed to the following:

- Defective registration process in many parts of the country;
- The nomination process (registration of candidates to contest the elections) was flawed, particularly in the Rift Valley where 16 ruling party candidates were returned unopposed;
- The lack of transparency on the part of the ECK;
- The widespread intimidation and violence throughout the election campaign;
- The partisan state-owned media; and
- The failure of the Government to delink itself from the ruling party.

Up to that point in election observation, the Kenyan election had posed the greatest challenge to 40 strong COG. There was almost an even split in the Group among those who thought the election was not free and fair and those who judged it to achieve just about pass mark. Those observers who would have handed down pass mark won the day and so the election was not adjudged to be invalid. The deciding factor was more political than technical, since in the deliberations often an argument was advanced that if the elections were to be adjudged to be invalid chaos might have ensued in Kenya at a time when Somalia next door had already disintegrated as a nation-State.

The doubters of the validity of the election were influenced by the obvious lack of transparency in the election organization, the absence of a level playing field, particularly uneven access to the publicly owned media, and the widespread occurrences of intimidation and open violence during the campaign. In addition to the fore-going negative factors, the nomination of candidates was afflicted by widespread kidnapping of prospective opposition candidates and stolen nomination papers on nomination day with the upshot that some sixteen candidates were returned unopposed, all of whom were form the ruling party.

So strong was the impact of the Kenyan election on the Commonwealth's observation methodology in adjudging election outcome that it was no longer appropriate to use the criterion of 'free and fair' to which many stakeholders attached too emotive a label, and so phrases like 'the voters had an opportunity to exercise their franchise freely', or that 'the voters turned out in large numbers' were subsequently used instead.

Post Script

Justice Telford Georges, the Chairman of the COG, served as Chief Justice of Tanzania and Zimbabwe, and also served as a member of the Judicial Committee of the Privy Council and so he was well respected in the east African region. He visited the then outgoing Chief Justice of Kenya and was apparently briefed about the circumstances under which Justice Chesoni, the ECK Chairman, had to resign from the Court of Appeal and he also obtained a copy of the Court papers on Justice Chesoni's bankruptcy case. Justice Georges came to the view that Justice Chesoni should not have taken the post of Chairman of the ECK and wanted to reflect that viewpoint in the report. I did not agree with Justice Georges, as I thought that a personal attack on the Chairman of the ECK would serve only to distract attention from the report as a whole. It split the COG and a compromise was reached whereby the papers on the bankruptcy case of Justice Chesoni would be put on the records of the Commonwealth Secretariat but would not be included in the report of the COG.

Guyana 1992

Guyana was known in the Caribbean and elsewhere for 'fixed' elections in favour of the ruling party, People's National Congress (PNC), until the wind of change reached that country in 1992. There were many known problems that listed as deficits of previous elections in Guyana. Among these was the registration of voters. Indeed, in the lead up to the 1992 elections, the register had to be re-visited after all sides expressed concern about the quality of the voters' register. The Parliament which was dissolved had to be recalled to address issues related to the re-opening of voters' registration.

Most of the other shortcomings were addressed, including counting at polling stations and not at polling centres as in the past. Despite the strenuous efforts of the Elections Commission to get the voters' register right, on polling day riots broke out at the Electoral Office due to the inability of voters to find their names on the voters' list.

In the preparatory stages, there were several hiccups. One such incident involved the printing of the ballot papers. The ballot papers were printed in Miami, Florida. When they were received a few days before the Election Day, it was discovered that there were a number of errors on the face of the ballot papers, the most serious of which was the omission of part of the shortened name of the opposition party, PPP/Civic. The 'Civic' part of the name was omitted from the ballot paper. The leader of the opposition party involved initially was uncooperative and insisted that he was taking the matter to court. In the meantime the COG and partners were trying to get the ballot papers reprinted in Trinidad & Tobago or in the UK. In time, the opposition leader recanted, but issued a statement that he reserved the right to challenge the election results. The election went ahead as planned.

Another interesting titbit that came out of the 1992 Guyana elections was the split in the Elections Commission. The Commission, after much agonizing, decided to replace the indelible election ink with a new type of ink and actually acquired the new type of indelible ink, but the Commission for more than six months could not agree how and when to dispose of the old indelible ink. The old ink was only disposed of a few weeks before the elections at the instance of members of COG who accompanied members of the Commission to dispose of the ink in the Demarara River. The reason why the Commission could not take quick decisions was because its membership of seven was evenly divided between government party and opposition parties-three each, with an independent chairperson who did not like the role of constantly having to break deadlocks between the two sides in the Commission.

The formula for establishing the Elections Commission of Guyana was known locally as the 'Carter formula' as it was developed with the assistant of former President Carter of the United States. It was credited with gaining the support of all sides and was instrumental in settling the thorny issue of the composition of the election management body at a time when the incumbent ruling party and the opposition parties agreed on very little electoral matters. The 'Carter' formula enabled the electoral process to start up, but the six political nominees who were appointed as Commissioners seldom agreed and so the decision process became inefficient.

Post Script
The Headquarters building of the Elections Commission was badly damaged by rioters on Election Day. I and a colleague from the Commonwealth Support Group were going towards the Elections Commission's building when just above the Central Bank Building

in Georgetown our car run into a hail of bullets from guns in the street. We did not know where the shots were coming from and so my colleague and I ducked on the floor of the car while the driver kept on driving. Fortunately, none of us in the car was injured, but we discovered that there were a couple of fatal injuries resulting from the shooting.

Pakistan 1993

The electoral environment in 1993 in Pakistan was unsettled. There was a Caretaker Government in place which was anxious to deliver free and fair elections. There were important changes to electoral field personnel to conduct the elections. Returning officers were recruited mainly from the judicial branch, particularly the magistracy. Stakeholders were unhappy with the state of the voters' register which was not up-to-date and did not adequately cover a number of qualified women due in part to the political environment at the time, but also due to cultural and religious reasons. Activists from human rights movements complained to the COG about the many obstacles that were placed against women voting in some parts of Pakistan, particularly in the Northwest Frontier Districts.

The election was boycotted for political reasons by a prominent but relatively small political party in the Pakistan Province of Sind. The COG sent a delegation, headed by the Deputy Leader of the COG, Dato Harun Din, Chairman of the Malaysian Electoral Commission and himself a Muslim, to meet representatives of the party, MQM, which was boycotting the elections, in order to ascertain their reasons for not taking part in the electoral contest.

The election campaign was relatively quiet. The Caretaker Government succeeded in created a relatively level playing field for the contestants. There were a few notable positive developments in the preparation for the elections. One was the framework for the swift and transparent disposal of election complaints and disputes. The Elections Commission itself dealt with immediate cases, and when time permitted, examined some of the urgent cases as they came in. The other notable feature was the transparent approach of the Commission to stakeholders and with respect to the preparatory processes as a whole. It was also admirable to see how the field staffs were able to use substitute materials to (improvise) make polling booths in polling stations from cloth and table and desks in school buildings.

On the negative side, some stakeholders felt that the presence of the security personnel was intrusive in many cases. This issue provoked a lively discussion which lasted a whole afternoon without being exhausted, in the COG. The arguments in favour of the presence of the security personnel was intrusive and should be commented upon in the report was being strongly supported by two observers, one from the United Kingdom and the other from Canada, both of whom happened to be journalists. The issue was settled by a set of words which bridged the divide between the two approaches. The issue which proved to be so contentious was whether the presence of the military in such large numbers was necessary to give confidence to the voters or whether it was so intimidating as to cause voters to stay away. The majority of voters who were asked about the presence of the military in the vicinity of the polling stations indicated that they found it to be reassuring from a security point of view. However a minority did indicate that at some stations the presence of the military was indeed intrusive and even intimidating. The two Western journalists who were insisting that what seemed like a minority view among voters, that the military presence was intrusive and not compatible with democratic elections wanted to send a signal that such military presence at polling stations should be avoided in future elections in Pakistan.

The COG concluded that the elections were credible.

Post Script I
The Chairman of the COG, a former Speaker of the Australian State of Western Australia Assembly, and I, leader of the Commonwealth Secretariat Support Team to the COG, were randomly examining polling stations on the eve of polling. We were on our way outside Islamabad along a roadway without any warning that it was close to foreigners when suddenly we came to joint police/army check

point. We were stopped and asked to produce identification, which we did, and explained our mission. We were then told that foreigners were forbidden to travel in that area. Despite producing identification, we were detained and interrogated by the police and the army for about 90 minutes before we were released. We protested to the Chairman of Elections Commission who apologised profusely for not informing us about the national security area.[5]

Post Script II
After the election, a member of the COG and I travelled to the Kyber Pass and then to the Afghanistan border as guest of the Governor of the border post on the Pakistan side. We had an escort of several vehicles. The Pakistani Governor invited us to cross the border into Afghanistan and while we were there, the head of one of the Afghan militia groups joined us for a photograph. Just as we finished taking the photograph a shell rang out in the valley behind us. No one was injured, but we hurried back to the Pakistan's Governor's office. The Governor did show us bullet marks in his office which occurred a couple months previously, before we crossed border, but assured us that the area was safe!

South Africa 1994
The 1994 South African transitional elections were historic in that they were intended to see off apartheid in that country. There were many countries and inter-governmental organizations which offered assistance. I negotiated technical assistance offer on behalf of the Commonwealth to the Electoral Commission through its Chairman, Judge Kreigler. He accepted the Commonwealth's offer in many areas, including training of election officers, voter education, election logistics, and polling procedures. The Commonwealth also sent an observer team to observe all aspects of the elections.

The South African election environment was almost unique in so far as its electoral structure was not geared to accommodate free and fair multiparty democratic elections. Consequently, several new

---

[5]   The security area was home to an atomic research laboratory, but we were not aware of that.

legal election managerial structures had to be introduced. Among these structures were an Interim Constitution, a Transitional Executive Council, an Electoral Act, an Independent Electoral Commission (IEC), an Independent Media Commission and an Independent Broadcasting Authority.

The Interim Constitution provided for a Constitutional Assembly, with a National Assembly, which was charged with the task of drawing up a Constitution within two years.

The National Assembly consisted of four hundred members elected in accordance with a proportional representation system. Two hundred of the seats of the National Assembly seats were allocated through the parties from regional lists in nine provinces. The remaining two hundred seats were allocated from nine lists, which were submitted by the respective political parties. The Senate consisted of ten Senators from each of the nine provinces, nominated by the party representatives in the provincial legislatures, according to their strength in the respective legislatures. A new Electoral Act came into force in January 1994 and it provided for the organization of free and fair elections. The main feature of the electoral legislative scheme was the creation of an Independent Electoral Commission whose principal functions were to generate confidence in the electoral process; to protect the secrecy of the ballot; and to conduct the elections.

The composition of the IEC had an international dimension to it aimed at strengthening its acceptance locally as well as internationally. There were eleven South Africans and five non-voting Commissioners chosen from the international community in a non-representative capacity. The State President appointed the Commissioners upon the advice of the Transitional Executive Council. A similar procedure was followed in appointment of the Chairperson and Vice Chairperson of the Commission. An International Advisory Committee was established under the IEC Act to advise the Commission with respect to matters relating to its functions.

The IEC Act set up a structure to deal with matters requiring adjudication of disputes. There was a system of Election Tribunals, Election Appeals Tribunals, a Special Electoral Court and an Election Adjudication Secretariat.

An Independent Media Commission (IMC) was established by an Act in 1993. It consisted of a Chairperson and six other persons, appointed by the State President on the advice of the Transitional Executive Council. The aim of the IMC was to create a level playing field for the parties contesting the elections. It was wholly independent of all state authorities and political parties.

An Independent Broadcasting Authority was set up to regulate broadcasting activities. Like the IMC, it was to be completely independent of the State, government and political parties.

On the whole, the transitional structures performed well. In a very unsettled election environment, the IEC handled its almost impossible task admirably. There was no voters' register and the infrastructure of election logistics was underdeveloped. The majority of the voters had no experience in voting. However, within a few months, the IEC transformed the electoral environment. The logistics, which seemed so impossible a few months before the elections, gradually were transformed with an aggressive voter education programme and an intensive training of election officers.

The election campaign experienced violence in some areas, particularly in Kwa Zulu Natal and Johannesburg, and with sporadic outbreaks in other parts of the country. There were 'no-go' areas in a few parts of the country and non-cooperation by individual farmers. There was considerable loss of life, especially in KwaZulu Natal.

The political disagreements continued throughout the campaign and the Inkatha Freedom Party (IFP) whose base was in KwaZulu Natal only decided to contest the elections a few days before

Election Day. As a consequence the ballot papers had to be altered by pasting on the IFP logo and party thereto.

There was suspicion that some of the election officers attempted to sabotage the distribution of polling materials on polling day. I observed the polling in Tokosa in east Johannesburg where several stations were not opened by mid-morning because of lack of delivery of ballot papers. It was reported that millions of ballot papers were 'lost' or mislaid only to be found days after polling. There was also a short strike in some areas after the poll and before the counting of the votes was completed.

On the technical side, there were mistakes made, particularly with respect to reconciling the ballot papers delivered to stations with the voting returns. There was complete chaos at the counting centre at the stadium in Sweto where the reconciliation process had to be abandoned. Many stakeholders however held that the election was more about politics than about good practices in democratic elections. Politically, the 1994 elections were a celebration of the demise of one of the most hated political regimes of the twentieth century.

The Commonwealth observer mission was led by former Prime Minister Michael Manley of Jamaica and the Support team was led by Max Gaylard, Director of the Political Affairs Division of the Secretariat, with me standing for Max Gaylard when he was called away from the South Africa mission to go to Lesotho.

I was with the COG when they paid a courtesy call on President DeKlerk of South Africa. He was affable and courteous with the COG, but when he was asked if he would rejoin the Commonwealth if his party won the elections, his response suggested that he was not sure.

The year 1994 was a watershed not only for South Africa with its first democratic general election, but also for Malawi and Mozambique all of which I offered technical assistance and participated in election observation. Moreover, immediately after the Mozambique general election in October 1994, the Commonwealth Secretary-General dispatched me to South Africa at their request to advise them on the organization for the local elections which were set for 1995.

Malawi 1994

In 1994 Malawi held its first multiparty elections in several decades. The movement towards dismantling the one-party regime and the President for Life status that existed in Malawi was gradual. A referendum was held on the issue of replacing the one-party with a multiparty system and after a positive result from the referendum, structures were put in place to serve as a transition to multiparty elections in 1994, and a new constitution was at the same time designed to come into effect after the government which emerged from the multiparty elections was sworn in. As the Commonwealth Secretariat's representative to the Interim Council considering the interim and some permanent structures, such as a new Constitution, an electoral law, including the establishment of an independent electoral commission, I assisted with legal advice with respect to those instruments.

When the members of the Electoral Commission were named, I went to advise the Chairperson, Mrs. Justice Msosa, on putting together an initial programme. On behalf of the Commonwealth Secretariat, I offered technical assistance to the Commission in the areas of a media adviser, voter education and training of election officers. The Commonwealth team did well because they were very experienced election experts. The United Nations had a technical assistance team in Malawi at the time, and the leader of that team, Mr. Michael Meadowcroft, was uncomfortable with the Commonwealth's efforts, the Commonwealth's small team of experts were very experienced professionals who were familiar with Commonwealth election procedures.

The preparatory arrangements for the elections went well, but there were hiccups with the voters' registration exercise. Initially, the traditional methods of communicating with rural population were minimized in favour of up-to-date voter education programmes, but the new method did not produce the results desired. The period for registration was extended and the traditional methods, including notices on trees which were located in some remote areas, but were used traditionally to bear messages to the local residents, were resorted to with positive results.

The campaign was competitive and experienced sporadic violence which was blamed on the youth wing of the ruling party. However, in the early stages of the campaign the youth organization of the ruling party fell out with the Army and at one incident some youths were killed. The youth organization was disbanded and many of the members fled to rural areas.

The Commission had considerable problems with managing the election logistics, mainly due to shortage of motor vehicles to transport election materials. There was also a problem with communications between some field offices and the Headquarters office. The Commonwealth sent an observation mission led by a former Deputy Prime Minister of Malaysia, Mr. Musa Hitam, and the Commonwealth Support Team led by me.

Polling day passed off relatively smoothly and the opposition candidate, Mr. Muluzi, won, and putting an end to the Life President's tenure.

Post Script I

A few days before the elections, the COG paid a courtesy call on the President Banda at one his palaces. He was 75 minutes late. He came into the conference room unaided and using a walking-stick. There were sixteen of us in the group. The first three persons individually greeted the President and he responded with a slight rise and bow. Then, as though he was blocked out, he never acknowledged any other greeting. When the greeting from the other members of the group ended, the President came alive again and asked his Information Minister to read his welcome address. When an assistant of the President thought it was time for the Commonwealth Group to leave, she reminded him that he had another appointment, in response he was heard to say out loudly that he did not know of it. At that point the Commonwealth Group politely bade goodbye.

Post Script II

I was visiting a polling station with the Chairman of the COG and our Information Officer. I had a few pins with the Commonwealth logo which I gave to some youngsters who were hanging around the vicinity of the station. Then shortly afterwards a long stream of other youngsters came on asking for more pins. The police had to step in and move them away. It was an embarrassing moment.

Post Script III

I knew Michael Meadowcroft, the UN Officer heading its technical assistance mission in Malawi at time of the '94 elections; we had lunch together on a couple of occasions and discussed how the UN and the Commonwealth might work together. It was therefore a surprise to me when I went back to London to hear from the British Foreign and Commonwealth Office that Mr. Meadowcroft had sent in a negative report on the Commonwealth's efforts in Malawi. I treated the report with the contempt it deserved and it made no impression in the Commonwealth Secretariat. In fact, the Commonwealth's team headed by me was operating from the inside and was far more experienced than the UN's Team. When I returned to Malawi, a couple of Ambassadors alerted me to Mr. Meadowcroft's concerns and organised a breakfast meeting between us at the British High Commissioner's residence. The High Commissioner asked me to open the discussion and I snuffed any life from the conversation by indicating that as far as I knew there were no differences between the Commonwealth and the UN on assistance to Malawi. I indicated that we had agreed to collaborate as far as practicable and that that was happening. The meeting noted the position of the Commonwealth and discerned that there did not seem to be any dispute between the UN and the Commonwealth. The meeting ended on that note and Mr. Meadowcroft was not even invited to put his case at the breakfast meeting.

Mozambique 1994

Mozambique was not a member of the Commonwealth in 1994. However that country was the beneficiary of two Special Funds from the Commonwealth and had received technical assistance there under in areas, including elections, of democratic development, as well as mineral contracts. Indeed, I had advised the Electoral Commission until the holding of the elections, and, before that, the Ministry of Justice on certain electoral issues. Many months prior to the elections, the Commonwealth Secretariat mounted an election training session in Maputo, and closer to the elections, John Syson, a Commonwealth Secretariat colleague, and I were instrumental in organizing a retreat outside of Maputo where the Mozambican Electoral Commissioners met selected peer Electoral Commissioners from the region-Kenya, Malawi, South Africa, Zambia and Zimbabwe—to discuss the identification of problems impacting the electoral preparatory process and advance possible solutions.

The Government and Electoral Commission of Mozambique invited the Commonwealth to send election observers to the elections, but since Mozambique was not yet a member of the Commonwealth, it could not send an official observer mission, instead the Secretary-General of the Commonwealth sent two emissaries, John Syson and me, to represent him in witnessing the elections.

The UN provided security and technical inputs for the election preparation and conduct. The elections were well organized with stipulated numbers of persons per polling station over two days. Pregnant women and mothers with young children were given preference at polling stations. Despite a temporary disruption caused by the main opposition party ordering a boycott halfway during the first day of polling which caused the polls to be extended into a third day, the polling went off smoothly. The incumbent Government and party won the election and although the main opposition party was unhappy about the outcome of the election, the result stood.

Post Script

Renamo, the main opposition party contesting the first post-conflict elections in Mozambique in 1994, decided to call a boycott of the elections during polling, and purported to call off its polling agents from polling stations. The grounds were not clearly spelled out for the boycott and it clearly was not thought through. The boycott message did not reach all the agents as some continued to work at the stations. Whatever the discontent that was alleged—whether rigging or partisanship by the Commission, it had little or no foundation, since all seven, or the majority of them, opposition Commissioners, subscribed to an official statement by the Electoral Commission, disapproving of the opposition party's allegations as baseless. Eventually, the boycott was called off. This strange conduct of the main opposition was ill advised as it must have cost them the loss of many votes.

Tanzania 1995

The multiparty elections of 1995 in Tanzania were an important event and brought the end of one-party regimes in Africa closer. I went on a planning mission with the then Deputy Secretary-General, Mr. Srinivasan, to see how the election preparation was progressing. We made contact with many stakeholders, including opposition parties, some of which were under the impression that the Commonwealth favoured the ruling party and government. They were however in favour of the Commonwealth sending an observer mission to witness the elections.

The Chairman of the Electoral Commission, Justice Makame, initially requested technical assistance from the Commonwealth Secretariat, but made it clear that his Commission would have to approve the request. The Commission's Chairman had requested some thirteen Commonwealth election experts, mainly in the training of election officers and one from an election commission to strengthen the credibility of the management. Apparently the Commission did not go along with the Chairman's suggestion concerning the request of Commonwealth's training experts. Only the Chairperson of Malawi was accepted as the person who would work with the Commission.

The election campaign was relatively peaceful on the Mainland, but less so in Zanzibar. The Chairman of the COG, Mr. Rasleigh Jackson, a former Foreign Minister of Guyana, and I, head of the Commonwealth Secretariat Support Team to the COG, travelled extensively through Dar es Salaam, the capital, observing polling stations prior to polling day. We also flew to the shores of Lake Victoria at Mwanza to see what the preparation was like.

The elections in Zanzibar were held a few days before those on the Mainland. The COG's mission to Zanzibar was led by the Deputy Australian Electoral Commissioner. The Team found that the Zanzibar elections were poorly organized and allowed many irregularities to occur. The statements issued after the counting of votes at the polling stations were not officially authenticated and the figures of those statements differed from the figures entered on the tallying records. When the discrepancies were brought to the attention of the Zanzibar Electoral Commission, the response was that the statements of the count issued at the stations were not official as they were not authenticated. Invariably, the changed numbers recorded fewer votes for the opposition candidate at the presidential level for the Zanzibar Legislature. The opposition and their supporters in Zanzibar claimed, with some justification, that the election was stolen.

The Mainland had its fair share of problems, albeit of a different kind from Zanzibar's. The election logistics management in Dar es Salaam had a complete breakdown. The Chairman of the COG and I visited a number of polling stations on Election Day which were not opened at mid-morning when we arrived, due the absence of polling materials and, in some cases, polling officers who apparently had gone off to chase up the missing materials. Outside of Dar es Salaam, there was a worrying complaint of shortage of presidential ballot papers. Other COG teams received similar complaints about ballot shortage, but we were unable to detect any pattern, or any indication that there was a national conspiracy. It appeared that inexperience in ordering ballot papers might have led to the shortages. The ballot papers seemed to have been ordered in batches of 100 and did not take account of stations with less than 100 voters where the 100 batches were also dispatched.

The disarray in Dar es Salaam was so bad that the elections in all seven constituencies were aborted and had to re-run. Thankfully, outside Dar es Salaam, only one constituency had to be re-run. After the re-run, the Mainland elections were considered credible.

Post Script

Seeing the weakness in the logistics management in Dar es Salaam during the elections, shortly afterwards, on behalf of the Commonwealth Secretariat, I renewed the offer of technical assistance to the Tanzanian Electoral Commission and they accepted. Dr. Afari-Gyan, the Chairman of the Ghanaian Electoral Commission, was recruited for a six-week stint in Tanzania to develop a structure and programme for election logistics management. The Mainland, Tanzania, has done better than in 1995 ever since.

Some General Comments

Mindful of the timely gentle push start which Malaysia gave to the Commonwealth in the endeavour of systematic election observation in 1990 and also taking account of the Commonwealth's pre-election observation mission to Namibia in 1989 to which I was the technical adviser, the years 1989-1995 were truly wonderful experience in election observation. Interspersed with a good measure of technical electoral assistance, during the space of six years I had the privilege of observing some ten major general elections which, among other things, saw the deplorable apartheid system swept away into oblivion in two cases (Namibia and South Africa), the one-party regimes in six countries officially abandoned (Kenya, Guyana, Malawi, Mozambique, Tanzania, and Zambia), and democratic elections put on show temporarily for the world to see in two countries (Malaysia and Pakistan). It had been an unforgettable and wonderful experience!

Bangladesh 1996

The Commonwealth Secretary-General was invited to send a Commonwealth election observation mission to the Bangladesh general election in February in 1996. However, the main opposition party decided to boycott the election. The Commonwealth's policy then was to observe elections only if the main opposition party/parties together with the ruling party agreed to accept Commonwealth observers. The Secretary-General decided not to send a Commonwealth observer mission, but rather to send a small team of emissaries headed by me to talk with representatives of NGOs and distinguished members of academia in Bangladesh, while witnessing the election.

The days leading up to the elections were tense with sporadic violence which made it unsafe to wander about Dhaka. A similar situation prevailed on Election Day with rumours of scenes of violence and intimidation. Our delegation was advised to stay at our hotel on polling day for our safety. We organized to meet with selected Commonwealth Ambassadors to Bangladesh at our hotel to be briefed on the political and electoral developments.

The turn out on polling day was low, but the ruling party and their supporters were alleged to carry out ballot stuffing in order to inflate the turn out figures. The ballot rigging attempts discredited the election results and had the effect of reducing the largely uncontested elections to a farce.

Guyana 1997

The Commonwealth sent an observer mission to the Guyana 1997 elections under the leadership of former President of Tanzania, Mr. Mwinyi, and the Secretariat's Support Team led by me. After the experience of the 1992 elections which saw a measure of violence and dissatisfaction with the election organization, it was hoped that this time the election would pass off smoothly. The Chairman of the COG and I observed the polling in Georgetown and its environs and there were no major incidents. We also observed the count at a station in Georgetown and it went well. Later that evening we met Mr. Hoyte, Leader of the Opposition, and he brought certain evidence of what he deemed to be irregularities during the tallying process to our attention. The concern of the opposition deepened when the tallying process seemed to have been compromised by poor organization. The COG found that the protracted period of verification during which the Commission announced partial election results created an environment in which each of the major parties claimed victory prematurely. The totals of the data spreadsheets did not add up accurately and did not tally with the party representatives' numbers and there had been manual overwriting of the totals in the computer system.

There was also dissatisfaction with the manner in which the Chairman of the Elections
Commission announced the results of the election on 19 December before the count was completed. On that date the Chairman announced that the ruling party had received the largest number of votes and its leader was declared the President of Guyana, although the tallying process was not yet completed. The Chairman explained that on the basis of the Commission's projection, even if all the remaining votes went to the opposition, PNC, it could not achieve a majority. The dissatisfaction led to the rejection of the results by the opposition and triggered widespread violence. Eventually, an inquiry into the organization of the election results was ordered and the votes were audited. Elections were set for a date two years ahead of the normal schedule.

The 1997 Guyana elections needlessly descended into confusion which triggered violence in part because the election was conducted in a manner that was not transparent, particularly the vote-tallying process. The Chairman of the Commission failed to consult with all his Commissioners in a manner which would facilitate collective responsibility to important decision-making with respect to the tallying of the votes and the announcement of the election results.

Nigeria 1998-99
Soon after the sudden death of President Abacha in 1998, a new Head of State was installed in Nigeria. The new Administration announced that it would return the country to civilian rule. The then Secretary-General, Chief Emeka Anyaoku, himself a Nigerian, dispatched me to Abuja to organize Commonwealth's technical assistance to the Nigerian Independent National Electoral

Commission (INEC). I worked closely with the then Chairman of INEC, Justice Ephraim Akpata and his staff.

In order to help the Commission along with improving the quality of election organization, Justice Akpata asked me to observe each of the series of elections that was set for 1998 and 1999 and make proposals to strengthen the weak points in the subsequent elections.[6] The Commonwealth provided a team of trainers of trainers of election officers prior to both the Local Government Councils Elections and the State Assembly and Gubernatorial Elections. The Commonwealth Secretariat also provided an experienced Indian election logistics expert to assist the Commission in planning the logistics arrangement for the elections.

I observe the two first stages of the elections for the INEC and the final stage, that is to say, the National Assembly and Presidential Elections, 20 & 27 February 1999 as a member of the Commonwealth Secretariat Support Team to the COG.

Given the circumstances in which the series of elections took place, they went off reasonably well. It took the INEC just about four months to organize the series of elections in a post-dictatorship regime and where for many years regular democratic elections had not been conducted. Nevertheless, throughout the series of elections the shortcomings were obvious—

- Shortage of electoral materials, including ballot papers and polling screens;
- Poor physical arrangements at polling stations which impacted adversely on the secrecy of the ballot;
- Failure to fold properly or at all ballot papers;
- Failure to use the indelible ink, as required by the rules; and
- Failure to lock ballot boxes.

---

[6] The series of elections were: Stage 1-Local Government Councils Elections, 5 December 1998; Stage 2- State Assembly and Governorship Elections, 9 January 1999; and Stage 3- National Assembly and Presidential Elections, 20 and 27 February 1999 respectively.

Many of these shortcomings reflected lack of adequate training of election officers. There was a high degree of motivation on the part of the electorate to return to civilian administration. The elections were a great success politically, but from the point of view of technicality the organization and conduct of the series of elections needed much improvement to achieve good practices.

Post Script I

On the polling day of the Local Government Councils Elections, towards the end of the accreditation process which took place ahead of the commencement of polling, two ballot boxes were brought into a station each about one third full of ballot papers. I drew the attention of the presiding officer to the ballot papers in the ballot boxes and suggested that she should investigate the matter. She did and discovered that the ballot papers were from a previous election. The next step was what to with those ballot papers and she turned to me for suggestions and I advised that she should publicly announce the position and dispose of the ballot papers publicly. That was done and the matter ended there.

Post Script II

At a polling station in the district outside Abuja, while the presiding officer was attending to the accreditation process a padlock was left unlocked on the ballot box. Unseen by anyone, an intruder came into the station, locked the ballot box with the key and went away with the key. At the end of the accreditation process the key could not be found and polling was held up while another ballot box had to be secured.

Zanzibar (Tanzania) 2000

The Zanzibar election 2000 was observed by a COG led by Dr. Gaositwe Chiepe and the Secretariat Support Team was led by me. After the outcry about the conduct of the 1995 elections, much assistance was offered to the Zanzibar Electoral Commission and the Zanzibar Government to improve the electoral process. The 2000 elections were disappointing. The COG was constrained to declare them to be not credible due to poor organization and rigging of the votes. The COG found that the conduct of the election fell far short of minimum standards. There was failure to deliver ballot papers in good time which caused cancellation of the election in 16 constituencies, and suspension of the elections in a further 34 constituencies. It concluded that the cause of these actions was either deliberate manipulation or gross incompetence. In addition, the COG expressed concern about the adequacy and credibility of the voters' register and the role of the sheha (government official) at registration centres. Further, the COG felt that the voter education programme was inadequate and that the imbalance in the state-owned media needed correction. The COG made a number of recommendations to improve election organization in Zanzibar.

Post Script

An enduring election anecdote was encountered in Stone Town in Unguja, Zanzibar, in 2000. It was a moonlit night at about 9.30 p.m. and many polling stations at the sports stadium were still open awaiting promised ballot papers which never arrived. Then suddenly appearing at the far end of the stadium was the silhouette of a man with a bed and mattress on his head making his way in silence across the stations to the one where he should vote. He made his point without saying a word. The ballot papers never arrived.

Trindad & Tobago 2000

The Commonwealth sent an observer mission to the 2000 general elections in Trinidad and Tobago led by Hon. Roy MacLaren, PC, a former Canadian Cabinet Minister and diplomat, and a Secretariat Support Team led by me. It was the first time that the Commonwealth was invited to send observers to elections in Trinidad and Tobago.

There were two incidents that occurred in the preparatory stages for polling. The first was a couple of cases where nominated candidates with dual nationality improperly but successfully stood for nomination. It was drawn to our attention but was clearly a matter for the courts.[7] The other incident allegedly occurred when

---

[7]   The two candidates were successful at the polls and were made ministers but were subsequently disqualified. –The Constitution of Trinidad & Tobago forbids

some members of the ruling party caused persons who did not reside in marginal constituencies to register therein. That act of cheating triggered an inquiry and several prosecutions.

Those incidents apart, the elections were close but went off smoothly.

Post Script

The rule requires a person to register in the constituency in which he/she resides, provided that he/she has resided in that constituency for a period of two months or more. Despite the apparently clear rules on the matter, there had been a longstanding practice in Trinidad & Tobago whereby persons vote at their ancestral home regardless of where they lived and the practice was followed by many voters from the ruling party as well as opposition parties. Because of this practice, both major parties were hesitant to mount challenges to persons suspected of voting in districts where they no longer lived, despite the improper registration in marginal constituencies. As a consequence, the well—publicised promise by opposition candidates to mount challenges to voters at polling stations on grounds of residence never materialized.

---

a person with dual nationality to sit in the House of Representatives.

CHAPTER IV

Election Legal Expert—Technical Assistance

Jamaica (National Gov.)
Kenya (Commonwealth Secretariat)
Malawi (Commonwealth Secretariat)
Zambia (Commonwealth Secretariat)
South Africa (Commonwealth Secretariat)
Sierra Leone; (Commonwealth Secretariat)
Nigeria (Commonwealth Secretariat/ UN/DfID)
Lesotho (DFID-ERIS)
Guyana, 2004-06 (USAID-RTI)
Tanzania 2004 (UNDP Central register)
Antigua Barbuda (Commonwealth)
Cayman Islands (National Gov.)
Liberia (European Commission)
Indonesia, Aceh, USAID—2006.

Jamaica 1979
Chapter I sets out the range of legal assistance which I offered to the reform of the Jamaican electoral programme in 1979. It covered the reform policy and modernization of the election management structure and various amendments to the election legislative scheme, which impacted positively on the procedures relating to the major election processes.

Kenya 1992
Through the Commonwealth Secretariat's electoral technical assistance programme to Kenya in 1992 prior to the elections of that year, I assisted the Attorney-General's Office in drafting a law relating to international election observers. I also advised the ECK,

through its then Chairman, Justice Chesoni, on a code of conduct for international election observers.

Zambia 1994

In 1994, at the request of the Zambian Government, the Commonwealth Secretary-General dispatched me to Zambia to advise the Government on ways to update the voters' register. I was asked specifically to address the issue of whether or not it was feasible to upgrade the national identification system into a voter identification system. Upon examining the national ID system, I came to the view that, although it was possible, the required safeguards to achieve best practice were such that the time available would militate against that approach.

Malawi 1994

As the chief liaison official of the Commonwealth Secretariat to the reform process relating to the interim constitutional and electoral regimes prior to the 1994 elections, I worked with the Interim Committee on the Constitution which came into force after the 1994 elections. I worked as a kind of sounding consultant on certain constitutional issues, for example, the nature of provisions that would shape an independent electoral commission and provisions that would allow for independent candidates to contest elections. I also worked with the Solicitor-General on the Electoral Law, including the provisions which would establish an independent electoral commission.

South Africa 1995—6

I advised and vetted some of the draft regulations for the Local Government Elections of 1995 as a part of the Commonwealth's technical assistance to South Africa. In a similar vein, I assisted with framing the electoral law and the Constitution, particularly those provisions relating to elections as well as the formula to make the electoral commission an independent entity.

Sierra Leone 1996

Under the Commonwealth Secretariat's programme to Sierra Leone, I reviewed the legal framework for elections when Dr Jonah took over as Chairman of the Electoral Commission. I prepared certain urgently needed regulations and identified an electoral legal expert to continue reform of the electoral legislative scheme for Sierra Leone.

Lesotho 2001 & 2004

In 2001, I embarked on my first private consultancy project (after retirement from the Commonwealth Secretariat) for the Electoral Reform International Services (ERIS) and funded by the Department for International Development (DfID). The project entailed advice to the Independent Electoral Commission (IEC) of Lesotho on an election complaint and disputes procedure and drafting suitable regulations there for. The terms of reference (TOR) also included the drafting of election rules and procedures for registration and for the MMP Model pursuant to draft regulations to the National Assembly Act 1992 and the National Assembly Regulations 2001.

In 2004, I did another assignment for ERIS-DfID in Lesotho. The TOR in part stipulated that the consultant was required to:

- Research alternative models of management currently employed in other IECs or similar quasi-autonomous organizations;

- Research existing elections and other legislation (Government and Public Sector) to clarify supporting or negating legislation that may need revision;

- Liaise with internal stakeholders—Commissioners, the Director of Election and Chief Legal Officer—in facilitating discussion and development of ideas; and

- Assist the Chief Legal Officer in the development of draft outline 'instruments' legal or internal for the revised framework.

These two projects were aimed at improving the operation of the new electoral system, the mixed member proportional (MMP), which Lesotho had then recently adopted.

Antigua/Barbuda 2001

As a private election consultant in 2001, the Commonwealth Secretariat secured my services to implement the COG's recommendations with respect to Antigua and Barbuda, made during an election observer mission to the 1999 general election in that country. The basic recommendations of the COG were that the Government should establish an independent electoral commission with mandate to create a new register, a system of identification cards, redrawing of constituency boundaries and review the electoral law. The Commission should have responsibilities to select and train electoral officials, who should reflect the independence and impartiality of the electoral commission.

The assignment was for approximately four months during which time I undertook the following tasks:

- Extensive amendments to the Representation of the People Act paying particular attention to the establishment of an independent electoral commission with security of tenure for its members and clothing it with legal ability to hire and fire its own staff; the amending Act strengthened the registration provisions and created stiffer penalties for breach of the electoral law; it also created a regime for disclosure of contribution to election campaigns.
- Preparation of a set of media regulations for the purposes of election coverage;
- Revision of election rules; and
- Revision of registration regulations.

The amended Representation of the People Act was passed by Parliament during my stay in Antigua/Barbuda.

Cayman Islands 2003
In 2003, the Government of the Cayman Islands awarded me three separate election assignments, namely, Chairman of the Election Boundary Commission; construction of a voter education programme; and review and modernization of the electoral laws. Only the latter will be considered here.

The modernization of the elections laws of the Cayman Islands entailed bringing of the laws in line with developments such as the recognition of computer printed documents-reports and other computer-generated documents such as lists of voters. The changes also reflected the changes which were taking place locally, for example, references to 'electoral districts' gave way to 'constituencies'.

There were also substantial changes in the electoral legislative scheme generally penalties for election breaches increased. A transparent and impartial regime for the registration of political parties was developed. The management structure of election logistics was strengthened and postal voting procedures were clarified and made more user-friendly. The regime for election expenses was expanded and made to apply to both candidates and political parties.

Nigeria 2003-04
Since the restoration of civilian rule in Nigeria in 1999, there had been a determined but unsuccessful attempt to construct an electoral legislative scheme that facilitated best practices in election organization in all tiers of government in that country. The first post—transitional national elections of 2003 were not well organized and so in July of that year, in collaboration with a number of partners an Electoral Review Team was established. The Report of the Review Team recommended far-reaching reforms, including the establishment of a truly independent national electoral commission.

In my capacity of an election consultant, I was recruited by the UN Election Assistance Division to draft the amendments proposed by the Report of the Review Team for the consideration of the INEC and the Nigerian Government. It was a significant challenge, but one that was well within my grasp as an election legal specialist.

In preparing the draft amendments to Electoral Act, I took account of the recommendations of the Review Team, but also of recommendations made by several seminars, international and local on the inadequacies of the 2003 elections. Many of the recommendations had implications for the Nigerian Constitution, particularly those provisions that related to elections.

The main focus of the reform was aimed at the INEC. It had to be made to be seen to be more independent of the ruling political party of the day. An optional formula for the appointment of the Chairman and members of the Electoral Commission, as well as the appointment of regional commissioners who were appointed directly by the President of Nigeria, was put forward for consideration to replace the existing formula. The INEC was established by a Decree of 1998 and needed to be reviewed. The new draft was aimed at improving transparency, non-partisanship and preservation of the integrity of the electoral system. It was inspired by the EMBs' schemes then in Commonwealth countries such as Australia, Canada, Barbados, Ghana, India, Malta, Namibia, and South Africa. The central attributes of the reformed commission would be its independence, the transparency and efficiency of its performance. In order to implement the reforms proposed, a few changes to the relevant constitutional provisions, namely, *inter alia,* selection and appointment of the chairman and members of the Commission; extended functions of the Commission; modification of the management structure of the electoral process; and restructuring of the funding of the Commission; needed to be made.

The draft reforms were extensive and along with consequential changes the entire Electoral Act was affected and so eventually the draft was included in a consolidated Bill, incorporating the INEC Act of 1998. The proposed changes to the Constitution were drafted separately. The proposed reforms encompassed changes to the major election processes such as delimitation of constituencies/

electoral districts; continuous voters' registration; registration of political parties; registration of candidates to contest elections (nominations); election expenses; election petitions; and increased penalties for breaches of the provisions of the Electoral Act.

I began the process of discussing the draft Bill with the President's Office, Ministry of Justice and with the Legal Adviser to the Assembly before my assignment ended.

In 2004, the Government produced a Bill to amend the Electoral Act of 2002. Wearing another hat, as it were, as a consultant employed by the International Foundation for Election Systems (IFES), I was engaged in March 2005 to carry out an on-going review of the INEC draft Election Bill 2004 and to provide a written analysis for consideration of Nigerian Stakeholders; and to highlight divergences between the law and international standards and regional best practices.

In perusing the 2004 Government Bill, I noted that it incorporated much of the draft that I had done on my UN assignment. However, crucial aspects dealing with the reform of the INEC and changes to the Constitution were not included in the Government Bill. Also the procedures dealing with the registration of candidates to contest the elections were not incorporated in the Government Bill. Apart from the issue of independence of the INEC which had not been addressed in the Bill, the nomination procedures were of practical significance since they were the cause of utter chaos at the 2003 elections. The reason was the absence of a firm cut-off date for the substitution of candidates to contest the election. Candidates' names or photos were not placed on the ballot paper and so the cut-off date for replacing candidates was 14 days before Election Day. The chopping and changing of prospective candidates until the last minute was facilitated by the farcical nature of the major parties' primaries where 'dummy' candidates' names were put on the list of nominated candidates to meet the legal requirements and subsequently 'withdrawn' when a 'suitable' replacement was found.

It was little surprise to election commentators familiar with the intricate workings of the Nigerian election environment when the subsequent general election in 2007 met a fate even worse than that of 2003 in terms of credibility.

Liberia 2004/2005/2006

During the years of 2004-06, I was engaged as an election consultant in Liberia pursuant to three service contracts, two with the European Commission and one with UNDP. The first of these contracts was signed in June 2004 with Channel Research Ltd on behalf of the European Commission and was for 90 days with the possibility for extension up to 120 days. The extension did materialize. The terms of reference (TOR) included the following: design of an election system for Liberia; assist in drafting an election law/electoral regulations for the 2005 elections and advise on issues as boundary delimitations, voter registration, and other crucial steps in election preparations.

Pursuant to this contract, much time was spent on reviewing the Constitution to find out what clauses could be suspended under the powers conferred under the Comprehensive Peace Agreement (CPA).[8] A number of the provisions of the Constitution had to be suspended in order to effect the changes necessary to organize democratic multiparty elections. The electoral system had to be reviewed and constituencies' boundaries be modified. New rules had to be designed for the registration of political parties and codes of conduct for parties and officials prepared. I worked closely with the Legal Department of the National Electoral Commission (NEC) of Liberia in discharging my EC mandate. (The UN had promised to send a legal expert but was late in doing so.)

The second consultancy service contract was entered into directly between the European Commission and me, and covered a 4-month period from March to June 2005. The TOR for this period included:

---

[8]   The Constitution of Liberia could only be amended through referendum.

- Preparation and conduct of voter education for registration of voters;
- Preparation and conduct of registration;
- Assisting with the drafting of regulations, guidelines, manuals and election procedures; and
- Preparation of demarcation of electoral districts.

The second phase of the second EC contract contained TOR as follows:

- Assist the NEC with the application of the formula for the allocation of seats for the House of Representatives;
- Assist with the amalgamation of electoral precincts into electoral districts which will each send one representative to the House of Representatives;
- Assist in finalization of the voters' roll;
- Advise NEC on management of election logistics;
- Monitor and advise on the effectiveness of the voter education programmes and the contribution of civil society organizations;
- Monitor the quality of services delivered on polling day, particularly to disabled persons;
- Furnish a report to EC's office on polling; and
- Monitor the counting of votes and announcement of results.

Emphasis was placed on certain specific tasks, namely, to:

- Advise the EC's Office in Liberia on the progress of the preparations for the 2005 elections;
- Advise the National Electoral Commission (NEC) on good practice in election organization, preparation and conduct leading up to the 2005 elections;
- Assist the NEC's Legal Section with the drafting of regulations with respect to registration of voters, elections, political parties, vetting manuals for training of election officers and voter education trainers; codes of conduct for NEC, political parties and media houses;

- Work closely with advisers of the principal donors, UNMIL and IFES-USAID, and the NEC on matters relating to the 2005 elections;
- Conduct seminars on specific issues of need in election preparation for NEC's senior staff;
- Work closely with other entities, namely, NGOs, multilateral and bilateral donors, as well as community-based bodies, where appropriate, to assist the full participation of political parties, candidates, and their representatives in all stages of the preparatory process for and conduct of the lections;
- Assist the NEC to set up a proper mechanism for the accreditation and operation of domestic and international observers.

UNMIL (United Nations Mission in Liberia) was the lead international organization offering aid and technical assistance to Liberia and so I worked closely with them and with the NEC and also with IFES-USAID which was another significant partner. I delivered on all the requirements of the EC's TOR to their satisfaction.

The EC contributed approximately equivalent of four million US dollars towards the election preparation, including voter education, through a Fund administered by the UNDP and supervised by a Committee of which I was a member.

The third consultancy service contract for Liberia was concluded with UNDP in Liberia from 10 July to 8 September 2006. The TOR included:

- Institutional review and capacity-building programs of NEC;
- Review existing organizational structure of NEC;
- Advise on a framework for electoral reform in Liberia;
- Advise on the training needs for NEC; and
- Preparation of a road map for holding local (chieftaincy and municipal) elections.

These terms of reference triggered a detailed examination and recommendations with respect to the needs of Liberia in its preparation for the second post-conflict elections. The under-mentioned summary of the findings and recommendations were indicative of Liberia's needs:

1. Institutional Review—There is urgent need for institutional review for the following reasons:

    *   The NEC that conducted the 2005 elections was a reconstituted body under the CPA. It lacked experience in election organisation and depended to a large extent on the advice of partners.
    *   Considerable reform to the election laws were introduced by NEC under the authority of the CPA in 2004-05 in order to deliver free and fair elections in 2005, but those provisions fell away when the new Government took Office in 2006.
    *   It is therefore necessary to review the current structures to ensure that they will in future be capable of delivering free and fair elections.

2. Capacity Building—During the preparation for the 2005 elections, NEC was assisted by a significant contingent of election experts from partners, particularly UNMIL, supported by EC and IFES. It is unlikely that partners will be as forthcoming with expert assistance to the same extent for future elections. NEC needs to train its own staff to the level required to enable it to organize free and fair multiparty elections to acceptable international standards.

3. Organizational Structure—The organizational structure of the reconstituted NEC in 2004 was done to meet the needs of the transitional elections in 2005. That structure was reviewed and modified, along with considerable down-sizing. The TOR for my assignment was fashioned against this background. Nevertheless, I identified areas where further down-sizing could be undertaken, and refinements could be made to the organizational chart. While NEC has accepted the latter changes,

it has shown reluctance to consider any further reduction in the permanent staff complement.

4. Electoral Reform—The electoral reform that is necessary falls into two broad categories, namely, (a) constitutional provisions touching elections and (b) provisions of the New Elections Law.

    (a) Constitutional provisions relating to elections fall into two categories, namely those provisions which were suspended under the Electoral Reform Law 2004 and which have now been restored, and those that were not suspended largely because they had much wider implications than electoral matters, for example, the term of the Presidency and of Legislators.
    The procedure to effect changes to the Constitution is different from that of amending the New Election Law, as while in respect of amendments to the latter, NEC may send its proposals directly to the Legislature, it has no such standing which respect to proposals for constitutional change.

    (b) With respect to reform of the New Elections Law, for convenience two categories of provisions could be taken into account, namely, the provisions which were amended by the Electoral Reform Law 2004 which now ceased to have effect, and those provisions which were not so altered, but are in need of review to see if they can be improved.

Electoral Law Reform Task Force—This entity is proposed to undertake as a matter of urgency the identification and drafting of changes necessary to the electoral legislative scheme of Liberia. The Legal Section of NEC would lead the Task Force, with inputs by the NEC's Legal Consultant and, if needed, assisted by an election lawyer with knowledge of international good practices.

Training Needs of NEC—The training needs of NEC are clearly spelt out in the Strategic Plan 2006-2011. It stated that 'currently, all the major divisions and department of the Commission require electoral management skills and competences relevant to their domain of operations. It is therefore essential to expose the Commission staff to continuous elections management skills and training.'

Consistent with the need expressed in the Plan, the Report has proposed an intensive program and action plan to be conducted over a 30-week period (not necessarily consecutively) and covering all facets of election organization. All categories of staff will be covered in their respective sphere of work, albeit with varying degrees of intensity.

Local (Chieftaincy & Municipal) Elections—A road map for these elections has been set out as required in the TOR. The proposed road map sets out the following principal election processes to be undertaken before these elections can take place:

- Promulgation of guidelines by NEC under section 1.7 of the New Elections Law.
- Identification and delimitation of the boundaries of cities, paramount, clan and zones chiefdoms.
- Registration of voters.
- Registration (nominations) of candidates (including independent candidates) to contest the elections.
- The conduct of appropriate public awareness programs.
- Mobilize funds for the preparation and conduct of the elections; and
- Preparation of an election calendar with respect to the preparation and conduct of the local elections.

The Way Forward-
Organizational Structure
With respect to the organizational structure NEC has agreed to minor changes to the organizational chart, but there seems to be little chance, except budgetary constraints, of NEC scaling back the complement of permanent staff as recommended in the report.

Electoral Reform
The Electoral Reform Task Force should begin work as soon as practicable, so that the appropriate amendments to the New Election Law can be passed in time to be used in the local elections.

Training Needs of NEC
Securing funds to launch this training action program is the starting point. The training facility needs to be secured and equipped. The facilitators will have to identified and engaged on a timely basis. The Personnel Section and the Procedures and Training Section will be responsible to get the program up and running.

Road Map for the Local (Chieftaincy & Municipal) Elections
The budgetary funds need to be mobilized so that the delimitation of the election units can be demarcated and registration of voters undertaken. The legal framework (promulgation of the guidelines) should be done by NEC.

Tanzania 2004
The UNDP, Tanzania, offered me a consultancy contract in 2004 to advise the EMB of Tanzania on amendments to the Electoral Law to enable a Permanent National Voters' Register to be created. It was a straightforward task which I completed in a few weeks, working out of the UNDP's Office in Dar es Salaam, Tanzania.

Guyana 2005/06
During the period 2005 to 2006 I was offered two assignments in Guyana funded by USAID. The first was with RTI International from July to October 2005. The particulars of that contract were clearly stipulated. The purpose of assignment was to redraft and modernize the elections laws of Guyana. The exercise was aimed at modernizing the election laws and make them transparent and accessible to all political parties, civil society and other stakeholders in Guyana. The task was to review phase I report; study good practice and international standards in electoral legislative designs; review regional and international legislative schemes; recommend inputs to relevant stakeholders; and draft a modernized law. The

implementation procedures were set out in the TOR as follows, the Consultant was required to:

- Meet with the Ambassador, USAID and relevant staff of the Mission;
- Meet with the Chairman of GECOM and other stakeholders recommended by him.
- Liaise with the staff of the GDCCR Project throughout the exercise;
- Consultant to meet all senior staff members of the Guyana Elections Commission ;
- Meet with all Commissioners;
- Review documents produced by Phase I consultancy;
- Review of the Reference Manual prepared by the consultants engaged to conduct Phase I which focused on reviewing and consolidating of the electoral laws of Guyana;
- Review requirements of GECOM (prepared by GECOM)
- Review all laws and Acts related to elections in Guyana
- Study good practices and international standards in electoral legislative designs and discuss information with GECOM
- Conduct comparative analysis of regional and international electoral legislative schemes and discuss with GECOM
- Redraft existing legislation and introduce new legislation to fill the gaps, clarify ambiguities, and eliminate contradictions in the existing laws (Special emphasis should be placed on the section of the aforementioned manual related to identification of the lacunae, ambiguities, contradictions and general deficiencies existing in the current legislation);
- Liaise; *inter alia,* with the Phase I Consultancy Group, Stakeholders, The Attorney-General's Office and, the Chief Parliamentary Counsel.

A collection of the relevant laws relating to elections in Guyana was done by a group of local consultants and my task was essentially to review those laws and propose reforms.

The second contract in 2006 was with Democracy International in March 2006. Its mandate was to review all training manuals of GECOM.

Aceh (Indonesia) 2006
I was offered an assignment under the Democratic Reform Support program (DRSP)-USAID in Aceh, Indonesia in 2006. The TOR was as follows:

Election Management Specialist for the
Independent Election Commission (*Komisi Independent Pemilihan*—KIP), Aceh

The Election Management Specialist will:

- Advise KIP on all aspects of administration of the local elections (*Pilkada*), for example: implementation of staff training; procurement of materials; polling station locations; timeframe for election implementation stages; voter and electoral participant registration; and development of case management system for handling cases of administrative violations;

- Advise KIP on the development of the Qanun regulating the Aceh *Pilkada* including but not limited to legal drafting of regulations, and inclusion of civil society input (e.g. NGOs, ulama, women's groups, students, academia, GAM, etc) into the Qanun;

- Provide technical assistance to KIP for their meetings with external stakeholders, such as: the national parliament, the Ministry of Home Affairs, and the local government;

- Assist DRSP partner organizations in the process of revising provincial regulations (*Qanun*) as they relate to the *Pilkada* process;

- Participate in partner and donor coordination meetings in Aceh and Jakarta.

- Provide regular and ad hoc reports to DRSP and USAID on activities conducted and on the local elections process in Aceh;

- Provide a comprehensive report of activities on completion of assignment.

This assignment was not very productive. I was expecting a six to nine-month stint; instead I spent only six weeks during which time there was very little to do as Parliament of Indonesia had not enacted the main election legislation pursuant to which the Provincial Regulations would be drafted.

CHAPTER V

Constituency delimitation involvement

Jamaica—review of constituencies/polling divisions;
Malawi local govt. wards/constituencies
South Africa
Liberia
Cayman Islands Chairman of Electoral Boundary
Commission—2003/10
Factors to take care of: fairness;
Demography;
Participation by stakeholders.

Introduction

"In order to hold an election, some political organisation of space is necessary. This may include delimiting electoral districts for electing representatives, determining questions of residence for voters and potential office-holders, creating voting areas and assigning eligible voters to the appropriate voting area or choosing the optimal location for voting stations."[9] The process of constituency boundary construction should be fair and conform to stipulated criteria consistent with recognised best election practices. Specifically, the boundaries of constituencies and other electoral districts should not be gerrymandered to favour any political party or candidate.

Some new and emerging democracies whose electoral system requires boundaries of electoral districts to be constructed

---

[9]   See paper by Lisa Handley of the ACE Project, *"The Use of GIS [geographical information system] for Redistricting", in* Electoral Reform in the Commonwealth African Countries, ed. Carl W Dundas, Commonwealth Secretariat.

frequently neglect to undertake such delimitation on a timely basis or at all. The result is often inequitable distribution of voters in constituencies or electoral districts. As a consequence of this frequent neglect, I have given a more lengthy background to the construction of fair boundaries of electoral districts. As will be seen later in this chapter, I have done considerable specialist work in this area and would like to see much more progress in this area in countries like Kenya, Malaysia, Nigeria and Zimbabwe.

Abuse in boundary making

The phrase *gerrymandering electoral districts' boundaries* signifies a first line of low-key election manipulation. It actually refers to the act of delimiting an electoral district in a distorted manner for political purposes. The phrase originated in the United States of America where it was used to describe the practice of one Elbridge Gerry, Governor of Massachusetts in 1812. The practice of gerrymandering has been expanded to encompass much more than distorted electoral districts. The ruling party of some States indulges in systematic manipulation of the variation of the size, shape and population of constituencies and other polling districts in order to secure political advantage.

In order to determine whether or not gerrymandering occurred in demarcating constituencies or other polling districts, not only its characteristics need to be identified, but also some issues of a legal and practical nature have to be dealt with. Straightforward questions may arise, for example, should all constituencies contain an equal number of voters? Or should each vote be of equal value?

General Approach

The boundaries of constituencies or other polling districts are usually constructed according to a formula in the constitution or electoral law of the country concerned. (Although there are jurisdictions where the polling districts' boundaries follow those of administrative districts and in the cases where certain proportional representation systems are used polling districts are unnecessary.) The provisions relating to the drawing of the boundaries of polling districts often revolve around the population or the size of the electorate in each district in the country. This primary consideration is frequently impacted upon by factors, such as topographical features, administrative boundaries, sparse population and poor communication means. The substratum of gerrymandering polling districts' boundaries resides in the disproportionate distribution of the electorate in those districts. In order to avoid unfair boundary delimitation, most jurisdictions provide for a deviation above or below the electoral or election quota, which is arrived at by dividing the population of country, or the political unit to be delimited, by the number of legislative seats allocated to that country or political unit. The level of deviation above or below the quota will be a factor in determining whether unfairness in the demarcation of the boundary was in play. The shape of the boundaries of the polling districts impacts on their fairness, for example, diamond shaped boundaries, that is to say, that they are not contiguous, may be evidence of unfairness in the boundary construction. The presence of any or all these factors in the delimitation of polling districts' boundaries is not necessarily proof of intentional gerrymandering. However their presence is an indication that the delimitation process should be carefully examined to detect any evidence of a pattern to manipulate the process.

Impact of Gerrymandering

Consistent with the search for fair boundary delimitation and the avoidance of gerrymandering of polling districts' boundaries, is the need to consider whether or not free and fair elections require that each constituency or polling district in a country or political unit should have an electorate of equal population. This issue was explored in Australia by the High Court in *McGinty & Others v The State of Western Australia*[10]. In that case the Court was asked to decide whether, in an election for the Legislative Council or the Legislative Assembly for the State of Western Australia, the number of persons eligible to vote for or required to elect a member in one

---

[10] McGinty et al v. The State of Western Australia (1996) in Compendium of Election Laws, Practices and Cases of Selected Commonwealth Countries, Vol. 2, Part 1 p.97 ed. Carl W. Dundas, (1998) Commonwealth Secretariat; see also [1995] HCA 46, (1996) 186 CLR 140.

electorate (constituency) should be approximately the same as the number of persons eligible to vote for or required to elect a member in another electorate (constituency). The plaintiffs contended that every legally capable adult was entitled to vote in such an election and that each vote, so far as it was reasonably practicable, should be equal in value.

The Court did not agree with the plaintiffs' argument and found that there was no constitutional requirement for each polling district to have an equal number of electors and that there was no right of each individual elector to participate in the electoral process on an equal basis. Some of the Judges in that case examined the practice and court rulings in other jurisdictions to assist their consideration of the issues raised. McHugh J, after reviewing cases in the United States of America and Canada on the matter of equal representation, stated that although the gap between the largest and the smallest electoral divisions in all Australian States had narrowed considerably over the last century, the governments of Australia had consistently legislated for inequalities, which had generally favoured the non-metropolitan areas.[11] Similarly, Gummow J, after reviewing a number of American and Canadian cases[12] on the question of equality of numbers of electors within electoral districts, concluded that the evolution of representative government in the United States which favoured a strict adherence to equal representation, was different form that of Australia and Canada. He express the view the "equal value" was not an essential or inherent feature of "representative government" as was historically understood in Australia.

The notion of equal number of voters in polling districts has been frowned upon in many countries and therefore the unjustifiable deviation from the electoral quota is difficult to determine. This

---

[11]   Ibid. At page 167.

[12]   See Baker v Carr (1962) 369 US 186; Wesbury v Saunders (1964) 376 US 1; Kirkpatrick v Preisler (1969) 394 US 526; Mahan v Howell (1973) 410 US 315; Brown v Thompson (1983) 462 US 835; Dixon v British Columbia (Attorney General) (1989) 59DLR (4th) 247.

situation is further complicated by the fact that many countries allow a generous margin of tolerance, up to 25%, above or below the electoral quota. Genuine deviation from the electoral quota due to geographical, population distribution, communications or communities' consideration is often included in the boundary delimitation formula. However, these factors, which may give rise to deviation from the strict application of the quota, frequently set the stage for manipulation of the drawing of the polling district boundaries through irregularly shaped districts. Excessive manipulation in this manner may create electoral disadvantage for some political parties, and may form a part of the plan of the beneficiary party to gain undue advantage from boundary construction.

Good Practice

In order to avoid the delimitation of polling districts' boundaries playing any part in stealing an election by stealth, good election practice exists to reduce the opportunity to create partisan or unfair polling districts' boundaries. The search for good practice must commence with an examination of the formula dealing with the delimitation of polling districts' boundaries and the body that applies the formula. Many of the formulae dealing with electoral boundaries are intentionally flexible in order to minimise complaints and, in some cases, to avoid legal action. The application of a clear and strict formula based on equal population is likely to result in multiple challenges both of a political and legal nature for which the American redistricting process is well known. A random selection of election boundary delimitation formulae drawn from Commonwealth countries serves to illustrate the imprecise nature of many of these formulations, which enable the electoral administrators to escape from legal consequences.

In the United Kingdom where there are four boundary commissions, one each for England, Scotland, Wales and Northern Ireland, established in 1986 to continuously review and distribute the seats at parliamentary elections, the rules for redistribution are wide and discretionary. The number of constituencies in Great Britain at the time of writing must not be substantially greater or less than 613. The number of constituencies in Scotland must not be less 71 and in Wales not less than 35, and not more than 18 and nor less than 16 in Northern Ireland. A Boundary Commission can depart from the strict application of certain of the rules if special geographical considerations, including size, shape and accessibility of a constituency, appeared to them to render a departure desirable. In applying the rules, a Boundary Commission has to take account of the electorate of any constituency and the electoral quota which is the number obtained by dividing the electorate for that part of the United Kingdom by the number of constituencies in it existing on the enumeration date. The Commission concerned can also take account of the inconveniences resulting from alterations of constituencies and any local ties, which would be broken by such alterations.[13]

The Malaysian Constitution requires that the Election Commission review from time to time the division of the Federation and the States into constituencies. In undertaking any such review, the Commission is required to apply certain principles including the stipulation that the number of electors within each constituency in a State ought to be approximately equal except that, having regard to the greater difficulty of reaching electors in the country districts and the other disadvantages facing rural constituencies, a measure of consideration in respect of size of area ought to be given to such constituencies. Other principles to be observed include the avoidance of constituency boundaries, which crossed Federal or State boundaries. Regard was to be had to the inconveniences attendant on alterations of constituencies and to the maintenance of local ties.[14]

The Zambian Constitution provides for a temporary commission to review the boundaries of constituencies. The boundaries of each constituency shall be such that the number of inhabitants thereof is nearly equal to the quota as is reasonably practicable. The number of inhabitants of a constituency could be greater or less

---

[13] See Schedule 2 to the Parliamentary Constituencies Act 1986
[14] See the Thirteenth Schedule of the Constitution

than the population quota[15] in order to take account of means of communications, geographical features and the difference between urban and rural areas in respect of density of population.[16]

In the case of Malta, an alteration of the boundaries of any electoral division has to be done in such a manner that the number of members to be returned to the House of Representatives for each division is as equal to the electoral quota as is reasonably practicable. However, the size of the electorate in any division cannot be greater or less than five per cent of the electoral quota, the deviation here is allowed for geographical and population factors. The phrase "electorate quota" means the number obtained by dividing the total electorate of Malta by the total number of members to be returned to the House of Representatives.[17]

The Jamaican formula provides that the boundary of a constituency must not cross the boundary of a parish (an administrative unit) and at least two constituencies should be in each parish. Taking account of these two stipulations, the formula states that the boundaries of each constituency should be such that the number of the electorate thereof is as nearly equal to the electorate quota as is reasonably practicable. However the electorate of a constituency can be greater or less than the electorate quota in order to take account of varying physical features and transportation facilities, as well as the difference between urban and rural areas in respect of the density of population. The deviation allowed for these reasons should not exceed the electorate quota by more than fifty per cent or be less than sixty-six and two-thirds per cent of the quotas. The "electorate quota" means the number obtained by dividing the total of the electorate of all the constituencies by the number of constituencies into which the country is to be divided.[18]

---

[15] "Population quota" is defined as the number obtained by dividing the number of inhabitants of Zambia by the number of constituencies into which Zambia is to be divided.

[16] Section 77 of the Constitution of Zambia 1991.

[17] Section 61 of the Constitution of Malta

[18] Second Schedule of the Constitution of Jamaica.

The general approach to electoral quotas in having a band of tolerance above or below the quota is widely recognised. Good practice suggests that the band of tolerance should be kept narrow, perhaps 5% to 10 %. Margins of up to 50% above or below the quota can quickly lead to licensed boundary manipulation. In jurisdictions where polling districts' boundaries are determined as administrative units of the State, the size of the electorate in a district may not take any account of any formula for applying an electorate quota.

Boundaries Management Bodies

The bodies that apply electoral quotas are not always equipped to take impartial decisions. In many countries, delimitation of electoral districts' boundaries is undertaken by the election management body and so the fairness or otherwise of the delimitation will reflect the general approach of the election management body to the conduct of free and fair elections. A few examples of the cases where the election management body undertake the task of boundary delimitation are Malaysia,[19] Malta,[20] Kenya,[21] Ghana,[22] Barbados,[23] Belize,[24] and Trinidad and Tobago.[25]

The cases where a body other than the electoral management body is responsible for the delimitation of polling districts' boundaries require close examination to see whether there is potential for partisanship or unfairness. The concepts of 'fairness' and 'unfairness' are imprecise and the criteria for measuring either are not well defined. However an examination of these bodies may throw some light on their potential to deliver fair boundaries delimitation. In the case of Singapore, the Minister responsible for

---

[19] Article 113 of the Constitution of Malaysia.

[20] Section 61 of the Constitution of Malta.

[21] Section 42 of the Constitution of Kenya.

[22] Articles 47 & 48 of the Constitution of Ghana, 1992.

[23] Section 41D of the Constitution of Barbados

[24] Section 88 of the Constitution of Belize.

[25] Sections 70, 72 and Second Schedule of the Constitution of Trinidad and Tobago.

electoral matters does the naming and construction of boundaries of electoral divisions for the purposes of parliamentary elections.[26] Zambia used to use a system of temporary electoral commissions created specifically to review constituency boundaries for elections to the National Assembly. Being a temporary body, its appointment and duration of tenure of office would instantly draw attention to questions about its independence and impartiality. Some of these anxieties were put to rest in one instance by the appointing authority, the President, appointing members of the Electoral Commission to constitute the boundaries commission.[27] There is a separate body, the Electoral Boundaries Commission,[28] in Mauritius, appointed by the President, acting in accordance with the advice of the Prime Minister after the Prime Minister had consulted the Leader of the Opposition. In applying the population quota, the Boundaries Commission has an open-ended tolerance level to allow for difficulty in means of communications, geographical features, and density of population and boundaries of administrative areas. (The "population quota" is arrived at by dividing the number of inhabitants of the Island of Mauritius by 20.) In Australia, each State and the Australian Capital Territory is divided into electoral divisions, each of which is represented by one member in the House of Representatives. The process by which electoral boundaries are drawn or reviewed is called redistribution and a redistribution committee appointed by the Electoral Commission did this for each State. The Electoral Commissioner, the Australian Electoral Officer for the State, the Surveyor-General for the State and the Auditor-General of the State are the members of the redistribution committee of a given State. The Electoral Commissioner determines the quota of electors for a State or Territory. An elaborate procedure provided for taking account of suggestion and comments by the public and another body, the Augmented Electoral Commission, hears objections to proposed redistributions and determines the

---

[26] Section 8 of the Parliamentary Elections Act 1954

[27] Section 77 of the Constitution of Zambia 1991.

[28] Section 38 of the Constitution of Mauritius.

names and boundaries of electoral divisions into which a State or Territory is to be divided.[29]

In New Zealand, the Representation Commission is charged with the responsibility of dividing New Zealand into general electoral districts from time to time. When the Commission is determining the boundaries of Maori electoral districts, it is enlarged from seven to ten members (the additional members are required to be Maoris).[30] In Papua New Guinea, there is a Boundaries Commission, which is responsible for the delimitation of the country into electoral districts or electorates (as they are called in that jurisdiction). The Commission consists of the Electoral Commissioner (who is the chairperson), the Surveyor-General, the Government Statistician and two persons appointed by resolution of the Parliament.

The Jamaican experience in delimiting the boundaries of constituencies is governed by the existence of a constitutional entity which is a standing committee of the House of Representatives consisting of the Speaker of the House, who is the Chairperson, three members of the House appointed by the Prime Minister and three members of the House appointed by the Leader of the Opposition. The function of the Standing Committee is to keep under continuous review the number and the boundaries of the constituencies into which Jamaica is divided.[31] This situation reflects the formal constitutional position, which had been considered flawed by some electoral commentators, since the Speaker was invariably from the side of the governing party. Reports of the Committee are not considered free of political partisanship. In practice, the views of the Electoral Commission were taken into account when constituency boundaries were being reviewed, but this had not yet been given formal constitutional recognition at the time of writing.

---

[29] See the Commonwealth Electoral Act 1918 sections 65-75

[30] Section 28 of the Electoral Act 1993

[31] Section 67and second Schedule of the Constitution.

This brief survey of a random selection of countries reveals that the approach to the delimitation or redistribution of electoral districts is done by different bodies, many of which are separate and apart from the electoral management bodies. The composition of some of these bodies gives rise to potential political partisanship, which might easily lead to gerrymandering of the recommended boundaries. Although partisanship in electoral districts' boundary-making is not frowned upon in some countries like the United States of America, it is believed that such practices sit ill-at-ease with the approach of a level playing field between contesting parties to an election, particularly in an emerging democracy.

Competence of the Courts

Some jurisdictions regard many aspects of the delimitation of electoral districts as falling outside the competence of the courts; in other words this issue is treated as a non-justiceable one. Other jurisdictions offer either partial or full judicial remedy to aggrieved persons or political parties. There is a growing tendency on the part of emerging democracies to create a level playing field in this important area of election preparation by providing for the intervention of the courts to redress gerrymandering or obvious unfairness in the delimitation of electoral districts. The absence of full or partial competence of the courts to intervene on behalf of aggrieved persons or political parties may be mitigated by the resort to non-judicial methods such as public inquiries and local representation on behalf of the communities affected by the delimitation.

In Australia, a well-developed procedure, which requires receiving and considering objections, precedes the redistribution of electoral divisions.[32] In addition, as the case of *McGinty & Others v The State of Western Australia*[33] showed, the courts have competence to deal with redistribution matters. Other countries where the courts have

---

[32]   Section 72 of the Commonwealth Electoral Act 1918.

[33]   See McGinty & Others v The State of Western Australia (1996) in Compendium of Election Laws etc. of Commonwealth Countries Ed. by Dundas (1998) pp97-232, Commonwealth Secretariat.

unfettered competence to deal with delimitation or redistribution or redistricting (as it is called in the US) of electoral districts include the United States of America, Ghana and Canada. Since 1962, the Supreme Court of the United States has become active in the redistricting process and has taken the opportunity to establish rules governing the process. In dealing with the experience of the United States of America, Lisa Handley and Wayne Arden cited many cases, which served to consolidate the courts' role in defining acceptable procedures and outcomes in respect of redistricting.[34] The Canadian experience thus far is one, which demonstrates caution on the part of the courts to embark enthusiastically on the road of intervention, although they are conscious of their competence and have from time to time invoked it. The limited role of the courts in Canada in entertaining delimitation actions is believed to be due in part to the fact that the Supreme Court of Canada has permitted both tolerance levels of deviation from the population quota of more than 25% limit and the rather open ended notion of "extraordinary circumstances". However other views have been put forward to explain the differences in approach to delimitation between the courts of the United States and Canada. Thus McLachlin J. while Chief Justice of the Supreme Court of British Columbia, in *Dixon v British Columbia (Attorney-General)* said:

> *"The American emphasis on a pure population standard for electoral apportionment may be seen as a product of that country's unique history and concept of democracy. The decisions upholding this standard are heavily influenced by the court's understanding of the intentions of the framers of the US Constitution . . .*
>
> *Democracy in Canada is rooted in a different history. Its origins lie not in the debates of the founding fathers, but in the less absolute recesses of the British tradition. Our forefathers did not rebel against the English tradition of democratic government, as did the Americans; on the*

---

[34]   See *Role of the Courts in Electoral District Delimitation* in 'Boundary Delimitation' 1998 ACE Project http://www.aceproject.org/main/english/bd/bdb06/default. htm

contrary, they embraced it and changed it to suit their own perceptions and needs.

What is that tradition? It was a tradition of evolutionary democracy, of increasing widening of representation through the centuries. But it was also a tradition, which, even in its more modern phases, accommodates significant deviation from the ideals of equal representation. Pragmatism, rather than conformity to a philosophical ideal, has been its watchword."[35]

In Ghana, there is a two-tiered approach to redressing grievances resulting from the delimitation of constituencies' boundaries. An aggrieved person could appeal from a decision of the Electoral Commission to a tribunal consisting of three persons appointed by the Chief Justice and the Electoral Commission is required to give effect to the decision of the tribunal. A person who is aggrieved by a decision of the tribunal can appeal to the Court of Appeal whose decision on the matter is final.[36]

The jurisdiction of the courts is sometimes excluded from dealing with some issues relating to electoral districts' boundaries delimitation, but not from dealing with others. This was the case in the Bahamas,[37] Dominica[38] and Jamaica.[39] Though these constitutional provisions are not identical, but their language and intent are similar. The Bahamian approach indicates that the question of the validity of any Order by the Governor General purporting to be made and reciting that a draft thereof had been approved by resolution of the House of Assembly cannot be inquired into in a court of law. However Parliament could, by passing a law, provide for an appeal to the Supreme Court against a statement or a recommendation submitted by the Commission.

---

[35]   Dixon v British Columbia (Attorney-General) (1989) 59 DLR (4th) 247, at 262.

[36]   Articles 47 & 48 of the Constitution of Ghana 1992.

[37]   See section 70 of the Constitution of the Bahamas

[38]   Section 57 of the Constitution of Dominica.

[39]   Section 67 of the Constitution of Jamaica.

A number of countries, among them India, Pakistan, Barbados, and Trinidad and Tobago, have ousted the jurisdiction of the courts from dealing with delimitation matters. In India, the Constitution has a clause, which seeks to bar the interference of the courts in electoral matters and it contains a specific reference to delimitation of constituencies. It states that the validity of any law relating to the delimitation of constituencies or the allocation of seats to such constituencies, made or purporting to be made under the Constitution cannot be called in question in any court.[40]It is not clear whether this provision would preclude a court action in respect of demarcated constituency boundaries, which are considered to be gerrymandered. The Pakistan approach prevents the validity of the delimitation of any constituency, or of any proceedings taken or anything done by or under the authority of the Commission, under the Delimitation of Constituencies Act from being called into question in any court.[41]

In general, judicial scrutiny of gerrymandered or unfairly demarcated electoral districts' boundaries is not widely accepted even in established democracy. This aspect of the electoral process requires greater transparency and public participation. Electoral districts' boundary making should contribute to the notion of having a level playing field for all the potential contestants in an election. The checks and balances in the delimitation process must be sufficient to prevent it from contributing to the theft of election by stealth. Where the deviation from the electoral quota allowed is large, as in Jamaica and Canada, abuse of the delimitation process is more difficult to detect. The purity of an election cannot be properly certified if the process of delimitation of electoral districts is seen to be unfair or partisan.

Gerrymandering in Perspective

In any assessment of the impact which gerrymandering of electoral boundaries may have on attempts to manipulate elections, it should be stated that in some electoral systems examined there is

---

[40]   Article 329 of the Constitution of India.

[41]   Section 3 of the Delimitation of Constituencies Act.

no need for electoral districts. This is so in cases where for national elections the whole country is a single constituency as in Guyana, Netherlands, Israel, Namibia and South Africa. At the other end of the electoral landscape are the countries where single-member constituencies reign supreme and where the delimitation of constituency boundaries becomes important. Between these two positions there is a third where each electoral district returns more than one representative to the elected body. These multimember electoral districts reduce the urge to manipulate the delimitation process through gerrymandering or otherwise to benefit a particular political party or candidate. An unfair delimitation process is more likely to impact on single-member constituencies.

The method of determining the boundaries of electoral districts may also have a significant impact on the fairness of the outcome of elections. An instance of this may be seen when the boundaries of electoral districts are aligned to administrative divisions. In some countries, for example, Cameroon, the administrative divisions are created by executive acts by the head of State or government and there is no scope for challenging their fairness. Similarly, there may be no limitation on the size or population of an administrative division. In short, not only may opposition parties be unable to make any input into the determination of an administrative division but also they may not be able to mount a challenge in a court of law.

My personal involvement with electoral boundary-making goes back to 1979 when I was Director of Elections in Jamaica and oversaw constituencies' boundaries' review. I advised on local government councils' boundaries in Malawi post-1994 elections and was associated with division of local government districts in South Africa in 1995, Cayman Islands in 2003 and 2010, and Liberia in 2005.

Cayman Islands Experience

In 2003, I was appointed Chairman of the Cayman Islands Electoral Boundary Commission and again in 2010. The task in Cayman Islands in 2003 was to divide the three islands in single-member constituencies. I chaired a Commission of three, included myself. The exercise was transparent as the Commission sought the participation of all stakeholders through oral and written submissions, as well as consultative public meetings in all three islands.

The opportunity, twice over, to chair the Electoral Boundary Commission which was tasked to delimit the small three-islands British Overseas Territory of Cayman Islands in the Caribbean was important for me, as chairman to demonstrate how fair constituency boundaries were constructed in practice. The Cayman Islands' Electoral Boundary Commission was a temporary constitutional body which was appointed by His Excellency the Governor and stood dissolved immediately after the Boundary Commission submited its report to the Governor, as in the case of the 2003 Boundary Commission, or to the Governor and the Legislative Assembly, as was the case of the 2010 Boundary Commission.

The particulars of the method of appointment of the boundary commission changed during the period of 2003 and 2010 due to constitutional changes in the Cayman Islands. In 2003, the Boundary Commission was constituted under the then Constitution whereby the Leader of Government Business recommended one person to be appointed to the Boundary Commission and the Leader of the Opposition recommended another person, and the Governor, in his discretion appointed the Chairman of the Commission. I was appointed chairman by the then Governor. The constitutional development in the Cayman Islands in 2009 meant that the incumbent governing political party was led by a premier and not the Leader of Government Business. However, the appointments to the 2010 Electoral Boundary Commission was constituted on principles similar to those of the 2003 Commission whereby the Premier recommended one person to be appointed to the Commission and the Leader of the Opposition recommended one person, and the Governor, in his discretion, appointed the third person and chairman of the Commission. I was again appointed chairman by the then Governor in place at the time of the appointment.

Except for the Chairman, in 2003 and 2010 the members of the Electoral Boundary Commission nominated by politicians, the Commission could not therefore be described as independent to that extent. However, in its operations, the Boundary Commission was completely independent of the Governor, the Government and the political parties. The Chairman and one member of the 2010 Electoral Boundary Commission had served on the 2003 Commission. The members of each of the two Electoral Boundary Commissions were of impeccable integrity and worked as a team in carrying out their tasks under the Constitution.

As an election expert who had always believed in the construction of fair electoral districts' boundaries, the Cayman Islands provided the perfect environment for putting ideal boundary construction into practice. In both times, 2003 and 2010, the major drawback was the lack of up-to-date population statistics and so the great reliance had to be placed on the register of voters which was revised regularly. Other elements to facilitate fair boundary-making were present.

Nature of Electoral Districts in Cayman Islands
The Cayman Islands consist of three islands, Grand Cayman, Cayman Brac and Little Cayman (amounting to about 100 sq. miles in area). The Overseas Territory elects 15 members to its Legislative Assembly distributed as follows: Grand Cayman 13 and Cayman Brac and Little Cayman 2 members. On Grand Cayman, the return of members to the Assembly is done as follows: two members are returned by two single-member constituencies (one each), and three multi-member constituencies in which each voter has as many votes as members returned by the district concerned.
The matter of one person, one vote, has been an issue in the Cayman Islands for some time because the two single-member districts where the voters have one vote only are dissatisfied with the existing 'districting'. The 2003 Electoral Boundary Commission was mandated to construct seventeen single-member constituencies. The report of that Boundary Commission was not implemented. The reasons for the failure to implement that report appeared to be political rather than technical. The issue behind failure to move

forward on the single-member constituencies has been the inability to resolve the issue of one person, one vote. The Cayman Islands' constitution conference in 2009 failed to resolve issue of one person, one vote, as well as the question of single-member constituencies. The upshot was that the mandate of the 2010 Electoral Boundary Commission merely stipulated that the Commission should divide the islands in a manner which allows the islands to return 18 members to the Legislative Assembly, but in a manner which allows the Sister Islands, Cayman Brac and Little Cayman, to return at least two members.

Good Practice

Registered and Unregistered persons

The 2010 Electoral Boundary Commission was committed to carry out its tasks in accordance with good practice in boundary-making. A vital issue for the Commission was to establish the number of registered persons, as well as persons qualified to be registered but have not registered. The regular population census was due to be conducted later in 2010. The Electoral Boundary Commission decided to use the electoral register which was updated regularly to secure the number of registered voters in the respective electoral districts or constituencies. With respect to ascertaining the number of qualified unregistered persons, the Commission held discussions with the Elections Office, the Planning and the Census Departments. One issue came to the fore was that a relatively high proportion of qualified persons refused to register because they do not wish to end up on the jury list. The Departments abovementioned confirmed the estimate of the Elections Office of the areas of growth throughout the islands. That approach helped the Boundary Commission to establish the distribution pattern of registered voters and unregistered persons.

Participation of Stakeholders
The Commission used various means to attract the participation of stakeholders in the delimitation exercise. There were public meetings in each electoral district, with two meetings in each of

the larger districts. Each public meeting was widely advertised in the electronic media and in the press. Several of the public meetings were broadcast live on Radio Cayman and the Chairman and members of the Commission appeared on radio phone-in programmes. Many members of the Legislative Assembly attended the Commission's public meetings in their respective districts. The public meetings served as inter-active sessions where members of the public put their concerns to the members of the Commissions who did their best to give answers and provide explanations as were considered appropriate. However, many stakeholders were disappointed when the members of the Commission explained that the mandate of the Commission did not allow it to deal with the issue of one person, one vote, which belonged more to the matter of 'electoral system' which had to be dealt with as a constitutional matter.

Stakeholders were also invited to make written submissions to the Commission and many did so. The Commission took all the submission into account, although some could not be given full effect in the construction of the recommended boundary lines.

Recommendations of the Commission
The interpretation of the Commission's mandate proved to be anything but straightforward, because it did not state whether or not the unit to be represented by a member of the Legislative Assembly was a district or a constituency, and it did not state whether or not each member unit was to be a single-member or multi-member unit. These ambiguities arose largely because the Constitution did not clearly deal with these matters. If the dual concepts of single-member and multi-member districts were to be retained, (and that appeared to be the constitutional position), some issues arose to be considered, for example, according to the distribution of registered and unregistered persons, the George Town, the largest concentration of people would have a third of the members of the Legislative Assembly. In order to reduce the number of votes which each voter in the George Town electoral district, the Commission proposed that a new multi-member electoral district be created which would reduce the number of

members elected by George Town from six to four. An argument in favour of the creation of a new electoral district was that in a small jurisdiction such as that of the Cayman Islands, there should not be inequality in the number of votes each voter has, (in other words while voters in single-member districts had one vote, hence one opportunity, multi-member districts had as many as four or six times as many votes and hence opportunities to influence the government of the day). This reasoning was also used to support the case for one person, one vote.

In its Report, the Electoral Boundary Commission recommended that the eighteen members to the Legislative Assembly should be allocated as follows: four members for West Bay; six for George Town; four for Bodden Town; one for North Side; one for East End, and two for Cayman Brac and Little Cayman. This allocation was consistent with the mandate of the Commission and the Constitution.

However, having regard to submissions made to the Commission and issues raised at the public meetings, the Commission offered two alternative approaches for the consideration of the Legislative Assembly, namely, creation of a new electoral district electing four members to the Legislative Assembly; and creation of eighteen single-member constituencies. In all three approaches, the precise descriptions each member's geographical unit's boundaries were set out along with illustrative maps of the respective areas.

This small jurisdiction shows an example of what may be entailed in the search for fairness and balance in the delivery of good practice in electoral districts' boundary-making.

Liberia
In Liberia, there was a significant challenge to retain the constituency system after almost 14 years of civil wars during which there was massive displacement of people, including the electorate, internally and as refugees outside the country. A process of delimitation was carried out in which, along with other partners, particularly the UN, I played a significant role. The delimitation was an interim measure,

being for the 2005 elections only, but even so the exercise was little more than a licensed gerrymandering process since the influence of local clans held sway and many boundaries of constituencies avoided linking areas of geographic proximity because of reported inability of neighbouring clans to get along with each other.

The long civil war had damaged the physical infrastructure throughout the country. The constitutional and legal environment was also damaged by the conflict to the point where large parts of the Constitution had to be suspended to facilitate democratic elections. The electoral system and the distribution of the voting population had to be reviewed in the light of massive displacement of the population inside the country, while thousands fled abroad as refugees in neighbouring countries.

In the circumstances, new approaches were created to facilitate electoral districts for the 2005 elections. Under the auspices of the United Nations and other partners of the National Elections Commission (NEC) a programme of village mapping was undertaken to establish the location of village and to gain a rough picture of the existing population. The village mapping exercise paved the way for the registration of eligible persons for the voters' register. The voters' register in turn provided a basis for the construction of constituencies within the counties of Liberia.

Liberia had adopted the first past the post electoral system with single-member districts to elect members to the House of Representatives. Unlike the Cayman Islands where the Constitution laid down a framework, albeit an imperfect one, for the delimitation, in Liberia there was no framework, legal or practical, and so the delimitation team had to create a practical frame work based on good international standards. The process was initiated by creating a number of stages for different tasks to be carried out. Stage 1 consisted of establishing guidelines for the delimitation process and gathering relevant information to support the process. This process encompassed the selection of the delimitation criteria to be used to construct the electoral districts, and the formula for allocation of seats in the House. The next stage was to allocate the seats for the House to counties on the basis of size of electorate. Then stage 3 entailed drawing electoral districts consistent with the regulations which had been promulgated and the general guidelines established by the NEC.

For the purpose of keeping the delimitation team up to speed with respect to electoral district boundary-making, the basic principles of fair delimitation were agreed as follows, that:

- The population of each electoral district should be relatively equal;
- Electoral districts should be contiguous;
- Geographical features such as rivers and swamps should be taken into account;
- Administrative boundaries, including, for example, administrative districts and tribal and chiefdom boundaries, should be kept intact as far as possible;
- Communities of interest should be respected as much as possible; and
- Old constituency boundaries should be taken into account as much as possible.

On the importance and role of population in delimitation, the team enunciated its guidelines as follows: that single-member districts should be relatively equal in population to ensure that voters have almost equal weight; and that the degree of equality of population is measured by the relation of each district's population proximity to the quota, (that is the population of the area to be delimited divided by the total number of districts). Probably more for political expediency than fairness, each county was allocated a minimum of two seats in the House.

The criterion of 'contiguity' was introduced into the delimitation scenario to avoid a known form of gerrymandering. Contiguity can be demonstrated when any part of the district can be reached from any other part without crossing the district boundary.

In the context of Liberia, administrative boundaries were important as they related to tribal and chiefdom boundaries which should not be crossed unnecessarily. It is believed that administrative boundaries provide electoral district recognition to voters. Also by taking administrative districts into account, a more homogeneous electoral district can be constructed. Efforts were made in Liberia to identify communities of interest where voters were united by shared characteristics, or shared values brought about through common racial, ethnic, cultural, or by shared language or religion.

It was also felt that it was appropriate to take into account, whenever possible, previous constituency boundaries, for example, those that were in place for the 1985 election, as they would assist voters and candidates with electoral district recognition.

The principle of equality of population per constituency was impinged upon by a political agreement that each county would have at least two seat allocated to it regardless of the county's population (size of electorate—no population census had been taken). The formula for allocating the seats threw up disagreement between some members of the delimitation team which was ultimately resolved by the political parties adopting their own formula. The upshot was that the allocation of seats per county in 2005 denoted a significant shift in the electorate from 1985, for example, Montserrado County moved from 10 seats in 1985 to 13 in 2005, while Nimba County moved from 9 seats in 1985 to 6 in 2005, and Margibi County move from 2 in 1985 to 5 in 2005.

The information that was acquired to complete the delimitation exercise included:

- The voter registration totals for each voter registration centre (VCRs);
- Paper maps of counties that contained the location of the VCRs, villages, administrative district, clan and chiefdom boundaries, as well as physical features; and
- Additional information collected through country magistrates and submitted to the NEC.

The process was transparent, but was short on full participation by stakeholders—one reason for this was lack of time and inadequate infrastructure to hold public meetings in the districts to extent that would facilitate fuller participation. The unexpected influence of clan boundaries on the delimitation boundary lines was surprising.

CHAPTER VI

Fashioning the Register of Voters

Jamaica (1979)
Kenya (observation of registration 1992)
Nigeria (1998)
Liberia (2005)
South Africa (local govt. 1995)
Malawi (1994)
Antigua/Barbuda (2001)

Principles of Voters Registration
The Register
I was involved in shaping through drafting electoral legislation or offering advice with respect to voter registration regimes in the seven countries listed above and discussed below. My approach to constructing voter registration legislative schemes (including rules and regulations) was to take account of good electoral practices in this area of election organization. In the paragraphs below, before proceeding to discuss assistance offered to individual countries, I set out in some detail my concept of good practice in voter registration currently. Some thoughts are also given to emerging trends concerning cost-effectiveness or otherwise, as well as measures to minimize complaints.

In delivering his report on the revision of the electoral rolls in 1991, the Chief Election Commissioner of Pakistan stated that he attached great importance to the authenticity and accuracy of the electoral rolls because the fairness of the elections depended on error-free electoral rolls.[42] Those remarks would no doubt attract the approval of most election managers. The accuracy of a voters' register is more often than not hotly contested by aggrieved prospective voters who fell victims to the omissions of the registration system and by political parties who fear that their supporters might be among the victims.

A genuine difficulty is to discover those complainants who were victims that had no opportunity to register themselves. Persons, who were in detention, but who, by law in the concerned country, could register, or the ill or disabled, for whom proper arrangements had not been made, may be justified in complaining, if the registration process passed them by. And so would anyone who was deprived of registration through clerical errors, negligence or fraudulent practices. Persons who were either unmoved by the awareness programmes or avoided registration intentionally would be less justified in complaining about being omitted from the voters' register.

Perhaps the question of how accurate can a voters' register be in a voluntary registration system will never be satisfactorily answered. However, the acceptable tolerance levels of inaccuracy, which may vary between 4%-7% in older democracies, can be reduced in emerging democracies by the introduction of better procedural rules governing registration. In particular, the rules dealing with publication of the provisional register and the period within which the public may inspect it are unsatisfactory in some jurisdictions. Also, the method of redress and the procedures relating thereto are often not considered to be user friendly, since claims to be entered on the provisional register are dealt with by the registering authorities or those to whom the authorities report. In most cases the courts have not been given a proper role to deal effectively with the concerns of the aggrieved. Public scrutiny of the provisional voters' register is vital in purging the records, while public access

---

[42]   Report on the Annual Revision of the Electoral Rolls 1991 by Chief Election Commissioner, Justice Naimuddin January 1993.

to the finished product is necessary to ensure that all corrections, additions and deletions are done faithfully.

The first phase in the preparation of a voters' register consists of a preliminary list of the names and other relevant particulars of all eligible persons recorded in the enumeration or registration exercise. The preliminary lists invariably contain a considerable number of discrepancies and inaccuracies, such as misspelling of names and addresses, names of ineligible persons, omission of the names of qualified persons, change of address or death of a person subsequent to the enumeration or registration exercise or lack of residential qualifications.

In order to remove the names of persons, who should not be on the preliminary list, and to insert names of persons who were omitted there from or correct incorrect spellings, a period for public display of the preliminary list is required to facilitate public scrutiny. Some jurisdictions allow only a restricted form of publicity at this stage on grounds of privacy and security. The period of scrutiny should be 14 to 21 days, which should be set out in the election calendar and given due publicity in the respective registration units or divisions. Usually a person whose name is on the list is allowed to ask for its removal, if that person is not qualified. A person, whose name is properly included on the list, may object to any other names on the list, giving reasons for the objection. A person whose name was omitted from the preliminary list can make a claim for inclusion in the list. Current election practice in many emerging democracies allows political parties, NGOs, election observers and even donor agencies to assist individuals or groups of individuals in making claims or objections.

Claims and objections are normally initially made to the registration officer of the registration unit or division, and if that officer is satisfied with the veracity of the claim or objection, the preliminary list is amended accordingly. Aggrieved persons should have the right of appeal from a decision of a registration officer or from the EMB, where it has power to deal with appeals. There is no standardization of the treatment of appeals at the present time.

Some jurisdictions use revising courts, others use the magistrate courts, or resort to the High Court or a Chamber thereof, while many have no process beyond the EMB's decision. In the context of modernization of election organisation, the right of the franchise is too important to be denied by an arbitrary or wholly administrative manner, and so a judicial or quasi-judicial procedure is preferred.

The hearing of appeals resulting from claims, objections or rejections by the registration officer, by aggrieved persons before an election may encounter difficulty, where registration takes place on polling day, or where in a continuous registration system the cut-off date is too close to polling day so that appeal procedures would not be able to take place.

By its very nature, the procedures governing a quasi-judicial or judicial determination of registration appeals have to be set out in the registration regulations, which have to safeguard the appellant rights to a fair hearing.

The final lists of qualified persons emerge from the purged preliminary lists and form the register of voters, voters' roll or voters' list, depending on the term used in the respective legislative scheme. In some large federal States, such as Australia, Canada, India and Nigeria, the trend is to create a national voters' register, which may be broken down into local or regional, provincial or State, and federal components. The format of the register may be determined by administrative and or geographic structure of the country concerned.

The final voters' register should be certified by the EMB before distribution according to the stipulations set out in the legislative scheme or in the registration regulations. The legislative scheme should permit addition or deletion to the final register to correct clerical and typographical errors, or to add or delete names, which may be so ordered by an appellate registration claims and objection tribunal. Some schemes place a cut-off date, after which no additions or deletions can be made before an election.

Voters' Cards

In his study on voter registration and identity cards in South Asian countries, Jafar Chowdhury noted that voter identity card programme was a service to Bangladesh in its journey to the strengthening of the electoral process for the institutionalization of democracy.[43] The study traced the progress of voter identification programme, which commenced in India in 1995, in Bangladesh in 1995 and Nepal in 1996, leading to the issuance of voters' identification cards. Other countries like Malawi, South Africa and Nigeria have upgraded their voter identification systems for their elections held in 1999. Voter identification cards are not standard; they vary in form, size, uses and the nature and amount of information they bear. Voters' cards have the real potential to assist in the fight against multiple voting and impersonation at elections. But the process of producing, controlling and distributing voters' cards has always had considerable attraction to election manipulators. Voters' cards have been known to be sold and bought, stolen, lost, destroyed, defaced, stored away with impure motives, undelivered and unused, with the intention of depriving the lawful owners of the right to vote. The voters' cards can be used, and indeed are often used, in the sordid aim of stealing elections, the very mischief that their use was intended to stamp out! The situation becomes grave in societies where it has not been customary to hold documents of value in safe custody for long periods, the nomad communities come to mind readily, but theirs is only the extreme case of a widespread problem in emerging democracies.

In some cases, voters' cards are issued immediately to each person upon registration.[44] There are certain advantages in issuing a voter's card to a person at the time of registration, including the following:

1.   Ensuring that the card is delivered to the rightful holder;

---

[43]   **Voter Registration and Identity Cards in South Asian Countries**, Jafar Ahmed Chowdhury, Deputy Project Director, Voter Identity Card Project p.51 Bangladesh 1997

[44]   For example, this is the procedure in Kenya and Tanzania.

2. Avoidance of large numbers of voter's cards remaining undelivered on polling day;

3. Cost effective in so far as costs associated with the distribution of the cards to the electorate throughout the country concerned and the issuance of a second document as proof of registration or identification as a voter, are avoided; and

4. The voter's card, when issued upon registration, serves two purposes, namely, as evidence of registration and certificate of identification of the holder as a voter.

There are disadvantages associated with the issuance of voters' cards at the time and place of registration, including the following:

1. The voter's card is much more likely to contain errors, since each person's data would not go through complete purging process to which the preliminary register is normally subject;

2. A prospective voter, whose particulars required correction, may have to return the voter's card or visit the registration centre in person in order to get the card corrected;

3. The procedure for issuing or cancelling voters' cards, as the case may be, upon the determination of the claims and objections process, as well as the appeals process, which may be instituted by aggrieved applicants, will require treatment subsequent to the initial registration exercise; and

4. Critically, the technical efficiency of issuing the voters' cards at the point of registration will depend on the information technology system and the ability of the technical staff to get acceptable quality information, including photographs, and produce good quality voters' cards instantly at the registration site.

Cost of Preparation

The cost of preparing the voters' register varies according to the complexity or otherwise of the process. For example, where thumb printing, photographing, bar coding and scanning are all or some only of these factors included in the process, the costs will reflect these added expenses. There may also be a sharp contrast in the costs between putting in place a new system where there was no proper structure for democratic multi-party elections and conducting registration in an on-going culture where multi-party elections are held regularly. Allowances should also be made for situations where a high initial capital outlay of funds are required to purchase scanners and computers to run GIS boundary data, read bar coded data and run the provisional and final list. The cost per person registered would be high if the total expenses were posted against their use at the first registration. A survey of registration cost per person in selected Commonwealth Countries undertaken in 1996 revealed that some countries like Dominica (US$0.07), Pakistan (US$0.11), Cyprus (US$0.18) and Sri Lanka (US$0.45), were at the lower end of registration costs, while Canada (US$ 1.61), Botswana (US$2.91), New Zealand (US$6.21) and Jamaica (US$7.49), represented the highest costs. Preliminary estimates indicate that since that survey was undertaken, South Africa for its election in 1999, followed by Jamaica, which used an expensive automated process for its election in 2002, ranked in the highest bracket of registration costs in the Commonwealth then. More up-to-date figures for the registration of each voter are emerging, for example, India recently released their latest cost at $0.62 per voter, the State of Oregon in the USA released its cost at $4.53 per voter, but put the cost of the registration transaction at $8.43 per voter in 2008. The Nigerian projected cost per registered voter for the 2010 registration exercise was US$8.6.[45]

Accessibility
The voters' register should be available to political parties and the public. It is the practice in many countries to make a stipulated number of copies of the register free of charge to recognized political parties. Further copies are usually made available on sale to parties. The price of the voters' register ought to be reasonable so that smaller political parties that are not well endowed with

---

[45] For a useful study on voter registration in Africa see Astrid Evrensel ed. Voter Registration in Africa-A Comparative Analysis, EISA2010.

resources can afford to purchase the extra copies that they need. Copies should also be made available to independent candidates. The registration rules normally require that the register be accessible to the public for inspection. This is an important element of the transparency that election management bodies should strive to achieve. In many jurisdictions, copies of the register may be sold to the public. This practice has prompted questions as to the use to which the registration information may be put, and there are a few cases where the election rules limit the use to purposes indicated at the time of purchase. An example of this may be seen in the case of Australia where the law states that if a tape or disk is provided under the relevant provisions of the law, a person must not use the information obtained by means of the tape or disk except for a purpose that is a permitted purpose in relation to the person or organization to which the tape or disk was provided. The law sets out the permitted purposes for which the information may be used.[46] In some countries, it is possible for a person who has been registered to request that their name and address be not included in the register for purposes of publication, inspection or sale.[47] Thus not all the names on the register will be included in the register at all times and for all purposes.

Maintenance
A voters' register should be properly maintained. As each day passes, a voters' register becomes less accurate through deaths, change of addresses, change of names through marriages or by deed poll, or incapacitation through conviction in a court of law. The combination of factors is enough to cause a register to deteriorate in accuracy by as much as 25%—30% over a four-year period even where annual revision takes place. This position is usually aggravated by poor maintenance of the register through a weak or even non-existent machinery to deal with the removal of the deceased names from the register and to correct the register where change of names or a change of address took place for whatever reason. In many

---

[46]   Section 91A of the Commonwealth Electoral Act 1918.

[47]   See Section 104 of the Commonwealth Electoral Act of Australia and Section 115 of the Electoral Act of New Zealand, 1993.

emerging democracies, the maintenance of the register is not done to satisfaction, partly because the supporting systems like the births and deaths registration may not be computerized or because the local custom does not allow for national reporting of deaths.[48] The lack of proper maintenance of the voters' register has created the potential for election manipulation by enabling persons to vote in deceased or other persons' names who have left their address, but whose names remain on the register. Where continuous registration is done and the register is properly maintained, inaccuracies are likely to be kept to a minimum of occurrence. Compulsory registration does not necessarily lessen the need for timely and thorough maintenance of the voters' register.

Manipulation of the Registration Process

A voluntary registration system offers many avenues along which manipulation can travel. The challenge for every election management body is to close off the avenues along which registration manipulation takes place. Completely free and fair elections can only be delivered where the voter registration process is beyond reproach. At present, the state of the registration process in many countries is unhealthy and is in need of corrective measures. In seeking to assess the extent to which manipulation or the stealing of elections occurs through the registration process, the negative reports by political parties, aggrieved persons, neutral interest groups and election observers, that flow from most elections suggest that the voter registration process finds itself in the dock more often than any other.

Perhaps, by its very nature, the voter registration process lends itself to perpetual political squabbles, since in the voluntary registration systems an unknown number of qualified persons will be left outside. Perhaps a realistic goal is to aim at a level of satisfaction that is acceptable to the chief stakeholders in the outcome of an election, namely the political parties, the general public and

---

[48] In Zambia, during the 1991 elections many voters turned up at polling stations to find their names removed from the voters' register with a notation "transferred" or just a blank space remaining.

election observers. A difficulty with voter registration approaches at present is that they lack a coherent strategy to achieve clearly stated goals. For example, in South Africa in 1995 there were those who liked to emphasise that the registration system was voluntary and so the onus was on the qualified persons to get registered. That approach did not highlight the need for any high-powered awareness programmes. Others in that country insisted on the obligation of the Electoral Commission to persuade qualified persons, through awareness programmes and other means, to get registered.

In some cases, the need to prevent manipulation is so overwhelming that regulatory checks overlook the need for balancing mechanisms, and the result is that the process is cluttered up with contorted procedural details and becomes unwieldy for persons seeking registration and registration officials alike. Some observers to the Jamaican elections in1997 reported as much about the system generally.

International help is needed to move along the quest for improvements to existing registration strands, ranging from acquisition of materials and equipment through to data capture and processing. The same level of attention that is attracted to the conduct of polling on voting day should be paid by both local and international observers to registration and the preparation of the register, since the outcome of some elections is already determined at the time when the register is compiled. A complete and accurate register should be the goal of every voter registration exercise.

Continuous or rolling registration

The foregoing account of the compilation and maintenance of the voters' register focused mainly on updating through periodic revision of the register, but there is a trend for EMBs to introduce continuous or rolling (as it is called in the United Kingdom) registration. Continuous registration may be provided for expressly in the election legislative scheme, or its procedure may be implied in the governance of election organisation. Whichever framework is adopted, continuous registration should be introduced with an adequate set of regulations governing, among other things, the following:

1. A firm commencement date, preferable fixed by the EMB;
2. Rules setting out the procedures, including the times and sites, where registration will take place;
3. Involvement of political parties through the presence of agents or representatives at the continuous registration sites;
4. Applicants should be required to appear in person at the registration sites;
5. Applicants should take along the documents stipulated for identification purposes;
6. The periods for continuous registration should be stipulated, that is to say, monthly, quarterly or yearly, as the case may be;
7. The information required to be supplied by each eligible person (for the registration database), and the forms required for registration;
8. The procedures for scrutiny of the names on the new list at the end of the given period, and appeals for aggrieved applicants, whose names have been challenged; and
9. Certification of the new list of names and incorporation into the existing certified register of voters.

Continuous registration refers to the tasks of registering eligible persons in the register of voters as and when they become qualified, instead of periodic registration or registration immediately before an election is due. At the same time as new prospective voters are being registered, the register is being purged of the names of deceased persons and the names of other persons, who have become disqualified or changed their address or their names.

The cost element of not only changing over from periodic revision to continuous registration, but also operating a continuous process in place of periodic revision, is often considered and compared to see which process is more cost effective. Experiences in Australia and Canada have shown that such comparisons may not be straightforward, as other factors, such as moving from local registers to a national register on or about the same time may influence initial costs, which may have to be discounted over a period of years in order to arrive at the true annual costs. The cost factor of continuous registration is sometimes complicated by costs sharing with other agencies, such as the post office, which may provide sites for continuous registration. In any event, the cost of registration, whichever procedure is applied, varies according to the nature of the checks and balances, which are built into the process, for example, voters' cards with photographs and biometric features, are likely to be much more expensive than a process without either or both features. In a similar vein, the use of high quality laminated voters' cards, though more durable than types of inferior quality, would increase costs initially.

Voters' register based on civil registry

The civil registry serves as a population register in some countries. Its contents vary from country to country, but the common feature is that the register contains vital information, such as name, address, citizenship, age, and identification number. In several Latin American and northern European countries, the voters' register is compiled from information contained in the civil register. This procedure sometimes does not separate the data collection for the civil registry purposes from the information for the voters' register and would perhaps fall short of the impartiality test associated with 'independent' EMBs, although many countries, which use the civil registry, have a separate entity to deal with voter registration.

The use of the civil registry data has the advantage of sharing the cost of registration of voters with the civil registry authorities, and thus it is a cost-effective way of producing the voters' register. However, unless there is an independent procedure, whereby the registry lists can be purged of errors, the voters' register may be less accurate than is required in the context of best electoral practices.

Compulsory registration.

Several countries have found it necessary to make registration of a voter compulsory. This means that failure of any qualified person to register is an offence and attracts a fine. One issue is how large the fine should be. Countries like Australia and Singapore impose a relatively modest fine for failure to register. Perhaps a more serious issue is whether it is in the spirit of democracy to compel a person to register. On this matter many reasonable persons differ. There can be occasions when a country faces a shrinking voters' register through the refusal of eligible persons to register, while deceased persons' names are being taken off the register.[49] In such cases, there may be a strong argument in favour of compulsory registration. Compulsory registration has the potential to increase the size of the voters' register to as much as 95 percent of the estimated number of qualified electorate. (In Australia the percentage is between 94-5). The effect of compulsory registration on attempts to manipulate the process through multiple registrations has not been reliably measured, but it is believed that it does reduce the incidence of that type of manipulation.

Voluntary registration

Voluntary registration places the onus on the qualified person to register. Such a person may choose not to apply for registration. However, when the legislative scheme does state that the onus is on the qualified persons to register, it is sometimes construed by election managers as weakening the case for vigorous awareness programmes with respect to the registration exercise.[50]

Unlike the compulsory registration procedure, voluntary registration requires a strong and even aggressive awareness programme to persuade wavering and disinterested eligible persons to register. The percentage of estimated electorate registered will depend on the level of political awareness and motivation, since persons have a choice whether or not to register. This situation

---

[49] This was the situation in the Cayman Islands in 2003-all efforts in voter awareness programmes failed to improve the situation.

[50] This was what happened during the local elections registration exercise in 1995 in South Africa, (although that occurrence was due in part to the lack of experience in conducting countrywide voter registration in South Africa at the time).

has led to constant accusation by opposition parties in emerging democracies that EMBs failed to conduct proper voter registration operations. The widespread behaviour of eligible persons not showing the necessary interest during the registration exercise and then subsequently, when the election campaign gets going, they complain of being omitted from the register, is frequently encountered in many countries.

Jamaica

The registration of voters in Jamaica is based on the voluntary approach and is undertaken by house-to-house enumeration of each qualified person. In 1979 the process had become flawed due to partisan enumerators and inadequate safeguards against multiple registrations. The reform of the process which I introduced as Director of Elections required improved screening of enumerators and improved identification through photographs and finger printing of qualified persons at the time of registration. Also the introduction of advanced computer programming allowed persons with similar particulars to be identified for further checks no matter where they were located in the island.

Of course, an accurate, complete and current register may be facilitated by additional measures, depending on the structure of the overall process; for example, in Jamaica in 1979 registration was carried out in units called polling divisions. Every qualified person was required to register in the polling division in which he/she ordinarily resided (except police and army personnel who could be registered where they were posted at the time of registration). Each polling division, as far as was practicable, would contain an average number of qualified persons between a stipulated minimum and maximum number. The size of the polling divisions had the potential to impact adversely or otherwise on the quality of election services delivered on Election Day.

Kenya 1992

I had the privilege to observe the Kenya registration in 1992 for a couple of weeks on behalf of the Commonwealth Secretariat. The Kenyan process then was wholly manual, an interesting contrast with the registration process which I had set up and presided over in Jamaica some thirteen years before. My Commonwealth team and I each day for a week began observation in the field at the commencement of registration and followed the registration officer until the close of the day's activities. We then followed the registration officer's returns after two or three days to the handing in of those days' output to the district office, and then followed the journey of the district's office partial returns to the constituency headquarters where the partial returns were cyclostyled and compiled to form part of what would become the preliminary list of voters for that constituency.

It was an experience even for me then who was an experienced election expert. The Kenyan approach to registration of voters was rather unprofessional; many registration officers were inadequately trained, there was no proper registration forms—registration officers used exercise books as registration forms, others used loose leaves, and yet others used shorthand notebooks. The unstructured field data collection was slow and resulted in lots on clerical errors in misspelling of names and loss of names which generated numerous complaints. The cyclostyled processing of the names to be placed on the preliminary list of voters was slow and messy, often requiring repeat printing to get legible copies.

With respect to the more substantive issues of registration, there was difficulty in establishing age, particularly of secondary school children many of whom did not have birth certificate to verify age claims. The requirement of possessing a national ID card in order to register to vote was a problem which some stakeholders maintained was one way which the Government and ruling party used to manipulate the number of persons who could register in given geographical areas. There was also the issue of non-issuance of voter's cards to registered voters, while there was credible evidence of significant trading in voter's cards; that is, buying and selling of voter's cards in some parts of the country.

Nigeria 1998

Nigeria's return to civilian rule was an important development in the democratization of the African continent and also for the Commonwealth. Although the military regime held the reins in Nigeria for a long time, there had always been an electoral structure of sorts in the country. Indeed, a national election which was said to be relatively free and fair was aborted by the military some five years previously. In 1998, when then opportunity again presented itself to organize democratic multiparty elections there were some old structures that could be dusted off and a good many electoral officers to be called into service.

Population census and voters' registration are two exercises which have always triggered controversy in Nigeria. One reason is said by stakeholders in Nigeria to be the north—south religious and economic divide in the country. Another reason is the perception on the part of many Nigerians that they must always register in the State where they were born in order that their home State would benefit from the increase in population by their inclusion, even if by doing so it would be a breach of the election law. This has resulted in large numbers of multiple registrations throughout Nigeria, although they may not necessarily result in multiple voting, unlike in many other countries. Indeed, I have met some senior officers in INEC who admitted that they were registered in their home State, sometimes involuntarily by their family, while they were also registered in Abuja where they voted.

In the short space of time (August to December 1998) to organize the series of elections (local, State and Federal) meant that there was not enough time to carry out full awareness programmes for voter education for registration of voters. However, at the invitation of the Chairman of INEC, Justice Akpata, I did participate in a couple of training sessions in Abuja for registration officers in September 1998.

South Africa 1995

I was instrumental in leading a Commonwealth Team which successfully negotiated technical assistance for the 1994 South

African elections with Judge Kreigler and his Commissioners. In October 1994, the South African Government requested Commonwealth technical assistance with the pending local elections. The Commonwealth Secretary-General requested my urgent return from Mozambique where I was representing him at the Mozambique general elections to discuss with the South African authorities the nature of assistance needed.

Initially, a Commonwealth team consisting of an Australian, Allan Wall, and I began by costing aspects of the local election in December 1994. Two main issues to grapple with in costing the pending elections were registration of voters, which had not been done for the 1994 general elections, and the delimitation of electoral districts, metropolitan districts and wards.

Here, I am dealing only with the registration of voters exercise. South Africa was facing for the first time the undertaking of registration of its entire electorate. Hitherto such exercises were confined to the white population only. I was a member of the committee dealing with the registration of voters for the local elections. The Registration Committee, to which I was an adviser, was made up largely of personnel from the Ministry of Home Affairs. We had brainstorming sessions and retreats to discuss strategy from time to time. Certain aspects of the preparatory activities were contracted out on tender to private firms and so elements of patronage associated with election services and acquisition of supplies were in play. On the whole, given the circumstances, the exercise worked well, but the registration awareness programmes were late in getting off the ground and qualified persons were not well informed about the registration requirements. Another attendant weakness was the interpretation which the authorities put on the nature of the process; they maintained that the onerous to register was on the individual and so persuasion by the authorities, through high profile awareness programmes, was inappropriate.

A particular weakness of the procedure was the lack of control of the registration forms and other registration materials that gave rise to an inability to account for the amount of registration form issued, used and unused.

Malawi 1994

Malawi was well placed in 1994 to have a smooth and lively awareness programme for voter registration exercise. I was advising the Commission, along with other partners However, certain partners, including the UN, advised on modern practices of advertisement on the electronic media and in the press to reach the eligible persons throughout the country. The new approach, which deliberately or otherwise unwittingly deemphasised the traditional manner of reaching the rustic electorate through notices on centrally located trees, where people gathered, and through the traditional leaders and churches, proved unsuccessful. After the end of the stipulated period for registration only about a third of the estimated qualified persons were registered. The period for registration was extended for a couple of weeks and all the traditional methods of communications with the rural population were opened up and soon the number of registered persons reached well over seventy percent of the estimated voters.

Zambia 1994

The state of play in Zambia in late 1994/5 was one in which the authorities had not updated the register on schedule and wished to convert the national identification process into the registration of voters process, or at least merge the two. At the request of the Zambian Government, I was sent by the Commonwealth Secretary-General to advise on the issue. After examining the issue and discussion with the Commission and with Ministers, my conclusion was that it would require extensive safeguards if the two processes were to be merged or if one were to be substituted for the other, if the register for the pending election were to be produced in that manner.[51]

---

[51] At the risk of repetition, I have included these projects which appeared under the chapter above on Technical Assistance for completeness.

Antigua and Barbuda 2001

In undertaking electoral reform in Antigua/Barbuda in 1991, dissatisfaction with the voters' register was a major issue. Improved safeguards against multiple registrations were provided for in the amended Act and stricter provisions dealing with the registration and voting by Antiguans resident abroad were enacted.

Cayman Islands 2003

In 2003 the Cayman Islands had a shrinking voters' register. Efforts to attract young voters by taking the registration exercise to dance venues and religious and other gatherings brought only modest results. I discussed changing the registration process from voluntary to compulsory registration and the authorities agreed and so failure to register attracted a fine of C$400.00.

Tanzania 2004

My involvement in Tanzania in 2004 with registration was in a legal capacity to draft amendments to the Electoral Laws which would facilitate the establishment of a permanent national voters' register.

CHAPTER VII

Designing election/civic/voter education programmes

Jamaica
Nigeria
South Africa
Cayman Islands
Liberia

Introduction

In framing this chapter, I have drawn largely on my recent experience in the African Union in which I assisted in setting up the Democracy and Electoral Assistance Unit (DEAU). There is a current view that election education should be ongoing. There have been insufficient election education programmes in many emerging democracies, particularly in the African Union. The need is unevenly spread, for example, throughout the African continent; but at best there has been a continuing need for more extensive election education at the national levels. Election education is primarily to enable voters to cast their ballot in accordance with the electoral rules and to encourage voters to go out and cast their votes. The discussion of educating primary stakeholders will here in be centred on election education which extends to political parties, candidates, representatives, agents, as well as the electorate. However, in the wider context voter education may be seen as a three-dimensional issue encompassing civic information relating to elections; information targeting politicians, parties, candidates, party officials, representatives, agents and the media; and information directed at the voters. At a meeting of EMBs from all over the African continent held in Accra, Ghana, in December 2009, there was a strong call for on-going election education across the continent. This issue was put forward with considerable emphasis by the representative of the Zambian EMB. This concept is not new. It had been recommended in the Commonwealth, for example, by the Commonwealth Observer Group (COG) to Antigua/Barbuda elections in 1999.[52]

Information designed to promote civic responsibility can be important in providing training in avoiding election conflict, violence and intimidation, corruption and election fraud. Election education designed to target politicians, that is to say, political parties, candidates, party officials, representatives, agents and the media, should include the election laws, rules, regulations and procedures, the role of the parties, candidates, agents, and behaviour on election campaign trail. Election information and training should also focus on the tasks of parties' agents and representatives during voters' registration, as well as during preparation for polling, during polling, and counting of the votes. Information aimed at the media houses and journalists should include glossary of election terms, relevant provisions of the election laws and procedures, as well as major events on the Election Calendar. The information aimed at the voters should focus primarily on the voting rules and procedures, particularly on new amendments to voting procedures. Other relevant information such as location of polling places, date and time of polling, and the protection of the secrecy of the ballot.

There is an urgent need to re-examine the scope of the 'traditional' voter education programmes to emphasize the compelling need for election education in new and emerging democracies in Africa and elsewhere, targeting voters as well as other primary stakeholders as political parties, candidates and their representatives and supporters. Election education should encompass, but not entirely subsume, civic education relating to elections. It should focus on the attributes of democratic elections such as tolerance towards other contestants, willingness to be prepared to win or lose and to accept the results of the election. Election education should target election campaigns to ensure that any code of conduct that

---

[52] See Report of the Commonwealth Observation Group of 9 March 1999 p.25.

may be in place is observed and that 'hate' speeches, intimidation and violence cease to be a feature of any election. The renewed approach to election education should highlight the acceptable behavioural conduct during election campaign, and conduct which ought to be unacceptable. The term 'voter education' connotes too narrow an approach in the context of most emerging democracies and should be broadened to embrace the candidates and political parties contesting an election.

Regardless of the scope, target groups or contents of election education, the real purpose of educating the stakeholders in democratic elections is to urge each voter to vote and demonstrate the power of each vote. As the American Association of University Women (AAUW) demonstrated one vote can make a difference in an election.[53]

My Approach to Election Education
My approach to the traditional voter education programmes is to broaden its scope and treat the content in a creative and user-friendly manner. I believe strongly that more emphasis should be placed on creating materials for use by and training of political parties, candidates, party agents and representatives in campaign (including financial) rules and procedures. I have set out in the paragraphs below some of my thoughts and concepts with respect to good practices in election education, followed by two

---

[53] In 1645, one vote gave Oliver Cromwell control of England. In 1649, one vote caused Charles I of England to be executed. In 1776, one vote gave America the English language instead of German. In 1845, one vote brought Texas into the Union. In 1868, one vote saved President Andrew Johnson from impeachment. In 1876, one vote gave Rutherford B. Haves the presidency of the United States. In 1923, one vote gave Adolph Hitler leadership of the Nazi Party. In 1960, a one-vote change in each precinct of Illinois would have denied John F. Kennedy the presidency. In 1968, Hubert Humphrey lost and Richard Nixon won the presidential election by a margin of fewer than three votes per precinct. In 2000, one vote in the US Supreme Court lost the presidential election for AL Gore and won it for George W. Bush. (AAUW's Action Alert. Sept. 2004).

short case-study illustrations, Liberia and Nigeria, in which I was involved.

The Architects of Election Education

The principal architect of election education ought to be the national EMB which should approve and coordinate all election education programmes in order to ensure that objectives are achieved and that partisanship is avoided. However, the legislative schemes of several countries do not vest primary responsibility for election education in the national EMB. Mauritius, for example, did not provide for civic and voter education in the electoral legislation and political parties and NGOs pay scant attention to educating the voters and other stakeholders as normally happens in most other countries. The explanation that has often been given for the unusual situation is that Mauritius is an established democracy and most of its citizens are familiar with the electoral system. The situation in Cameroon has not been as extreme as in Mauritius, but only limited civic and voter education had been dispensed to stakeholders in the past by the EMBs, namely, the Ministry of Territorial Administration and Decentralization (MINATD) and the National Elections Observatory (NEO) on the grounds that key responsibility for civic and voter education rested with the political parties. In Nigeria, the National Orientation Agency (NOA), a Government-run agency, which was set up during military rule, had primary responsibility for civic and voter education. The Independent National Electoral Commission (INEC) did a good job in co-existence with NOA in mounting programmes in educating voters concerning voting procedures and location of voting places. There are a number of other countries in the African Union whose national EMBs are not mandated to deal with civic and voter education including Botswana, Namibia and Seychelles. In the SADC region the majority of the countries' EMBs had a mandate to deal with voter education including Angola, Democratic Republic of Congo, Lesotho, Madagascar, Malawi, Mozambique, South Africa, Swaziland, Tanzania, Zambia and Zimbabwe.

Election Education Targeted Groups

In the context of the African Union, for example, certain groups need to be targeted in order to optimize the impact of election education (encompassing both civic and voter education) throughout the territorial jurisdiction of the Member States concerned. In large multi-ethnic, multi-religious and multi-lingual States such as Democratic Republic of Congo, Nigeria, South Africa and Sudan, all entities must be catered for in planning, preparing, and disseminating election education materials. People in remote rural districts should be included in the programmes. So should nomadic peoples where appropriate. Gender may be singled out for special treatment where tradition, custom or religion warrants it. Faith-based groups may also attract particular treatment in appropriate circumstance. In conflict or post-conflict areas there may be the need to develop special programmes for refugees in neighbouring countries with the permission of those host countries.[54] Internally displaced persons (IDPs) may need special election education focusing on where to register as a voter (if qualified to vote), and where and how to vote. Other groups of people such as the sick in hospitals, the old and infirm in hostels, prisoners serving time in prisons and persons in detention and not yet tried, all these groups may require election education

The Role of the Media in Elections Education

The general impression one gets of the media and elections in the emerging democracies is that the information environment has always been dominated by the media, despite that the landscape is always filled with messages from parties and candidates on billboards, posters on vehicles, buildings, trees, and balloons in the sky. The media has many dimensions so far as elections and election education are concerned. The electronic media, that is, television, radio, the Internet and mobile phone (text messaging)

---

[54] It is important for the country planning elections to ensure that neighbouring countries give permission in good time for election processes including election education be carried out on their territory. It ought not to be taken for granted. In 2005, some of Liberia's neighbours indicated that election processes should not be conducted on their territory.

are assuming increasing importance in the emerging democracies. Perhaps the radio has been the medium with the greatest outreach in most of these countries and so for the purposes of election education, perhaps the most valuable medium. Nevertheless, the print media remain popular in some countries with the literate electorate. For the purposes of election education the print media, that is, the national as well as the regional and local newspapers are important for disseminating election education messages.

Publicly Owned Media

The publicly owned media has been the most controversial so far as elections are concerned. The contention has centred on the near monopolization of access to the publicly owned media by the governing party and government. With few exceptions, the general perception is that there has been a failure of the publicly owned media to remain non-partisan and report in a balanced manner during election campaigns. There are many new and emerging democracies in which the public media, both electronic and print, are moderating their partisanship and moving to more balanced reporting and even access for opposition parties. The steady progress in the move to balanced reporting by the publicly owned media in election campaigns is under scrutiny in African Union Member States such as Benin, Cape Verde, and Botswana, Ghana, Mauritius, and South Africa and points to the future direction. In some countries, like South Africa, there are structures which provide the framework for equitable, and Malawi where the law requires equal free time on the publicly owned electronic media for political parties, the electorate is assured of a balanced party election education. Other countries, like Kenya and Zimbabwe, preferred to issue regulations dealing with access to publicly owned media during the campaign period.

Privately Owned Media

The privately owned media has shown no less partisanship than the publicly owned media, but is usually under less scrutiny than the publicly owned media which benefits from taxpayers' funds. Some private media sometimes opts to forego broadcasting of election campaign materials and so is not bound morally or voluntarily by a legal code of conduct. Most media codes of conduct have not been directed at the privately owned media, but it is always opened to the private media to enter into a voluntary code of conduct with respect to elections.

Election education may be promoted by both public and private media through political parties airing their manifestos, and CSOs promoting civic and voter education programmes.

The Role of Civil Society Organizations (CSOs) in Election Education

Civil society organizations have provided invaluable assistance to national EMBs and particularly in the area of civic, voter and election education. Support to civic, voter and election education often take the form of funding local NGOs' and national EMBs' efforts in producing education materials and providing training of election education officers. CSOs have been instrumental in designing their own voter education programmes or jointly with the EMBs concerned. My experience has shown that for the partnership between CSOs and EMBs to be successfully executed, there must be close collaboration between the two sides. Issues such as the budget, programme design, and texts of messages for advertisements should be in line with the broad approval of the EMBs concerned. A minority of EMBs often display non-cooperation or even hostility towards CSOs engaged in election education. However, with a growing trend to the recognition of the role of CSOs in elections, an increasing number of EMBs are showing a willingness to work with CSOs in election education.

The work of CSOs has come under the spotlight from time to time. Their work in many countries has won high marks, for example, in Zambia in 1991, in Kenya in 1992, South Africa in 1994, Malawi in 1994, and more recently in Liberia in 2005, Angola in 2008 and Rwanda in 2008. However, occasionally CSOs encounter difficulty in operating in some countries, for example, many CSOs and NGOs were expelled from Ethiopia in 2005, and the activities of local and foreign CSOs were severely restricted in Zimbabwe during the 2008 elections.

The NGOs and CSOs, taking account of the political situation and the social and cultural traditions of a given country, use a range of election education techniques including non-partisan posters, pamphlets, voter awareness kits, radio and television announcements and dramatizations, voting simulations and candidate forums.

The Content of Election, Civic and Voter Education

The content of election education in emerging democracies, particularly in the African Union Member States was always fascinating and had shown great adaptation to local needs. The diversity in tradition and local customs had also revealed itself in a variety of ways through local song and dance and indigenous plays. However, in designing election education programmes, the traditional contents should not be ignored although local modifications should be taken into account. Election education (voter and civic education) programmes are designed to educate primary stakeholders, particularly voters and political parties and candidates, to participate properly in the electoral process. The primary thrust of election education is to enable the main stakeholders to understand and appreciate the user-friendly campaign and polling procedures. In some Member States, like Ghana, the Constitution pointed to the nature of voter education which should be provided by the Electoral Commission, that is, to educate the people on the electoral process and its purpose.[55] Similarly, Electoral Commission of Malawi was mandated to promote through the media and appropriate and effective means the civic education of the citizens concerning the election.[56] The Nigerian structures were framed to cater for a broader need than voter education, although designed for purposes less worthy than the promotion of democratic elections. The INEC (Independent National Electoral Commission) shared the mandate with the NOA (National Orientation Agency) to educate the electorate. However, the NOA was established back in 1993 as an agent of Government (during the Military Administration) to ensure, among

---

[55] See article 45 of the Constitution of Ghana, 1992.

[56] See section 5 of the Parliamentary and Presidential Elections Act.

other things, discipline, patriotism, integrity and accountability. The main rationale of the agency was the need for orientation, sensitization and mobilization of the populace. The methodology used included, workshops, lectures, seminars, rallies, drama sketches, community theatre and interactive sessions. The NOA mounted election education programmes jointly with agencies of foreign governments, as it did for the 2003 elections, (although NGOs and other foreign partners were reluctant to work with NOA on the ground that it was partisan in favour of the Government and ruling party).[57]

In designing an election education project for a large African country as Nigeria, there are many factors to be taken into account. Nigeria has the largest electorate by far in the African Union-over 70 million. The ethnic and religious diversity is very pronounced. The territory is relatively large with minority ethnic groups interspersed within larger ethnic groups. Radio has for some time been the medium with the greatest geographical reach. If the election education budget is limited (and that is always the case), the radio with its greatest reach across the territory of the country offers the most cost-effective medium for the purposes of reaching the largest number of voters. The television has substantial reach in the urban areas, and the lively press has considerable reach, particularly regional papers. The production of materials for election education in a large African country as Nigeria encompasses a range of materials such as messages in the form of jingles for television and radio, plays relating to elections for radio and television, interactive sessions at town halls and in villages. Visual materials such as posters, sketches, fliers, billboards, and advertisements in newspapers have always been used throughout Nigeria.

In emerging democracies, the election education programmes need to be tailored to meet the local needs, for example, in Democratic Republic of the Congo, the Independent Electoral Commission along

---

[57]   In 2003 the author worked closely with NOA as a Consultant with the Department for International Department (DfID) to design a civic and voter education programme for the then pending elections in Nigeria.

with the UN and NGOs like the International Foundation for Electoral System (IFES) introduced the boîte á images or picture box. The picture box contained some 27 pictures that illustrated important concepts of democracy, free elections and civic responsibility. The target was primarily illiterate voters. In the Gambia where the voters used marbles to cast their ballot, the voting procedures were different and hence the content and requirements of election education were different from the rest of the African continent.

Cost of Election Education

The cost of mounting an effective election education programme designed to cover the entire territory of the State has often proved to be beyond the resources of the EMB or other entities responsible for educating the electorate and other stakeholders. Election education has been a high-cost activity in many emerging democracies. This has been the case because of the topography, conflict or post-conflict situations, for example, the Democratic Republic of the Congo where the election budget as a whole was $432 million of which some $46 million was pledged for the election education in 2006. Though there had never been enough resources to undertake a complete and effective national programme, international partners play a prominent role in funding and training election education officers in many countries. Election education usually generates considerable local expenditure engaging artists who produced plays, jingles and posters.

In managing these activities, patronage develops and sometimes gives way to petty corruption. The majority of the expenditure on election education usually goes on television slots for jingles or advertisements in many countries, including mature democracies. Radio always had a wider reach in most African countries and so it is the main medium for election advertisements.

Election education should be applied to many electoral processes and should not be seen as confined to the polling process. Substantial election education is required to support registration of voters, as well as the delimitation of electoral districts (where delimitation is required). The costs of these programmes of election education should be factored into the overall costs of election organization. Hence election education should embrace all these processes and target stakeholders other than the voters, such as the political parties, candidates, their representatives and agents. An appropriate wider definition, or perhaps more apt description, of election education might be a process by which qualified citizens are educated on how to register and vote, develop adequate knowledge of the electoral process, as well as the civic duty to participate in the electoral process and the commitment to abide by the result of legitimate elections.

Way Forward for Election Education Programmes

My hope and involvement with election education is that it will continue to be designed to clothe qualified citizens with the knowledge and appreciation of the values which will strengthen participation in the political process. It has been primarily concerned with programmes addressing the voters' ability to take part in the electoral process with confidence. Addressing the key role of primary stakeholders as the political parties, candidates, their representatives and agents, and voters, election education should make these persons targets of not only programmes with respect to registration and polling procedures, but also to emphasize the importance of the vote and enhance the sense of civic duty and knowledge of democratic principles, as well as commitment to accept electoral outcomes. The growing working relationship between EMBs and CSOs and NGOs will continue to generate confidence of stakeholders in the electoral process. Conflict and post-conflict situations, of which there are many throughout the world, will continue to pose a threat to comprehensive territorial coverage through degraded infrastructure and poor security.

Measuring the Impact of Election Education

The emerging democracies, including African Union Member States, need to take a number of measures to ensure that election education continues to develop steadily and improve in quality. The national EMBs need to intensify their involvement with election education programmes in partnership with NGOs and

CSOs. In general, election education will need more resources and commence earlier prior to polling day.

Election education programmes should be designed with verifiable or measurable indicators which aide post-election peer reviews and facilitate lessons learned. Each activity of such programmes should be justified for the approval of the EMB, NGOs or CSOs concerned. There could be verifiable interim indicators in appropriate cases to measure how well the activity or programme as a whole was performing in order to effect remedial actions. Indicators of election education will vary according to the election process being addressed, for example, in a voter registration exercise an indicator would be the number of qualified persons registered. With respect to the preparation for the poll and for polling, appropriate indicators would be the turn out of voters on polling day, and the number of spoiled ballots at the polls.

Selected Examples of Election Education

I have designed election education programmes in Jamaica, South Africa and Cayman Islands, as well as Liberia and Nigeria. The main features of the latter two countries are set out below:

Liberia 2004-05

Liberia in 2004-05 was in a post-conflict mode. I was European Commission's election consultant. We had a significant sum of money available for assistance with election education programmes. There was a newly reformed EMB which was ably assisted by a number of partners including the UN, European Commission, and IFES-USAID in the organization of the 2005 general elections. Election education was generously assisted by the main partners, as well as others. Several million dollars were made available towards election education programmes for the registration of voters and polling.

In post-conflict Liberia, election education was particularly important as many hundreds of qualified persons were dispersed either as refugees abroad or displaced internally. Furthermore, fourteen years of conflict had degraded or completely destroyed the infrastructure in many parts of the country.

Unlike the case of Botswana in 2004 where the IEC spearheaded the election education programmes, in Liberia the CSOs and NGOs played a prominent role, although the programmes were coordinated by the National Elections Commission (NEC).

Activities-Advertisements

Radio had the greatest reach in Liberia and so the bulk of the election education messages were presented through advertisements on the radio. There were several radio stations and so the stations which were most popular were selected to broadcast election messages and jingles. There were experienced local entities in designing and producing election messages and jingles. The costs were modest and the programmes were effective with respect to polling, but less effective during the registration of voters because the programmes were mounted late and not effectively monitored. It was also due to unfriendly and damaged physical infrastructure and insufficient knowledge of how to deal with such obstacles.

The press in Liberia was limited in reach serving mainly urban areas, but it performed well and was mainly non-partisan.

Visual Forms of Advertisements

Visual advertisements such as posters, fliers and billboards played an important role in the rural parts. However such was the state of the roads and the difficulty in organizing transportation that it took several weeks to get the billboards out to the designated locations. Vehicles, trucks and buses were also used to carry election messages from the NEC to the countryside.

Drama

There were several experienced drama groups of which probably the best known was *Talking Drums* which were able to produce plays and other presentations to audiences around the countryside. Those groups were employed by the NGOs and CSOs to take their shows on the road.

Oversight

The NEC approved the election education programmes proposed by NGOs and CSOs and kept a monitoring vigil in order to move in complement programmes where necessary.

Evaluation

The election education programmes performed below requirements and expectations of the stakeholders. Stakeholders quickly complained about the inadequacies of the election education programmes during the registration of voters and the complaints were acknowledged by the NEC and the partners. There were improvements with respect to timing and quality of messages that were broadcast during polling preparation and in particular with respect to the election logistics. There was significant improvement in the quality and the coverage afforded during polling preparation compared to what was available during the registration of voters. The joint efforts between the NEC and NGOs/CSOs were successful and could point the way forward with election education in emerging democracies, particularly in the African Union Member States.

Nigeria 2003

Nigeria has the largest electorate in Africa and occupied relatively large territory geographically. The Nigerian authorities had for sometime even before democratic government was restored in 1999 sought to extend election (civic) education beyond mere voters to wider sectors of the community. In 2003, I was retained as an election consultant by the British Department for International Development (DfID) to work with the National Orientation Authority (NOA) to design an election education programme for the pending elections. The NOA which had responsibility for election education was also mandated to deal with a range of civic and nationalistic education. The NOA and INEC worked closely with NGOs and CSOs to mount education programmes for the 2003 and 2007 elections.

Activities

Election education in Nigeria has had the potential to be very expensive because the need was always great and the country is large with many languages and ethnic customs. There were many television stations and radio stations, as well as a multitude of daily newspapers. NOA always had limited budgets to mount advertisements on television and radio. NGOs and CSOs also of necessity had been able to mount limited programmes because of the lack of resources. Nevertheless, television and radio election education messages, together with jingles and plays, were broadcast to stakeholders. While like many other African countries, television had a wide reach in the urban areas, radio had greater reach among the electorate in rural districts. The press also had a relatively wide reach in Nigeria and was used by the NOA, INEC as well as NGOs and CSOs to disseminate the election education jingles and other messages.

Interactive Sessions

Interactive sessions were used to get across messages to the rural population. It was a popular method used by NOA to get across its messages through participation at meetings in town halls or elsewhere in rural areas. A typical interactive session in the rural areas may be announced by the equivalent of the village crier. The session would be accompanied by entertainment and refreshment for the participants. Those popular gatherings were designed for impartation of messages to the rustic masses.

The Stakeholders Election Forum Committees

The stakeholders' election forum committees at the national level consisted of representatives of the political parties; NGOs and CSOs; INEC; agents of the government with direct relevance to the electoral process; security agencies such as the police and state security service; professional associations such as the Nigerian Bar Association, Nigeria Union of Journalists; representatives of the Legislature; the National Orientation Agency; the media; and international organization. The forum was designed to meet periodically.

Public Enlightenment Tours

The enlightenment tours were proposed mainly for the Federal Capital Territory and were designed for the election 2007 as a kind of pilot project to develop informal ways of stimulating voter interests. It intended to encompass live drama performances, meetings with community-based organizations and other stakeholders, courtesy visits to traditional rulers, and seminars for political editors and correspondents.

The Nigerian authorities had shown significant creativity in designing election education programmes. The NOA organized interactive sessions in rural areas as well as stakeholders forums that sought to cast a wider participatory net than even civic and voter education. While the NOA role and history might have been rightly frowned upon, the election education that NOA and the stakeholders forums represented pointed to wider scope that election education might take in the future in given situations.

CHAPTER VIII

Emissary of Secretary-General

Grenada unconstitutional change of govt.—Sir Paul Scoon—Chief
Justice Nedd;
Trip with SG to see CARICOM heads & Canadian Foreign Minister
McIntyre in Geneva, message from McIntyre to Delhi CHOGM
Grenada-Interim Govt.—preparation for elections Blaize—
Constitutional Commission
Eminent Persons Group Search—Chairperson—Manley—Ms. Barrow
President Moi
Mozambique elections 1994
Bangladesh February 1996
Nigeria 1998
Cameroon (Twice)
Guyana, Jagdeo 2000

Introduction
During my employment with the Commonwealth Secretariat, I
was privileged to undertake many special missions as an emissary
of the Secretary-General. These were missions with an electoral
or governance flavour and varied from a single purpose event
such as conveying a message to a head of government or State,
to a multipurpose mission with multiple goals as the Grenada
missions in the 1980s. The nature of some of my early special
missions drew adverse criticisms from the Office of the Deputy
Secretary-General which felt that I was doing tasks that properly
fell within the terms of reference of that Office. In a similar vein,
the Political Affairs Department of the Secretariat was unhappy for
not dissimilar reasons. I would have none of the complaints and
immediately advised the complainants to raise their concerns with

the Secretary-General, as they all knew that I was merely doing the Secretary-General's bidding.

Grenada 1983-85

Perhaps the most fascinating special mission which I undertook was to Grenada as an emissary of Secretary-General, Sir Shridath Ramphal, soon after the American invasion of that country in 1983. I was tasked with the responsibility to call on the Governor-General of Grenada, Sir Paul Scoon, and Chief Justice Nedd, and get a report from each distinguished officials of Grenada and report back to the Secretary-General.

The meeting with Governor-General Scoon was cordial. He related the events which led to the killing of Prime Minister Maurice Bishop and the movements of army tanks and other army vehicles which he saw from his residence. He confided to me that when the invasion started he hid under his bed for several hours for fear of being shot by sniper bullets from one side or the other.

My discussion with Chief Justice Nedd was largely about the legal and constitutional situation and his thoughts about an interim administration. I reported to the Secretary-General and conveyed messages from the Governor-General and the Chief Justice. My report to the Secretary-General triggered a search for a suitable Grenadian national who had the necessary standing to head an interim administration and who would not be wholly beholden to the Americans. The ideal person for the task was thought to be Mr. (as he then was) Alistair McIntyre, who was the Head of UNCTAD in Geneva.

I was mandated (to remain in Geneva as long as it took), to secure the agreement of Mr. McIntyre to head the Grenadian interim administration. After two visits to Geneva from London to discuss possible terms and conditions for the Grenadian assignment, McIntyre agreed and I took the good news to the Secretary General in New Delhi, India, where the Commonwealth Heads of Government were meeting.

When I reached New Delhi, a message had preceded my arrival to the effect that on his doctors orders Mr. McIntyre was not fit enough to assume duties in Grenada. That development upset the Commonwealth's plan for Grenada, which was one of the main issues being discussed at that Commonwealth Heads of Government Meeting. I accompanied the Secretary-General to the Heads' retreat in Goa where Mrs Indira Ghandi was in the Chair and Mrs Thatcher was leading the UK delegation.

The retreat was a very sensitive environment as the Caribbean Heads, unlike the Secretary-General who was also from the Caribbean, supported the American invasion of Grenada. My task in the face of the retreat plenary meeting was to lobby quietly the Heads to support a Commonwealth Resolution which did not enthusiastically offer support for the invasion. The Caribbean Heads at the Commonwealth retreat were not united. The two most vocal in support of the invasion were Prime Minister Tom Adams of Barbados and Prime Minister Charles of Dominica. President Forbes Burnham of Guyana appeared low key on the issue at the retreat and so were Prime Minister Chambers of Trinidad and Tobago and Prime Minister Seaga of Jamaica. Prime Minister Charles felt so strongly in favour of the American action that when I was quietly lobbying another Head of Government near to her to support the draft Resolution on Grenada, she started repeating aloud in the meeting that "I do not support this resolution". The comments of Prime Minister Charles were aimed at the resolution and not at me, the lobbyist. I had known the Prime Minister rather well for I was then her chief negotiator in ongoing maritime boundaries delimitation talks with respect to Dominica and France, relating to Martinique and Guadeloupe since 1981. The Chairperson of the retreat, Mrs Indira Ghandi, was not impressed with the Caribbean Heads' position in supporting the American invasion, nor was Mrs Thatcher, although she was low key on the issue at the retreat.

After the Commonwealth Heads' retreat in Goa, I went back to Geneva to ascertain whether or not McIntyre was indeed off the radar for Grenada and to trade thoughts on possible replacement. McIntyre confirmed that in the light of his doctors' advice he was no longer available. Towards the end of December 1983 and the beginning of January 1984, I accompanied Secretary-General Ramphal on a trip around the Caribbean to meet the Heads of Government to mend fences as it were, since the Secretary-General was not on the same page as most of the Heads of Government of the Caribbean on the issue of the American invasion of Grenada. We visited Prime Minister Pindling of the Bahamas, Prime Minister Vere Bird of Antigua/Barbuda, Prime Minister Tom Adams of Barbados, President Forbes Burnham of Guyana, Prime Minister Milton Cato of St. Vincent and the Grenadines, Prime Minister John Compton of St. Lucia, Prime Minister Eugenia Charles of Dominica, and Prime Minister Edward Seaga of Jamaica, and then on the see the Foreign Minister of Canada. In the meanwhile the search to find a suitable head for the interim administration had resumed until Mr. Nicholas Braithwaite, a former consultant to the Commonwealth Fund for Technical Co-operation (CFTC) and a Grenadian, agreed to take up the assignment. The Interim Administration was constituted of prominent Grenadians and it ran the affairs of the island until elections were held. I continued to be the Secretary-General's liaison officer with the Interim Administration. Subsequent to the Delhi Heads of Government meeting and the Secretary-General's trip around the Caribbean and to Canada, the Foreign Relations Committee of the British House of Commons requested the Secretary-General's appearance before the Committee. I accompanied the Secretary-General to that meeting.

The post-conflict elections were held, Mr Herbert Blaize became Prime Minister. So soon as Mr. Blaize was sworn in as Prime Minister, the Secretary-General sent me to meet him and to assist him in setting up a Commission to draw up a new constitution. I met the new Prime Minister of Grenada (whom I had met on several occasions before) about 9 a.m. on a Saturday morning. I delivered a message from the Secretary-General and welcome him and Grenada back into the Commonwealth. Prime Minister Blaize looked at me rather sternly and asked me, "What is the welcome for? I never left the Commonwealth!" he said. Nevertheless, my meeting went well and I managed to secure the agreement of Professor Ralph Carnegie to serve on the Commission. I had hoped that Prof. Carnegie would be asked to chair the Commission, but the Prime Minister resisted suggestions and offered Sir Fred Phillips, an old friend of his, the Chairmanship.

Eminent Persons Group Chairperson

In the late 1980s, the Commonwealth Secretary-General was putting together a group of eminent persons to undertake a mission to South Africa and he wished to have a prominent West Indian national to lead the group. He sent me as his special emissary to the Caribbean to find a person to fit the occasion. The Secretary-General had in mind Michael Manley as his first choice and so I went to Jamaica to talk with Prime Minister Seaga if he would agree to Mr. Manley leading the group of eminent persons. Prime Minister Seaga told me that he had to mull over it and he would let me know his decision through his Permanent Secretary, Mr. Don Brice. I must have been pestering Brice a bit too much for a quick response from the Prime Minister, and so quite out of character he lost his cool and told me that he had his work to do and I had mine. After about four days I was informed that Prime Minister Seaga would not give his consent to Mr. Manley joining the Commonwealth group of eminent persons to go to South Africa. No reason was given for Prime Minister Seaga's refusal, but informal soundings led me to believe that since a general election was not too far off, the Prime Minister feared that Mr. Manley might use such an appointment to emphasise his prominence in the Caribbean and the Commonwealth.

I conveyed my failure and disappointment to secure Mr. Manley in Jamaica to the Secretary-General who mandated me to carry on to Barbados to interview Ms. Barrow with whom I was satisfied and I recommended her for the position. An offer was made to her after consulting the Secretary-General and she accepted.

President Moi 1992

In 1992, I was embedded in the Electoral Commission of Kenya (ECK) on a Commonwealth technical assistance programme, while at the same time liaising with the Commonwealth Secretary-General, H.E. Emeka Anyaoku on the overall progress of the preparations for the pending multiparty elections, the first in many years in Kenya. There was widespread dissatisfaction among opposition parties and other stakeholders that the Electoral Commission was partisan and that the Commissioners were all appointed by the President without consulting the opposition. I conveyed the developing discontent to the Secretary-General and recommended that he should visit President Moi to discuss the matter. The Secretary-General agreed and I accompanied him to discuss the matter with the President. The President was persuaded that something should be done to improve the electoral environment and so he increased the number of Commissioners to eleven from seven in consultation with the opposition.

As the pace of the election preparation in 1992 increased, it became apparent to many that the Chairman of the ECK, Justice Chesoni, was not steeped in the electoral culture of transparency and so he seldom met with representatives of the media and of the opposition political parties. Again, the electoral environment was perceived as unfriendly to stakeholders. I had drawn the attention of Chairman Chesoni to the uneasiness of the media about the untimely release of information about the elections to the media and the general public, but he was not moved to do much to remedy the situation. I drew the deteriorating relationship between the ECK and the media and opposition parties to the attention of the Secretary-General and recommended that he paid another visit to President Moi and Chairman Chesoni. The Secretary-General agreed and I accompanied him to see President Moi and then Chairman Chesoni. They both were persuaded that the public relations strategy of the ECK needed strengthening and that regular meetings would be held between the ECK and the political parties, including opposition parties, and with the media.

Mozambique 1994 and Bangladesh 1996

Mozambique enjoyed a special relationship with the Commonwealth since its independence in 1975. It benefited from Commonwealth assistance in a number of areas and in 1995 was granted membership of that Association. Many months before the first multiparty elections in 1994, I was offering advice on electoral matters to the Commissão Nacional de Eleições (CNE) of Mozambique. On an occasion, Secretary-General Anyaoku visited Maputo and a colleague, John Syson, and I joined the Secretary-General at dinner with President Chissano. The Government of Mozambique and the Electoral Commission of that country invited the Secretary-General of the Commonwealth to send a Commonwealth election observer mission to the 1994 multiparty elections, the Secretary-General sent me and a colleague to represent him as it would not be appropriate to send a Commonwealth mission, since Mozambique was not yet a member of the Commonwealth.

In 1996, the Secretary-General sent me as his representative to the Bangladesh elections, when he was requested by the ruling party and Government to send a Commonwealth election observation mission. The main opposition party, however, decided to boycott the elections and so under the Commonwealth election observation guidelines, the Secretary-General could not send a Commonwealth team of observers and so he sent a small team headed by me to talk with prominent persons in Dhaka and witness the conduct of polling day.

Nigeria 1998
In 1998, as soon as it became clear that a return to civilian rule in Nigeria was in contemplation, H.E. Chief Emeka Anyaoku, Secretary-General of the Commonwealth and himself a Nigerian, called me in and mandated me to take charge of arranging Commonwealth technical assistance towards the transitional multiparty elections. He further charged me with the task of advising the Independent National Electoral Commission (INEC) and to liaise with him on all significant developments. I was dispatched to Abuja without delay to meet the Chairman of INEC, Justice Akpata, to ascertain his electoral needs. Training of registration and polling officers was high on his list, and so was election logistics management. The Commonwealth's response was modest but pivotal at the outset. The Elections Commission of India contributed one its experienced election logistics managers to be based in Abuja for several months. The Commonwealth Secretariat contributed my technical services to INEC for which

I arranged orientation sessions for Commissioners, and assisted many of INEC's Departments, including the Legal, Administrative, Operations and Public Relations Departments. INEC provided me with transportation and free accommodation at the Sheraton Hotel in Abuja. Canada and Australia also provided assistance to INEC.

I organized two groups of trainers of trainers drawn from several Commonwealth countries, one pre-local election in December 1998 and post-local elections to cover the six geographic regions of Nigeria. During the period leading up to the elections two Nigerian Commissioners attended a capacity-building elections course conducted the Commonwealth Secretariat in Zimbabwe for senior Commonwealth African election officers. I was instrumental in organizing and conducting that course which was one of a series that were being held in Africa. I was also the chief instigator of the two female Commissioners from INEC attending the election workshop in Harare, Zimbabwe.

I believe that the technical assistance that I was able to organize in such a short time made a difference and INEC and the Secretary-General were pleased with the results.

Cameroon (1996 & 98)

Secretary-General of the Commonwealth, Chief Emeka Anyaoku, was instrumental in Cameroon's successful bid to join the Commonwealth association. He was also interested in seeing Cameroon set up an electoral structure that would deliver credible multiparty elections. With that position firmly fixed in his mind, the Secretary-General, with the agreement of President Paul Biya, dispatched me as his special emissary to discuss with the President's Office and the relevant Ministers and the Attorney-General the way forward in establishing an independent electoral management body. The opinions of the Ministers and officials with whom I spoke were divided. Some were sympathetic to the idea, but others saw it as an Anglophone approach and did not like the idea. Some of the officials felt the President was not against an independent electoral management body, but that his senior Cabinet Ministers would not buy into it for fear of weakening their political hold on power.

I reported back to the Secretary-General in a cautiously optimistic manner as the President's Advisers and Ministers indicated to me that they would convey the Secretary-General's message to the President and he would be in touch with the Secretary-General. As it turned out, there was no positive development. A couple of years passed and the Secretary-General again raised the matter with President Biya and matters seemed to have advanced as the President again agreed to my visit to Cameroon this time with a draft instrument for the establishment of an independent electoral management. I was again dispatched as the Secretary-General's emissary accompanied by a French-speaking colleague from the Secretariat. Like the first visit, we were well received by the President's Office and by relevant Ministers. The response was similar—they would study the documents and convey the Secretary-General's message to the President who would speak to the Secretary-General on the matter. It was many years after my second visit that the Cameroon authorities finally established an Independent Electoral Commission.

Post-1997 Guyana Elections

I was the leader of the Commonwealth Secretariat' Support Team to the COG that observed the Guyana elections in 1997. The count and tallying processes did not go well and the opposition parties did not accept the election results which went in favour of the incumbent President and Government. Serious disturbance followed the announcement of the election results. The CARICOM Heads of Government stepped in and got the ruling and opposition parties to come to an agreement to end the stand-off. The agreement was embodied in the Herdmanston Accord which brought forward the following election to 2001 and provided that the 1997 election results be audited by independent persons. In the meanwhile the Accord also provided for a CARICOM Facilitator to work with the political parties to achieve constitutional and electoral reform. I led a team with an English Local Government Specialist and myself to deal with possible changes in the Guyana electoral system and reform of the Local Government system.

After some months, the relationship between the CARICOM Facilitator and the political parties became strained and movement between the parties came to a halt. Secretary-General Anyaoku and I went to Guyana to talk to the senior members of the ruling party and opposition parties about resuming contact under the terms of the Agreement brokered by CARICOM. We also had breakfast with former President Hoyte who was the leader of the main opposition and who outlined the reforms he was seeking, particularly with respect to local government. The Secretary-General succeeded in getting the two sides to agree to resume talking to each other.

Guyana 2000

I undertook some eleven missions as emissary for Secretary-General Ramphal, about twelve on behalf of Secretary-General Anyaoku and one for Secretary-General Don McKinnon. The lone special mission I undertook on behalf of Secretary-General McKinnon was in December 2000 to see the President of Guyana, Mr. Jagdeo, to get an update on the Herdmanston Accord from the point of view of the Government. I was well received and I found the young President to be friendly and forward looking. He was positive and optimistic about the implementation of the Accord.

CHAPTER IX

Assessment and Planning Missions

Nigeria '98   Malawi '94
Sierra Leone '96   Pakistan 1993/2000
Kenya '92   Guyana 1998
Pakistan 2000   Namibia '94
Liberia 2006
Tanzania 1995

Introduction
This chapter may be conveniently treated in two related parts; the first part deals with request for electoral technical assistance to the Commonwealth Secretariat and the second deals with planning missions when an invitation was received by the Secretary-General to send election observers to a national election in a Commonwealth country. The two missions are similar but the objectives are different in so far as assessment missions which follow a request for technical assistance concentrates on the technical electoral needs of the requesting country, while an assessment (planning) mission which precedes election observation which is triggered by an invitation to observe an election is directed mainly at establishing that the contesting parties would welcome Commonwealth observers. The secondary purpose of a planning mission is to sort out the logistics, for example, hotel, transportation, names and addresses of persons to meet, for the deployment of observers.

1. Assessment Missions
I led many needs assessment missions (NAM) of the Commonwealth Secretariat to assess the needs of EMBs up on their request for electoral technical assistance.

(a) Kenya 1992.

In 1992 when the Government of Kenya was transitioning itself from a one-party to a multiparty system, it sought technical assistance from the Commonwealth Secretariat. I accompanied the then Deputy Secretary-General, Sir Anthony Siaguru, to assess the needs of the Attorney-General's Department with respect to electoral legislation and the technical assistance needs of the Electoral Commission of Kenya (ECK). With respect to the electoral legislation, the assessment mission identified the need for a legal regime for election observers, domestic and international, which I subsequently assisted in drafting.

With respect to the ECK, there was need to review the costing of the election, since donors did not think the budget prepared by the ECK was credible. I subsequently organized a team with an English specialist in costing elections to review the budget of the ECK. Our review trimmed the budget substantially. The assessment mission also identified the need for a code of conduct for election observers taking account of the amended legal provisions with which I had assisted the Attorney-General's Department.

(b) Sierra Leone 1996

In the mid-1990s, I was dispatched to Sierra Leone to assess the EMB's electoral needs in an environment that was not very conducive to democratic elections. There was a military regime in power and the country was in between conflicts. On the positive side, reform was being done to the Electoral Commission and one Dr. Jonah, a former Assistant Secretary-General of the UN, had recently taken over as Chairman of the Commission. My assessment mission was keen to identify deficiencies and communication infrastructure for the purposes of voter/civic education. There was need for urgent legal action with respect certain electoral notices and regulations. I went back to Sierra Leone to assist Dr Jonah with the urgent matters and quickly got the Commonwealth Secretariat to secure the services of a competent Caribbean born election/legal expert to carry on assisting the Electoral Commission with what I had started.

I visited all the radio stations, AM and FM, in Freetown and Mckenna, in order find out whether or not, for the purposes of voter education, there was full radio coverage of the country. Radio coverage did not extend to the whole country.

Tanzania 1995

In 1995, prior to the first multiparty elections in Tanzania for many years Deputy Secretary-General, Mr. Shrinivasan, and I went on a dual assessment and planning mission. An invitation was received by the Commonwealth Secretary-General to send Commonwealth election observers to the pending general elections. At the same time, the mission was mandated to consider any request for Secretariat technical assistance from the Electoral Commission.

In discussion with the Tanzanian Electoral Commission, the Chairman, Justice Lewis Makame, requested thirteen experts from the Commonwealth Secretariat, twelve trainers of trainers and one adviser to the Commission. Chairman Makame did clearly state that the request was subject to the approval of the Commission as a whole. As it transpired, only the adviser to the Commission was taken up, presumably the Commission did not approve the other requests.

Nigeria 1998

The Nigeria electoral environment in 1998 was positive despite the fact that the country was under military rule. The newly installed military regime had resolved to return the country to civilian rule within about eight months. The EMB which was restructured was mandated to hold a series of three sets of elections between December

1998 and February 1999. The newly constituted EMB, the Independent National Electoral Commission (INEC) was in place in August 1998 and towards the end of that month, I visited the INEC to ascertain their technical electoral needs. Nigeria is a big country with approximately sixty million voters at the time. Their needs were great. In my discussions with Justice Akpata, then Chairman of INEC, we identified the management of election logistics, training of trainers for election officers, orientation course for Commissioners and general assistance with good practices in election organization, as areas with which the Commonwealth could assist the INEC.

Tanzania [Zanzibar]

In January 2000, I coordinated three teams of consultants under the auspices of the programme of action agreed to by the Inter-Party Committee (IPC) of the two main political parties in Zanzibar to ease political tension on the islands. Each team of two consultants was mandated to review stipulated areas of the judicial, constitutional and legal structure of Zanzibar. I was asked to coordinate the teams largely because I was the Commonwealth's representative and member of the electoral team of consultant. The consultants completed their work and submitted a report to the Inter-Party Committee which consisted of the representatives of the ruling Chama Cha Mapinduzi (CCM) political party and the opposition party the Civic United Front (CUF) on 6th February 2000. The Government and ruling party did not enact most of the recommendations contained in the report of the consultants.[58]

---

[58] The consultancy teams were: team 1 –Professor Issa G. Shivji and Mr. B. Pollard to review the Constitution of Zanzibar; team 2-Mr. Mark Bomani and Mr. Carl W. Dundas to review the Zanzibar Electoral Commission and the electoral laws; and team 3-Professor G. Mgongo Fimbo and Justice T. Doherty to review the Judiciary.

Pakistan 2000

In 2000, I led an assessment mission to Pakistan. While the mission was to assess the electoral technical assistance needs, the real intention was to find out from the Elections Commission whether or not the revamped local elections were being organized in a democratic manner. My mission did propose the strengthening of the election administration, but I was unsure how much of the proposals were implemented.

Liberia 2006

In 2006, I was recruited by UNDP (Liberia) to undertake a comprehensive assessment of the electoral technical needs of Liberia in preparation for the second post-conflict elections set for 2011. It was a wonderful opportunity to deal with some of the problems which I had identified during 2004-5 when I was the European Commission's Election Consultant to Liberia. During the period 2004-5, I was closely associated with the constitutional and legal changes made to facilitate the transitional elections. Moreover, as the EC's sole election consultant in Liberia during 2004-5, I had some influence on how the EC's contribution of the equivalent of US$4 million to Liberia's electoral budget, was spent towards election programmes.

I made extensive recommendations regarding the provisions of the legislative scheme and the Constitution that needed to be amended, including reviewing the electoral system and the delimitation of constituencies. I addressed other issues such as comprehensive training for all electoral staff, including field staff, campaign financing, political party registration and registration of independent candidates to contest elections.

This exercise was not only concerned with identifying the technical needs of the National Elections Commission (NEC), but also indicating how they might be met, including drawing up a detailed programme, as was done in the case of training of NEC's staff.

2. Planning (Assessment) Missions

A typical planning mission mandate of the Commonwealth read as follows:

"The purpose of this Mission is to meet with the election authorities, with representatives of the major parties, non-governmental organizations and other groups with an interest in the election in order to assess the level of support for a Commonwealth observer presence, and to review the conditions under which the election will take place. The report of the Assessment Mission will form the basis for the decision on whether the circumstances conform to the parameters under which Commonwealth election missions are conducted".

The African Union Guidelines for Election Observers and Monitors placed considerable emphasis on what they called 'Exploratory Missions' which precede AU election observer missions. I offered advice to the Department of Political Affairs and the Democracy and Electoral Assistance Unit (DEAU) of the Commission of the African Union.

I undertook many planning missions ahead of Commonwealth election observation missions of which the under-mentioned are examples:

(a) Pakistan 1993, I headed a planning mission prior to a Commonwealth election observation mission later that year. There was a Caretaker Government in place in Pakistan at the time and so my team met with Head of the Caretaker Government and with representatives of the main parties that were contesting the elections. The electoral environment was positive and except for boycott by a significant opposition, the MQM, in the Sind Province, the campaign was mostly free of violence. The Planning

Mission reported positively on the election preparation and recommended to the Secretary-General to send Commonwealth election observers to Pakistan.

(b) Malawi 1994

In 1994, I led a planning mission to Malawi to examine the electoral environment and to ascertain whether or not Commonwealth election observers would be acceptable to the major political parties. The Commonwealth did not send observers to the Referendum many months previously because the Secretary-General did not think that it was necessary for the country to vote on the introduction of multiparty elections which were the necessary precursor of democratic governance. The pending elections then were the first multiparty elections after the Life Presidency and one-party regime had been dismantled. The Life President and his one-party regime had been discredited, but were putting up a strong challenge. Some of the opposition political parties' personalities were not happy with the idea of Commonwealth observers, pointing to the return of President Moi to power two years previously and fearing that the Commonwealth observers might lean in favour of the incumbents. They did not wish to look at Zambia in 1991 when the COG did not hesitate to endorse the victory of opposition candidate, Chiluba.

Notwithstanding the less than enthusiastic endorsement by some opposition personalities, the Planning Mission reported positively. The Mission had identified the logistics needs of the observer mission, including deployment centres. The Secretary-General decided to send Commonwealth observers in accordance with the recommendation of my Planning Mission. I was named leader of the Commonwealth Secretariat's Support Team to the COG to the Malawi elections in 1994.

(c) Namibia 1994

In 1994, I led a Planning Mission to Namibia to examine the electoral environment leading up to the first post-independence multiparty elections in that country. I was the technical adviser to the Commonwealth pre-polling election observer mission in 1989 and led a Commonwealth Secretariat technical assistance mission after the election to see the President designate, Mr. Nujoma.

The Planning Mission met with the Electoral Commission and the Directorate of Elections, as well as with representatives of the parties and many other stakeholders. There were many aggrieved stakeholders mainly of small opposition parties which felt that they were not getting sufficient public funding to mount meaningful political campaigns. However, they were all in favour of Commonwealth election observers observing the pending Namibian election.

Tanzania 1995

I related above the dual nature of this mission which was undertaken by Shrinivasan and me to Tanzania in 1995. The main focus was undoubtedly the election environment not only in the Mainland but also in Zanzibar which had its own EMB. The mission met representatives of the main parties and President Mwinyi. I paid a visit to Zanzibar to talk with the Electoral Commission there and representatives of the political parties there. The Mission found that all the parties happy to have the Commonwealth observers at the Tanzanian elections.

CHAPTER X

Election Adviser to the African Union

Setting up of DEAU/DEAF
Work programme 2008/09
Prognosis

Introduction

I spent three delightful years in Addis Ababa with offices on the premises of the African Union Commission. My mission was to assist the African Union Commission to set up a Democracy and Electoral Assistance Unit (DEAU) in the Department of Political Affairs (DPA). I was recruited by the International Foundation for Electoral Systems (IFES) as Chief of Party (CoP) of an African Union Support Program funded by USAID. I arrived in Addis in April 2007 under the impression, some what erroneously, that there was a sort of election unit in place in the DPA, but that was not so. Things move rather slowly at the AU and it took a year to get the Elections Unit up and running.

I was excited about the prospects of advising on democratic elections in the African Union where I could get an overview of the state of democratic elections on the continent. I had done election-related work in Liberia and almost all the Commonwealth African countries, including Zimbabwe then. I relished the challenge posed by the diverse democratic practices in the AU. I was also aware of the stubborn resistance to democratic practices in preparing for and conducting elections by some national election management bodies (EMBs).

Background history to the DEAU

Since 2002, the DPA had been working towards establishing an election unit, but the procedures were lengthy and slow. The OAU/ AU had taken a decision to set up such a unit and the DPA followed up that decision with two feasibility studies, one on the elections unit and another with respect to a fund to support the activities of the elections unit. The recommendations of feasibility studies were approved by the AU in Banjul in 2006. It took almost two years after the approval in Banjul for the Democracy and Electoral Assistance Unit (DEAU) and the Democracy and Electoral Assistance Fund (DEAF) become operational. When I assumed duties as CoP in April 2007 my urgent task was to help accelerate the recruitment process of staff for the DEAU and DEAF.

The feasibility studies, supported by the two groups of experts and accepted by the Department of Political Affairs, had examined the issue of personnel for the DEAU/DEAF exhaustively and recommended that a staff complement of seven with the Head of Unit to be recruited at P.5 Level and the Election Officers at P.3 Level. The Sub-Committee on Structures[59] reduced the grade of the Head of Unit to P.3 and the Officers to P. 2. The initial staff complement was set at three-Head of Unit and two Election Officers. Indeed, the Sub-Committee had only recommended the post of head of unit and no other. The two Election Officers were approved by the PRC in Accra, Ghana, during the Summit of 2007.

I was able to instigate a fast track procedure for the recruitment of the initial staff of the DEAU/DEAF with the consent of the Commissioner of the DPA. Nevertheless, the recruitment took almost nine months, September 2007 to April 2008. The three staff members of the DEAU/DEAF assumed duties at the beginning of May 2008.

---

[59] The Sub-Committee on Structures is a sub-committee of the Permanent Representative Committee (PRC) of the African Union which is charged with the responsibility of staffing of departments and units of the African Union Commission which services the African Union.

Besides assisting the DPA with the recruitment of the staff of DEAU/ DEAF, I spent much time during the first year preparing the various 'deliverables' contained in the Statement of Work (SOW) prepared by USAID and which formed the basis of the contract with IFES. The SOW did not envisage that the program would be late, perhaps as much as a year late, and so the 'deliverables' which were set against firm project deadlines had to be met, albeit in the abstract, as there was no Unit in place. 'Deliverables', including short term activities to be delivered within 20 days of the project coming on stream; work plan for a year within 60 days; indicators within 90 days; and performance monitoring plan had to be done even though there was no Unit in place during that timeframe.

The 'deliverables' were discussed in principle with the DPA and so the work plan did form a part of the 'inherited' programme by the DEAU when it became operational. In general, the DEAU's work plan was based on the second 'deliverable', which was a year's work plan for the DEAU. The main goal of the Support Program was to strengthen the capacity of the DEAU to enable it to effectively support national and sub-national institutions. My responsibilities were to deliver the following:

- Enhanced electoral monitoring and observation with respect to the AU;
- Establishment of an effective operation of a Special Fund to finance the activities of the DEAU;
- Establishment of an election expert network;
- Development of electoral process standards; and
- Reporting on program progress, challenges and opportunities.

The work plan which the DEAU adopted was based on the second 'deliverable', that is, the draft one year work plan. The draft was refined and approved by the DPA as an on-going work plan through to 2010. The on-going work plan was modified and refined by the DEAU in consultation with me. There were six broad areas of activities, namely, 1) election observation, including training of observers, 2) improving election process standards, 3) offering technical assistance to national EMBs, 4) creation of an AU electoral database, 5) development of a public relations strategy for DEAU, and 6) mobilizing resources for the DEAF.

1) AU Election Observation

Election observation organization was a key activity of the DEAU. The AU, and the OAU before it, had placed importance on election observation. Between 1990 and 2007, the OAU and the AU sent election observers to approximately one hundred and thirty-eight elections.[60] The process of selecting the elections to be observed was governed by AU rules which required an invitation to be sent to the Chairperson of the AUC at least two months prior to Election Day. Whether by coincident or otherwise, a number of important Member States sent their invitation to the AUC's Chairperson a few days late and so avoided election observation by AU missions. That happened in the case of Kenya in 2007 when the invitation to observe was received late by the DPA and so the AU did not send observers. The elections were followed by serious violence in which many people lost their lives, the AU was severely criticised for not having a presence at the elections. The DPA took the administrative decision that thereafter the AU would send observers to all national elections.[61] The DEAU had to deal with many dimensions of election observations in the AU in order to raise standards in procedures, quality of observations and the style of writing mission reports and the presentation thereof. The DEAU with my assistance reviewed and made changes to the observers' briefing book, the format of reports, with

---

[60] OAU observed 2 elections in 1990, 3 in 1991, 10 in 1992, 14 in 1993, 8 in 1994, 8 in 1995, 15 in 1996, 5 in1997, 6 in 1998, 11 in 1999, 4 in 2000, 6 in 2001, 8 in 2002; AU observed 4 in 2002, 8 in 2003, 9 in 2004, 8 in 2005, 5 in 2006, 4 up to June 2007.

[61] Exceptions to this rule can occur if a Member State violate certain democratic practices, as when Niger, in 2009 held a referendum to change the country's Constitution to allow a third term for the incumbent President, the AU did not send election observers to the parliamentary elections in that year.

emphasis on improvements of the contents and secured the departmental approval to publish mission reports.

The DEAU organized twelve AU observation missions in 2008 (including run-off elections) and about sixteen (including run-off elections) in 2009. Exploratory election missions were sent to Guinea Bissau and Côte d'Ivoire in 2008 and to Algeria, Malawi and Sudan in 2009 and 2010.

The DEAU's task was facilitated by the AU Guidelines for Election Observers and Monitors and by a study of AU's election observation missions' reports which was commissioned by the DPA from Prof. Tessy Bakary in 2007. The AU Guidelines, which contain a Code of Conduct for Observers, are sound and were endorsed by Prof. Bakary, but, as he pointed out, the DPA, before the DEAU came on stream, was not implementing the Guidelines fully.

In addressing these issues, I set about reviewing the country profiles which formed the background information in mission reports in respect of given countries. Observers' briefing book was reviewed and improved. The scope and depth of mission reports were reviewed to include issues such as gender, disability, nomadic conditions, as well as giving a full account of the role of the media in election campaign, a comprehensive account of campaign financing, and a full account of the major election processes, such as management of election logistics, counting and tallying processes.

The AU has been trying to rationalize election observer missions by merging missions from the Pan-African Parliament (PAP) with those of the AUC. However, initially the proposed merger was being used by the PAP to extend the number of members they may be allowed to send on each merged mission, which remained an AUC's mission.

An important part of the DEAU's programme to raise the quality of AU's election observation was the orientation refresher course for AU election observers. For this aspect of their work plan, the DEAU worked with IFES' partners' under the USAID Program, the Carter Center (TCC) and the Electoral Institute of Southern Africa (EISA) to conduct orientation courses for the different Regions of the AU. The first orientation course was held in September 2009 in Nairobi, Kenya, for election observers from the Region of East Africa and the second course was held for observers from West Africa in Dakar, Senegal, in March 2010.

The orientation-course materials were prepared by TCC and EISA and consisted of eight teaching modules and a toolkit. The orientation courses opened up the way for long-time observers to refresh their minds of developments in election observations, while at the same time the process created a measure of standardisation of election observation practice.

The AU Election Database which was designed by a UN Database Expert in 2009 has four sections, one of which deals with AU election observers. By the end of 2009, the database section on observers had over eight hundred and eighty entries, only thirty-six of whom had undergone orientation refresher exposure. The database, when purged and the orientation refresher course is conducted in all five regions of the AU, and extended from fifty to a hundred observers per region, should have a reserve of 800 to 1000 observers who have undergone orientation refresher course. The prognosis for increased credibility of election observer mission reports is good so long as the orientation refresher courses continue and the observer section of the database consists of trained persons exclusively.

2) Raising Election Processes Standards

The issue of raising election processes' standards is the key to improving the quality of election organization and conduct of elections in the AU Member States. The stakeholders in African elections in the new and emerging democracies understandingly placed great emphasis on election observation, but true improvement in election organization and conduct can best happen through assisting national EMBs to improve the quality of major election processes.

I am of the view that raising elections' processes' standards activity of the DEAU's work plan will benefit national EMBs enormously. This is the surest, if not the quickest, way to improving the ability of national EMBs to prepare for and conduct democratic elections. In the AU, raising elections' processes' standards in 53 countries in respect of 12 or more issues areas is a significant exercise. The selection of the topics may vary, but the core issues should include the following: review of electoral systems; review of the legislative scheme; delimitation of constituencies/electoral districts; compiling of a proper voters' register; proper election campaign rules, including campaign regulations; and clear rules governing the management of election logistics.

The strategy which the DEAU and I agreed was to commission studies in the majority of countries in a particular economic community region, but avoiding the inclusion of any individual State twice, and have the recommendations contained in the studies discussed at a regional seminar which would address its recommendations to the EMBs and Member States of that regional grouping. The activity started off with the SADC Region in which ten countries were selected at random with five of the ten countries assigned to one consultant and the other five assigned to the other consultant. The first seminar was set for June 2010 in Lesotho, but that target date was easily missed.

The DEAU and National EMBs

A continental meeting of EMBs was convened by the DEAU in Accra, Ghana, in December 2009 to discuss matters that affect all EMBs in the AU, and to create a vehicle for ensuring and maintaining closer contact with each other. The meeting had been a long time in planning and so when it was held, it was a great pleasure to me. I believe that there is great merit in EMBs meeting periodically, though not necessarily annually as recommended by the EMBs at their December meeting. The attendance at the December 2009 meeting was not as large as was expected-only 29 representatives from 23 EMBs were able to attend, largely because the invitations were sent out late and indeed the meeting was being convened the week before Christmas. Nevertheless, it was a useful start to a process that, it is hoped, will lead to AU EMBs collaborating as they see fit. From my viewpoint, as adviser to the DEAU, the continental meeting of EMBs was also intended to enhance the public relations profile of the DEAU.

The meeting attracted the attendance of the senior officers of the Department of Political Affairs, namely, the Commissioner of Political Affairs, Mrs. Dolly Joiner, the Departmental Director, Ambassador Emile Ognimba, and Divisional Director, Dr. Mamadou Dia. The meeting heard from many EMBs' representatives about the challenges facing them and proposals to formulate solutions to those problems. However, some useful problems-solving mechanisms, such as an AU EMBs' network or facilitation mechanism and a set of procedural provisions to prioritize requests for technical assistance from DEAU, were not presented because the DPA had not yet cleared them.

3) Technical Assistance to National EMBs

The technical assistance programme to national EMBs is crucial for the improvement of election organization in the AU. The raising of elections' processes standards will assist in heightening the awareness of the need for technical assistance to improve the quality of election organization and conduct. The area of technical assistance to the EMBs of the Member States of the AU offers a great challenge to the DEAU because of the diverse needs of the almost fifty EMBs. Technical assistance may be requested in the areas in which work has been done with respect to raising standards, as well as in any other areas in which EMBs request assistance.

It is anticipated that in time the DEAU might have to prioritize requests for technical assistance if requests are more than it might be able to accommodate on a timely basis. I prepared a draft instrument setting out the possible procedures that the DEAU might follow in considering requests for technical assistance by EMBs and the cases that might attract priority consideration in awarding technical assistance.

4) Election Database

The AU election database was designed with the help of a UN expert and initial inputs provided by EISA and IFES at the AUC Headquarters in Addis. The construction of the database design was done in consultation with me. The database has four sections, namely, AU Election Observers; African Election Experts; AU EMBs; and African CSOs involved with elections. The database, which will be an important tool in election management throughout the continent, had over eight hundred and eighty election observers in the election observers section and an initial entry of two hundred and eighty election experts at the time of writing. There were forty-three entries for EMBs, and the criteria for entry of African CSOs had been settled and would be largely based on the CSOs' membership criteria[62] in the Economic, Social and Cultural Council of the African Union (ECOSOCC).

5) Public Relation Strategy

I assisted the DEAU in formulating a public relations strategy. The DPA had not been particularly savvy with respect to public relations in election observation missions and related matters. The establishment of the DEAU in the DPA aimed to change that perception so far as elections were concerned. The first proposal was to have an information officer embedded in each observation mission but it was not accepted until 2010. The other aspect of the P.R. strategy was to have observation missions' reports

---

[62]   Proposed requirements for CSOs to be Included in the AU –DEAU Database

African civil society organizations (CSOs) which are ***involved in election organization and conduct*** and which meet the under-mentioned requirements may apply to be listed in the database:

- Be national, regional or continental CSO without restriction to undertake regional or international activities;
- Have objectives and principles that are consistent with the principles and objectives of the Union as set out in Articles 3 & 4 of the Constitutive Act;
- Be registered in a Member State of the Union and/or meet the conditions set out in Part 1 of the Criteria for Granting Observer Status to the AU applicable to non-governmental organizations;
- Show a minimum of three years proof of registration as an African CSO prior to the date of the submission of the application, including proof of operations for those three years;
- Provide annual audit statements by an independent auditing company;
- Show proof that the ownership and management of the CSO is made up of not less than fifty (50%) of Africans or peoples of African origin;
- Provide information on funding sources in the preceding three (3) years;
- For regional and continental CSOs, show proof of activities that engage or are operative in not less than three (3) Member States of the Union;
- CSOs that discriminate on the basis of religion, gender, tribe, ethnic, racial or political basis shall be barred from registering with the database; and
- Adherence to a code of ethics and conduct for civil society organizations affiliated to or working with the Union.

published. After some hesitation, the DPA gave its consent to have the mission reports published. The third aspect of the DEAU's PR strategy was to have a continental meeting of EMBs soon after it commenced operations. However, the continental meeting took place in December 2009 almost 18 months after DEAU commenced operations. At that meeting, the EMBs decided that they should meet annually. They made a number of recommendations, including the following that:

- DEAU promote the idea of creating an interactive mechanism through which experiences can be shared and support between EMBs can be strengthened;

- pursuant to its mandate the Unit should endeavour to build the capacities of electoral commissions through the provision of training, material and financial resources;
- to enhance the level of cooperation in the area of election observation and election networking with the RECs (Regional Economic Communities);

- AU puts into place key mechanisms that would enable interactive debate on electoral processes;

- AU should contribute to the strengthening of the autonomy and independence of EMBs;

- the cost of running elections should be examined and more effective ways of organizing and conducting less expensive elections be explored;

- AU should conduct a study to assess the effectiveness of electoral commissions work and to take stock of electoral commissions successes and failures;

- the possibility of ensuring continuous voter education should be examined as part of citizen education campaigns, especially in schools;

- for funding of elections the sovereignty of the state must be safeguarded. However, the opportunity to ask for and receive aid from partners should be jointly examined by the competent authorities and EMBs officials;

- Promote exchange of experiences between EMBs by organizing annual meetings.

6) Mobilization of Resources for DEAF

The Head of the DEAU and I were responsible for mobilizing resources for the DEAF. The mobilization exercise was successful in so far as we were able to secure pledges of over five million U.S. dollars during the first two years of the DEAF's operations with several indications of pledges still in the pipeline then. The funds were needed to help finance the activities of the DEAU. The cost of the DEAU's project activities was relatively high, particularly the election observation missions, each of which may cost up to US $300, 000, more or less, depending on the size and duration of the missions. There may be an average of fifteen national elections in the AU per year, which may cost approximately $4,500,000.00. Selected elections may attract an exploratory mission, each of which may cost approximately $20,000. The orientation course for election observers and the seminar on raising election processes' standards costs about 200,000 to 250,000 for fifty participants in each Region of the AU.

Measuring Election Standards in the AU Member States

It is not easy to evaluate standards across the range of activities undertaken by the DEAU. In some cases, like training of observers, number of attendees might be a useful indicator, but in many cases, numbers cannot be used as indicators and other values have to found. The performance of an election observation mission, for example, has to be assessed more on the quality of the report and recommendations; and so will be the seminars on raising standards. Periodic evaluation of each of the activities of the DEAU by independent consultant is necessary to ensure that best practices or at least accepted international standards are being followed.

Prognosis

Despite the clear evidence that many Member States of the AU do have problems with the organization of democratic elections, there is no doubt that the quest to have credible elections is slowly being accepted as a shared value across the AU generally. The DEAU's work plan, particularly the activities with respect to lifting the standards of conducting election processes, coupled with technical assistance to national EMBs will, in the longer term, make a difference in election conduct in the AU. The DEAU has the potential and the opportunity to change the culture of accepting second or third rate standards in election preparation and conduct to settling for nothing less than transparent and credible democratic elections throughout the majority of the Member States of the Union.

Through the creation of basic relevant tools, such as the AU Election Database, to assist its operations, the DEAU will in time be equipped to respond to its administrative needs and those of regional institutions which wish to draw on such tools. The quest for good quality information that is easily retrievable will enhance the efficiency of the DEAU and the DPA.

The presence of the DEAU has made a difference and is expected to continue doing so in the foreseeable future with respect to election observation. The publication of AU observation missions' reports, having an information officer in each AU observation mission and training of observers will undoubtedly raise the awareness and standard of election observation in the AU. In addition to the improvements in the administrative arrangements relating to the selection of observers, the AU's decision to merge its observation efforts with that of the Pan-African Parliament's will further strengthen election observation in the Union.

The DEAU has considerable potential to weld those institutions of the RECs connected to democratic elections to the central activities being carried out by it. Having periodic (annual) meetings and exchange of work plans can be helpful in this regard. The DEAU's potential to improve on the AU's cooperation with CSOs which are entered into the database is a challenge, but since those entries will be filtered and screened, the task will be straightforward. This will also be of considerable benefit to national EMBs.

The DEAU has a great challenge ahead of it. With an average of twelve to fifteen national elections (not including run-off elections), coupled with several exploratory missions each year, the DEAU will have ample opportunity to influence positively the quality of AU election observation. The orientation courses for election observers introduced with my assistance as the CoP of IFES, and supported by Carter Center and EISA, will further enhance the overall quality of AU observer mission reports, and impact positively on the credibility of these reports.

The decision by the DPA to implement my recommendations on the public relations strategy to publish observation mission reports and include an embedded information officer in all AU observation missions will undoubtedly raise the P.R. profile of the DEAU and the DPA.

The AU Election Database has great potential to provide timely information in critical areas. However, the sections need to be completed and maintained so that they are up to date. In order for the database to be properly maintained a dedicated officer should be tasked with that duty. The various sections of the database can serve as a link with entities contained therein, for example, the section on EMBs will ensure constant contact with national EMBs; similarly, the section on CSOs will create frequent interaction with CSOs in the different regions of the AU.

Perhaps the greatest potential of the DEAU lies with its activities in the fields of raising election processes' standards, coupled with technical assistance to national EMBs. The priority in selecting topics which need to be tackled may be determined with the help of EMBs, individually or at continental meetings. Some regions may be more deficient than others in particular topics and so, funds permitting, it may be possible to organize two regional seminars concurrently or back to back, as the case may be. Technical assistance may be administered to individual national EMBs or regionally or sub-regionally. Attention needs to be paid to cost-effectiveness along with the priority assigned to particular requests.

The prospects for mobilization of resources should improve since the DPA had given the clearance to solicit resources from Member States of the AU.

The DEAU has been operating with its initial staff complement of three which was wholly inadequate for the workload. However, in 2009 the Permanent Representatives Committee (PRC) at a retreat in July in Mombasa, Kenya, based on briefing which I did for the DEAU, the PRC decided to increase the staff complement by two additional staff and to raise the grades of the incumbents according to what the Feasibility Study had proposed, that is, P5 Level for the Head of DEAU and P3 Level for the Election Officers. No date was set for the implementation of this decision.

My Second Stint at the African Union

The IFES-USAID Election Support Program was coming to its end in March 2010. Without any lead as to what IFES intended to do with the Office at the AU, I resolved that I would resign from that organization and go back to my private consulting. In late 2009 while I was contemplating my future after the end of the IFES-AU Election Support Program, I got a call from the Governor of Cayman Islands, His Excellency Governor Jack, who invited me to chair the Electoral Boundary Commission of the Cayman Islands, an office which I had held in 2003. I accepted the offer on the understanding that I would not be available until the end of March 2010 when I was due to leave Ethiopia. I notified IFES of my intention to resign at the end of March 2010 when the Program was due to close. I was planning to take vacation leave during the second half of March 2010 before my resignation took effect, but that was not allowed under IFES' rules and so my resignation took effect on 12 March 2010. The IFES Office at the AU Ethiopia was left in care of the Administrative Officer, a young bright Ethiopian woman who was well able to carry on for a few months.

As it turned out, there were sufficient funds available from the budget to extend the Program until September 11 2010, largely with a view to holding a third orientation course for AU election observation. After discussion with IFES and USAID, I indicated that I would be interested to re-join IFES to continue the Program until it was closed off.

I assumed duties as the Chairman of the Cayman Islands Electoral Boundary Commission on the 4 April 2010 and hoped that the Commission would complete its work by the end of May 2010. The delimitation exercise proceeded smoothly and on schedule, except for overseas travel by the Caymanian Commissioners at different times, which caused the Commission to conclude its work a week off schedule.

During my absence from Addis Ababa, the USAID undertook an evaluation of the Program. The evaluation was carried out by Mr. Jean-Marc Gorelick and he found that the objectives of the Program were met. On my way back to England from Cayman Islands, I went to IFES' Office in Washington to discuss the re-hire terms with the Africa Section and to meet with Mr. Gorelick, Democracy Officer, Bureau for Africa and Ms. Sarah Swift, the Program Officer, USAID, AFR/DP/POSE, Washington, and discussed the Evaluation Report.

The paperwork for the IFES rehire was completed in Washington on 9th June 2010 and I arrived in Addis Ababa to resume duties as Chief of Party on 28 June 2010. This was envisaged as a quiet period during which support would be offered to the DEAU in the form of technical and administrative back up.

CHAPTER XI

Impressions of Heads of Government I Met Concerning Elections

I met many Heads of State/Governments on electoral and related matters, including those of Namibia (Nujoma); Kaunda of Zambia; De Klerk of South Africa; Dr. H. Banda, Malawi; Daniel arap Moi of Kenya; Messrs Manley and Seaga of Jamaica; Forbes Burnham of Guyana; Jagdeo of Guyana; Ms. Charles of Dominica (Goa incident); Tom Adams of Barbados; Herbert Blaize of Grenada; Chambers of Trinidad & Tobago; Lester Bird of Antigua/Barbuda, Sir Linden Pindling of Bahamas; Milton Cato and Son Mitchell of St. Vincent; Mrs I. Gandhi of India; Mrs. Thatcher of United Kingdom and Ms. Johnson-Sirleaf, President of Liberia

Introduction
This chapter seeks to sketch my impressions of Heads of States or Governments in an environment related to matters of governance or elections. These impressions were formed when making contact about election-related matters, some times briefly, other times over a period. The environment is sketched out, where possible, to create an appropriate physical and mental picture of the politicians' behavioural posture.

The Late Michael Manley, former Prime Minister of Jamaica
I first met Michael Manley in 1962 when he successfully presented a case for me to get an increase in salary at the Jamaica Railway Corporation. He was a type of serious personality, a bit impatient by nature, but quick to see another's point of view. My next encounter with Mr. Manley was when I became Director of Elections in Jamaica in 1979. He was rather displeased that I did not re-employ

the returning office in his constituency. I had no particular reason other than the fact that the gentleman did not come across as sharp as I wanted for that somewhat high profile constituency.

There were many interesting inconsequential incidents between Prime Minister Manley and myself, as when he phoned me to congratulate me on the successes of the voters' registration exercise and I thanked him but added that I wanted to wait until the election process was over before resting on congrats. He was not very pleased with my less than enthusiastic embrace of his congratulations, and straight away he said "as Prime Minister, I extending congratulations to you". Then I said 'thanks Prime Minister', and we both put up the phone.

I had periodic meetings with the Prime Minister in the lead up to the 1980 elections; sometimes I met him with the Prof. Mills, Chairman of the Electoral Advisory Committee. The Prime Minister was very helpful to me in securing a standby power generator-I think from the Army; also in beefing up security, army and police, at the Electoral Office; and in securing additional printing machines to print the voters' lists. On an occasion approaching the time when the election date was imminent, Prime Minister Manley asked for my prognosis on the state of preparation and I said I would be ready by the 4 November 1980 and he said that's no good that is America's polling day. He asked if I could do it around the 30 of October and I said that it was possible if I got two more printing machines and he said, "okay, I will ensure that you get the two additional machines". We then came to an arrangement whereby he would telephone me on the following Sunday afternoon at 4 p.m. to get the signal that I was ready and he would make the announcement later that evening. He caused the two extra machines to be delivered to the Electoral Office as requested and the lists were completed. When the Prime Minister telephoned me from Montego Bay, I was ready, and there he was on his own to set the date he wanted for the elections.

Outside of the elections arena I had encountered Mr. Manley many times, including in 1990 when I led a team of British customs specialists to reform the Jamaican Customs machinery. His briefing to the group suggested that he had a good grasp of the custom machinery which was nearing the breaking point.

My final encounter with Mr. Manley was in 1994 when he led the Commonwealth Observer Group to the South African democratic elections. I was second in charge of the Secretariat Support Team to the COG. The person in charge of the Support Team was Max Gaylard, Director of the Political Affairs Division of the Secretariat. Max Gaylard had to leave temporarily on mission to Lesotho, and I took over as leader of the Support Team with Mr. Manley as the leader of the COG. I was part of a small group of the COG members who went to meet President De Klerk. When briefing Mr. Manley, I drew his attention to some technical flaws in the preparation, but he took the view that the South African election was more about politics than technical niceties about election organization. In any event, he must have remembered my days as Director of Elections in Jamaica; he was not impressed with my adherence to technicalities in election organization. Nevertheless, he was not unimpressed with my approach to elections, as he was reported as telling Sir Sonny Ramphal, then Secretary-General of the Commonwealth, when I joined the Secretariat that he was satisfied with the conduct of the Jamaican elections in 1980 which I directed and which he had lost. He had however grown even more prickly in temperament, as may be seen from this incident—we had an informal meeting while in South Africa in 1994, I was giving him copies of a couple of election books which I had written, and when I entered the room, I said 'good morning, Mr. Chairman', Mr. Manley retorted that he did not like that felicitation, he preferred "Michael" or "Mr. Manley".

Mr. Edward Seaga, former Prime Minister of Jamaica

I first met Mr. Seaga in 1979 when I was advising the Joint Select Committee of the House and Senate on Constitutional and Electoral Reform. I noted that the opposition MPs on the Joint Select Committee were very respectful of Mr. Seaga's position as Leader of the Opposition and would address him formally as "yes sir, no sir", when speaking to him. We met later in 1979 or early 1980 when I was Director of Elections at the Nuttal Hospital in Kingston when one of my returning officers, who was the returning officer in the constituency, which Mr. Seaga represented, had a mishap and was in that hospital. I went to look for the officer and we met up at the hospital. We had a chat and he made a few jokes about multiple registrations in the registration exercise which was taking place at the time.

My next encounter was in the late 1980s when I was a special emissary of the Secretary-General to search for a prominent Caribbean national to chair the Commonwealth eminent persons group to carry out a fact finding mission to South Africa. I put a case in favour of Prime Minister Seaga's political rival, Michael Manley. He listened patiently to my submission and said he would think about it, and he would let me know through his Permanent Secretary, Don Brice. I waited three or four days and received a negative reply.

Mr. P.J. Patterson, former Prime Minister of Jamaica.

I knew PJ (as he was affectionately called) for a long time. His former wife, Ms Shirley Field-Ridley, taught me in 6th Form at secondary school. I once took his children from Georgetown, Guyana, where they were staying with their mother to PJ in Kingston. At the time I was Legal Counsel at CARICOM and based in Georgetown, Guyana. When I became Director of Elections PJ always gave me encouragement whenever there was a positive development as when the registration exercise went off reasonably well. Perhaps, surprising to many, PJ like most of the experienced politicians from the two major parties abided by the elections procedures and seldom had any problems with me as the Director and my staff. It was that example that gave me much hope in the Jamaican political system, despite the antics of some of the parties' functionaries in attempting to rig some major processes of the elections.

Ms. Portia Simpson-Miller, former Prime Minister of Jamaica

When I was Director of Elections in Jamaica 1979-80, I never met Ms Simpson, as she then was. However, she was often in contact with me on the telephone. She frequently complained about the violence in her constituency and the fact that she often bore the cost of burial of her murdered constituents. She was very respectful of the office of Director, but there was always a twist to her telephone calls. She would offer congratulations on my performance up to the time of the call and added that her party was monitoring my actions; then she would say that she noted that I ruled against her party four times and three times against the JLP, as the case may be. I surmised then that the PNP were keeping a close check on my daily activities.

Mr. Bruce Golding, Prime Minister of Jamaica (at the time of writing)

When I became Director of Elections in 1979, Bruce Golding was one of the two representatives of the Jamaica Labour Party (JLP) on the Electoral Advisory Committee (EAC) of which I was a non-voting member. We came to know each other well. I respected him, but he was too much of a savvy young politician for me. This was borne out by this minor incident—I had just left a meeting of the EAC, which Bruce attended, for my Office; as soon as I reached my Office it was brought to my attention that Mr. Golding had made a release to the media that a candidate in a certain constituency was improperly nominated as he was convicted for fraud some years earlier, and that he (Golding) had written to the Director of Elections to take action. I inquired of my staff if there was any communication from Mr. Golding or the JLP'S Office and there was no such communication to be found. In the meantime, representatives of the media hived down on my Office, while others telephoned in. It was funny, but I was not amused. I had to make many holding statements explaining that I had not received any such communication from Golding or the JLP. The JLP's Office had always communicated with my Office through courier service and not by postal service. Two days later, I got a letter through the post from Mr. Golding raising the issue. The storm had already passed, but Golding and the JLP made their point.

Mrs. Indira Gandhi, Prime Minister of India

I met Mrs Indira Gandhi at the Commonwealth Heads of Government Conference in New Delhi in 1983 and at the retreat of the Heads in Goa during the conference. I was the 'liaison officer' between the Grenadian authorities and the Commonwealth Secretary-General during the post-American invasion crisis that beset that country. The Plenary Session of the Conference opened with Prime Minister Gandhi in the Chair. The Grenada issue was one of the main issues for discussion at the Conference. Chairperson Gandhi was by no means a passive bystander. She was against the American invasion of Grenada and made it known. Then the discussion drew in Tom Adams, Prime Minister of Barbados, who was a supporter of the American invasion. Prime Minister Adams was rather loquacious in his intervention and made reference to Mrs Gandhi's alleged reaction when a neighbouring country had threatened to bomb the Taj Mahal. Mrs Gandhi was not amused and excused herself momentarily from the Chair and gave Prime Minister Adams a dressing down. The stand-off between the Chairperson and Prime Minister Adams carried over to the Retreat, but Prime Minister Adams never re-visited his provocative remarks to the Chairperson

Mrs. Margret Thatcher, former Prime Minister of the United Kingdom

I met Mrs Thatcher at close range at the retreat of the Commonwealth Heads of Government in Goa, India, in 1983. Indeed, I was staying in the cottage of the Secretary-General Ramphal and Mrs Thatcher was staying in a cottage next door. During the retreat sessions my task was to lobby the Prime Ministers individually to agree a resolution on Grenada. Mrs Thatcher was known to have been opposed to the way the Americans handled the invasion without notifying the British. The Secretary-General suggested that I should ask Mrs Thatcher to allow me to see her notes on the discussions at the retreat. I asked Mrs Thatcher to see her notes and to my surprise she was so kind and approachable; she not only gave me her notes to read, but also her entire brief on the Grenada to read and make notes. It was a wonderful gesture and I appreciated it immensely at the time.

Mr. Forbes Burnham, former President of Guyana

I met President Burnham many times when I was Legal Counsel of CARICOM in the 1970s. Indeed, once he rushed to my defence when, as Legal Counsel, I advised a Heads of Government meeting that a vote did not constitute a Decision under the CARICOM Treaty, Prime Minister Barrow of Barbados launched an attack on Legal Counsel.[63] At the Commonwealth Heads of Government meeting in Delhi, the Caribbean Heads of Government were having an informal drinks session. I had the nod of Secretary-General Ramphal to hang around. The atmosphere between the Caribbean Heads, who supported the American invasion and the Secretary-General who had opposed it, was frosty. President Burnham then promptly invited me into the drinks session to have a brandy. Prime Minister Chambers of Trinidad and Tobago did not like the idea of me being in the drinks session-I believe he felt quite rightly that I was eves-dropping on the discussion for Secretary-General Ramphal. Prime Minister Chambers kept asking me, why are you here: until he could take it no more he came out and said you better leave now. I was there long enough to have a couple rounds of brandy and to assess the tempo of the dialogue. President Burnham kept a low profile at the Conference and the retreat. When the Secretary-General and his team (including me) visited Guyana in early 1984 as a part of the fence-mending mission, President Burnham put his private plane at the mission's disposal to travel from Guyana up the islands and to Jamaica.

Ms Eugenia Charles, former Prime Minister of Dominica

I knew Prime Minister Eugenia Charles rather well. I was her chief negotiator on Dominica's maritime boundary with France with respect to Martinique and Guadeloupe from 1981 to 1987. I had a working breakfast with her at her hotel while she was visiting London in the mid-1980s. We travelled to Martinique and Guadeloupe to negotiate with the French on maritime boundaries between Dominica and France. Prime Minister Charles was always a no nonsense personality.

When the Grenada episode broke in 1983, it was a bit awkward for me, as well as for Prime Minister Charles; for she was a

---

[63] The occasion was when Sir Garfield Sobers, a renowned Barbadian cricketer was being considered for a CARICOM sports' post, the vote did not carry as some States had voted against or abstained.

staunch supporter of the American invasion of Grenada and Secretary-General Ramphal was a strong and influential opponent of the invasion. At the Commonwealth Summit Retreat in Goa, India, in 1983, Grenada was a leading agenda topic and my task was to lobby the Commonwealth Heads of Government in support of a resolution that bridged the gap between those Commonwealth Heads who were sceptical about the American invasion, including Chairperson Indira Gandhi and Prime Minister Thatcher, and the committed supporters who included most of the CARICOM Prime Ministers. When I was lobbing some Prime Ministers who were sitting near to Prime Minister Charles, she could be hear muttering aloud, indeed loud enough for the Chairperson and Secretary-General Ramphal who were sitting at the 'head table' to hear, that she did not agree with the draft Resolution. So when Ramphal mounted his fence-mending mission to see the CARICOM Heads of Government individually in early 1984, I was on that mission and I knew the encounter with Prime Minister would be interesting. The shrewd legal mind that was the Prime Minister, spared me any embarrassment for as soon as the delegation reached her home, she signalled to Secretary-General that I should go for drive around the town, while she and the Secretary-General conducted their not so smooth dialogue.

Mr. Tom Adams, Prime Minister of Barbados

I did not know Prime Minister Adams well. Whether intentionally or otherwise, he got on the wrong side of Prime Minister Indira Gandhi, while chairing the Plenary Session in New Delhi, prior to the Retreat in Goa, India, and she gave Prime Minister Adams a thorough dressing down and so he kept a low profile at the Retreat. Knowing his staunch support for the American invasion of Grenada, not unlike Prime Charles' position, I did not spend much time lobbying his support for the Grenada Resolution at the Retreat.

Mr. George Chambers, former Prime Minister of Trinidad and Tobago

I met Prime Minister Chambers many times while he was Prime Minister and even before he became Prime Minister when he was Minister of Finance while I was Legal Counsel at CARICOM. My encounters with him and my general impressions of him were somewhat unwelcoming. He was fond of using four-letter words in my presence. Perhaps he was perceptive, for he appeared to be the Caribbean leader who was unhappy with my presence at a get-together drinking session of Caribbean leaders in New Delhi at the Commonwealth Conference of Heads of Government in 1983. My impression of Prime Minister Chambers' fondness for use of the four-letter words was confirmed when the Secretary-General of the Commonwealth sent me on a Special Mission to a CARICOM meeting in the Bahamas, in part to introduce the in-coming Managing Director of the Commonwealth Fund for Technical Cooperation (CFTC) Mr. Bob McLaren, to the CARICOM Heads, and to discuss Commonwealth-CARICOM matters with certain Heads of which one was Prime Minister Chambers on a one to one basis. We had a fruitful discussion and the Prime Minister was warm and friendly, but the occasional four-letter words were always forthcoming during the conversation.

Mr. Nicholas Braithwaite, former Prime Minister of Granada

I knew Nicholas Braithwaite before became Head of the Interim Administration of Grenada after the American invasion. When Alastair McIntyre withdrew on medical grounds as designate of the head of the interim administration of Grenada in 1983, Nicholas Braithwaithe's name came to mind as a possible replacement for McIntyre. He was consultant to CFTC and was not a politician. He fitted the role and was perhaps close to the Commonwealth. He served as the Head of the interim administration from 1983 to 1984. I visited him many time during his stint as the head of the Grenadian administration. After his tenure as head of the Grenadian administration, Nicholas Braithewaite eventually became Prime Minister of Grenada, but only after years had elapsed after democracy had returned to that country.

Mr Herbert Blaize, former Prime Minister of Grenada

I was first introduced to Mr. Hebert Blaize, who suffered from a form of disability, at a reception hosted by Mr. Braithwaite, when he was Head of the Interim Administration of Grenada. Mr. Blaize, who was also a veteran politician of Grenada, was already tipped as a possible

Prime Minister of the post-conflict Grenada. When the election was held, Mr. Blaize did emerge as the victorious candidate. I was sent by Secretary-General Ramphal as his emissary to greet Prime Minister Blaize and to work with him on the composition of a constitutional commission to prepare a new constitution for Grenada. Apart from the humourous side of the Prime Minister, which I discovered on one of visits, we got on well. The constitution commission concept took shape quickly and we worked on its composition and funding. Prime Minister Blaize had his own thinking on who should be the Chairman of the constitution commission, I favoured Professor Carnegie, but the Prime Minister stuck with an old friend, Sir Fred Phillips.

Mr. Jagdeo, President of Guyana

In 2000, I went on a mission for the Commonwealth Secretary-General, Mr. Don McKinnon, to see President Jagdeo of Guyana and discuss the state of the brokered arrangements between the ruling party, PPP/Civic and the main opposition party, PNC (Reform). The President was polite and came across to me as a thoughtful and balanced young leader. He felt that the relations between the two major political parties would improve and Guyana would continue to develop steadily. His desire was to see the brokered agreement between the ruling and main opposition party get back on track and work smoothly.

Mr. Lester Bird, former Prime Minister of Antigua/Barbuda

I knew Prime Minister Lester Bird for a long time since he was Deputy Prime and the CARICOM Council Minister while I was Legal Counsel of CARICOM Secretariat. I was on his maritime boundary delimitation team in negotiations with France for St. Bartholomew and Guadeloupe. The political admirers, as well as detractors, in Antigua/Barbuda sometimes referred to Prime Minister Lester Bird as Machiavellian in thought and behaviour and so it was a surprise to many in Antigua/Barbuda and elsewhere in the Caribbean when he agreed to electoral reform based on the recommendations of the Commonwealth observation mission report on the 1999 elections. I was awarded the assignment by the Commonwealth Secretariat with the approval of the Government of Antigua/Barbuda. It was my second assignment as a private election consultant. I was based in Antigua/Barbuda for 4 months while I carried major amendments to the election laws in consultation with the Attorney-General. Although I knew the Prime Minister, the only time I saw him while I was in Antigua was when Parliament was debating the amending Bill to the Representation of the People Act. I had no improper interference from the Prime Minister or the Government. I was free to consult the then leader of the opposition, and I did so. There were some recommendations which the ruling party and Government did not take on board, such as the formula for appointing the independent Electoral Commission members.

Ms. Ellen Johnson-Sirleaf, President of Liberia

I met President Johnson-Sirleaf when she was on way up as a candidate to the presidency. She used to attend meetings of the joint political parties and the National Elections Commission (NEC). At one of the meetings of joint committee of parties and NEC, when the meeting was discussing the campaign financing regulations, Ms. Johnson-Sirleaf was heard to be muttering aloud that regulations were too advanced for Liberia. Although initially she was somewhat tardy in meeting the requirements of the campaign financing regulations, she did comply fully with the requirements.

Mr. Sam Nujoma, former President of Namibia

I was technical adviser to the Commonwealth pre-election observation mission to Namibia in 1989. Shortly after the election, and before Namibia achieved its independence, I led a Commonwealth technical assistance mission to Namibia to discuss an assessment of Namibia's needs and what the Commonwealth Secretariat might offer. During a week of discussions in Katatura, my team met the President Designate, Mr. Nujoma, at his residence, where we had lengthy talks about the assistance that Namibia would need after independence. We agreed on a package of assistance which the Commonwealth would offer, including assistance with the country's Constitution which was being formulated in the Constituent Assembly which was constituted after the elections.

In the late nineteen nineties, I attended an elections conference in Windhoek and was a member of a small representative delegation from the conference that called on the President Nujoma. It was as though the President was on the war path, for he made sure that the visitors were comfortably seated in his official residence, before he launched on a soliloquy-type of tirade complaining that the intellectuals who were discussing democracy in Windhoek had not spoken out about the land issue in Zimbabwe or the conflict in the Democratic Republic of Congo. The President went on venting his feelings for many minutes until he calmed down and discuss some electoral matters.

Dr. Kenneth Kaunda, Former President of Zambia

Dr. Kaunda was President of Zambia for over 27 years during which time he was leader of a one-party regime. Multiparty elections were introduced in 1991. The Commonwealth sent an observer group (COG) to observe the elections. I was the leader of the Secretariat Support Team to the Observers. In travelling throughout Zambia's capital, Lusaka, and its environs, it was clear to many of us that the ruling party of President Kaunda was facing stiff competition from opposition parties.

I was a member of the COG and Support Team which called on President Kaunda at State House on the eve of the elections. Despite dire prediction of the informal opinion polls for the ruling party, the President sounded supremely confident of winning another term in office. Indeed, he was proudly recapping the history of his party to the Group. When the early elections results were announced there was no doubt that the President was disappointed for he was clearly on course to be beaten by rival opposition candidate, Mr. Chiluba. When I conveyed the projections of the early results to Commonwealth Secretary-General Anyaoku that President Kaunda would lose power, he repeated that it was the end of an era.

Dr. Hastings Banda, former Life President of Malawi.

Dr. Banda was facing his last presidential elections in 1994. It was the first multiparty elections in a couple of decades. He had put the issue of one-party versus multiparty elections to a Referendum and lost out some eighteen months or so previously. Many changes were made to the Constitution and the electoral legislative framework in order to usher in the first multiparty elections in many years. I was heavily involved in the reform of the electoral law and certain aspects of the new Constitution that would come into effect after the elections. The electoral environment had undergone considerable changes in the lead up to the 1994 elections.

I was part of a 16-member group of Commonwealth Observers and Secretariat Support Team who called on President Banda at one of his several Palaces on the eve of the elections. He kept the Group waiting for about seventy-five minutes before he appeared unaided but using a walking-stick. He was clearly much advanced in age, although there was lack of clarity about his exact age, which some reports at the time put at late eighties and others at early nineties. We all stood up and the President took his seat, followed by a lady, who was said to be the niece of his Official Hostess, and the Information Minister. Members of the Group then began to rise individually to introduce themselves. After each of the first three members of the observer group rose to introduce themselves, President Banda slowly rose to acknowledge the introduction. Then when the fourth observer rose the President sat firmly and just stared, as though his mind went blank, and for the rest of the thirteen introductions that was the state of play. When the introductions were through the President sprung from his stare and handed his Information Minister his welcoming statement and uttered mutterings to the effect of 'read this'.

After the statement was read, there was no dialogue; the atmosphere was clearly not conducive for that. As if to break the silence and to signal us to say goodbye, the Lady Hostess, whispered to the President that he had another appointment, in response the President said aloud something to the effect that he was not aware of that. The Group then thank the President for receiving us and said goodbye.

After several decades in office, mostly under a one-party regime and under the title of Life President, the incumbent lost the Presidency in 1994.

Mr. Daniel arap Moi, former President of Kenya

I met Mr. Moi several times during the lead up to the 1992 multiparty elections. The electoral environment in Kenya at the time was not really conducive to the conduct of democratic elections. President Moi had openly expressed the view to the Diplomatic community that he did not favour multiparty elections in Kenya. President Moi was evidently a tough political adversary for from the reports of stakeholders he seldom gave way to the pleas of political foes. Nevertheless, he was a good listener and always generated some movement in favour of Secretary-General Anyaoku's requests. When the Secretary-General and I saw the President about the need to consult the opposition with respect to the appointments of members of the ECK, the President agreed and increased the membership of the ECK from seven to eleven. Similarly, when during the campaign period, the Secretary-General and I saw him concerning the need for the Chairperson and the Members of the Commission to operate more transparently with respect to the press and opposition parties, the President agreed and took action, the results of which immediately led to increased communication with the media and opposition parties.

I was a member of the Support Team to COG which met President Moi at the State House in Nkuru shortly before the 1992 elections. He openly and voluntarily admitted to the Group that he was not in favour of multiparty elections and considered it to be provocation when the opposition candidates campaigned in areas where his support was strong. Members of the Group expressed concern to the President about the widespread violence during the campaign, particularly in the Rift Valley. The issue of unevenness in access to the publicly owned media was also drawn to the attention of the President.

Former President De Klerk of South Africa

As the temporary leader of the Secretariat Support Team to the COG, I accompanied Chairman Michael Manley and a representative body of the COG to meet President De Klerk at his Office in Pretoria shortly before the 1994 elections. Mr De Klerk was courteous but rather humourless on the occasion. When he was asked by a member of the COG if he would like to see South Africa return to the Commonwealth after the elections, he hesitated and said he was not sure. Perhaps it was due to the circumstances, but the atmosphere of the meeting with President De Klerk was less than relaxed.

Mr. Mwinyi, former President of Tanzania

I first met President Mwinyi when his second term as President was coming to an end and I was on a planning mission to Tanzania to see if the political parties would receive a Commonwealth election observation team. During that mission, the Commonwealth Secretariat delegation paid a courtesy call on President Mwinyi. He was a pleasant personality with a quiet disposition.

In 1997, former President Mwinyi was Chairman of the Commonwealth Observer Group to the Guyana elections and I was leader of the Commonwealth Secretariat Support Team to the COG. The Chairman of the COG and I got on well. The election was relatively smooth, but the main opposition party leader, former President Hoyte, alerted the Chairman and me that certain serious discrepancies with tallying process had come to his attention and he would be pursuing the matter. The post elections developments erupted into violence and led to a long-standing rift between the main political parties.

Chapter XII

Capacity Building of EMBs

Jamaica, Commonwealth-Oxford, Cambridge, Bangladesh & St. Lucia; African workshops—Windhoek, Botswana (twice), Zimbabwe and Mauritius. Liberia, DEAU, Nairobi, Dakar and Ghana's EMBs' continental meeting.

Introduction
An election management body (EMB) may lack capacity through inadequate core staffing, or through shortage of temporary field workers, or both. But lack of capacity may also be due to inadequate training of some or all categories of staff with respect to the election tasks that they have to perform. The key to a successful EMB is adequate staffing and thorough training of the full staff complement. In some jurisdictions, the selection of good quality election staff may require rigorous screening, at certain levels of recruitment with the help of the major political parties, although in many countries the competition is so fierce among political parties that the participation of parties may not be feasible.

In some States, such as the small island States of the Caribbean and in the erstwhile one party States of Africa and elsewhere, screening of prospective registration and polling staff may be necessary in order to indentify prospective recruits who are prone to display partisan inclinations. Proper screening of recruits and rigorous training of new election staff should mitigate the incidence of partisanship and incompetence of election workers.

Identifying the true needs of an EMB is not easy; there are those election advisers who favour a lean and efficient election management entity to the extent of having a very small core staff and an increased number of temporary field staff during election periods. In this same trend of thought, some election advisers favour part-time members of EMBs, or even a temporary EMB which is only convened when elections are due. Often the scaling back of the number of an EMB's members is due to lack of resources, but the trend currently is to place efficiency and competence to deliver credible elections ahead of all other considerations. Thus because temporary EMBs are less likely to accumulate good institutional memory and undertake continuous research to solve electoral problems, they are likely to be discarded.

To some election commentators, capacity building of EMBs points to staff development and training. Staff development sits uneasily with situations where EMBs rely on staff co-opted from the civil service. This is because in small jurisdictions, EMBs find it difficult to create full career opportunities that can compete with the civil service for their staff. Nevertheless, even for small EMBs some measure of staff development is necessary in order to impart to co-opted staff the culture of impartiality, non-partisanship and fairness that should go with election preparations and conduct. EMBs' staff development programmes should involve not only officers who are directly involved with election processes, but also deal with the finance and general administration related to election preparation and conduct.

Electoral Reform and Capacity Building in Jamaica in 1979
A significant aspect of the electoral reform in Jamaica in 1979 with which I was instrumental in advising on and subsequently responsible for implementing had to do with staff recruitment, development and training. The considerable amendments to election law (the Representation of the People Act) meant that the election rules and procedures were redesigned and as a result new manuals for returning officers, as well as other field officers, were re-written by me who had a legal background. Moreover, the electoral reforms meant that the senior field staffs were asked to resign and re-apply for their jobs if they wished to do so, subject interview. I spearheaded the recruitment of new staff, re-writing of the training manuals and the training of returning officers, and

through the cascade methodology, the low-ranked field officers. Training election officers is an exciting, but exacting exercise; for in addition to the written manuals, there may be practical tips that the trainers have to impart to trainees, such as protection of election materials against inclement weather, or what a presiding officer might do if the ballot box lock does not work properly.

In the case of Jamaica in 1979, capacity building was not confined to training field officers to use their new manuals; it was extended to training computer processing workers to process registration field data. Election tasks require capacity for detail and competency, but the key to bringing all these elements together to deliver success is the timely application of proper training. Election capacity building is usually all embracing but is only truly tested when its application is put into practice in the field.

Capacity-Building through Orientation Courses for Commissioners
I was instrumental in organizing and actively participating in orientation retreats for election commissioners and senior members of election commissions. The concept of orientation retreats for election commissioners and their peers was to foster a way for commissioners to benefit from the experience of commissioners who were seen to have conducted successful elections. In other words, those retreats were informal training and problem-solving meetings for the highest echelons in electoral management.

Orientation retreats were held at several locations, including 'Warm Baths' in South Africa in 1994 leading up to the multi-party elections of that year. The South African experience of 1994 was followed by a retreat of the twenty-one Electoral Commissioners of Mozambique a few weeks before the October 1994 national elections at a location a short distance outside Maputo. This retreat was organized by the Commonwealth Secretariat and I was a principal resource person who organized the informal agenda and led the discussion on some election issues.

During the preparation for the local elections in South Africa in 1995, many retreats were held, some with the dual Chairmanship of the local election management then, and others with senior officials only. There were retreats on voter registration officials of which group I was an adviser, and also of the electoral districts delimitation group with which I was also associated, as well as a Legal Regulations Group with which I was also associated.

I was invited by the EMB of Botswana, on behalf of the Commonwealth Secretariat, to organize jointly with a SADC delegation led by Justice Makame, Chairman of the Tanzanian Electoral Commission, an orientation course at a retreat for the newly constituted Electoral Commission of Botswana. I put together a small distinguished group of Commonwealth Electoral Commissioners and Justice Makame did the same and we met for a week in Francistown, Botswana's second city, with the newly appointed Commissioners. The orientation retreat was successful.

Later in 1998, on behalf of the Commonwealth Secretariat, I was invited to conduct an orientation retreat for the members of the INEC of Nigeria. A distinguished group of Commonwealth Election Commissioners was put together and visited Nigeria. However, due to the lack of time, the orientation retreat was conducted in the offices of the INEC in Abuja, not exactly an ideal location for an informal retreat of the kind intended.

Capacity Building through Workshops
The full potential of workshops and seminars to contribute to election capacity building has not been evaluated in emerging democracies, but it is believed that these events have potential to contribute positively to EMBs' capacity building. The main thrust of capacity building through workshops and seminars is the presentation of issues papers followed by discussions in 'break-out' groups or in plenary sessions. By this means, ideas are traded between EMBs and other election experts, experiences are shared in the process and problem-solving solutions discussed. The benefits of workshop-type discussions increased when the mix of experiences involves mature, new and emerging democracies. This mix was often found in the Commonwealth Chief Election Officers' periodic election workshops.

I was instrumental in organising and participated in six Commonwealth Chief Elections Officers' workshops between 1993 and 2000, commencing with a workshop at Oxford University, England, in July 1993; then followed up in Accra, Ghana (1995), and subsequently in Honiara, Solomon Islands (for the Pacific region), Dhakka, Bangladesh; Cambridge University, England; and Castries, St. Lucia. The agendas and contents of the workshops, though not identical, followed a similar pattern, that is to say, that they were designed to elicit experiences and articulate the problems confronting EMBs. Twenty-three EMBs sent representatives to the first workshop in Oxford.

The general thrust of what became a series of Commonwealth Chief Elections Officers' workshops was to facilitate the exchange of experience and information amongst Commonwealth electoral officials. In general, the discussions centred on practical concerns with respect to the administration of elections. The meetings presented an opportunity for the participants to compare electoral systems and practices. The initial workshop heard many participants' presentations which focused on the broad aspects of the electoral process as set out in the relevant electoral laws and rather less emphasis was placed on the implementation or application of the legal provisions. However, the ensuing discussions did throw up a good measure of analytical and critical observations by participants. One interesting feature of the Commonwealth Chief Elections Officers' workshops was the mix of election commissioners who were largely policy-makers, and electoral officers who managed election operations.

In setting the tone for future workshops, the Oxford workshop recommended that the initiative should continue either on a smaller scale with limited topics or on a regional basis. The meeting noted that there was need to keep the cost of elections down. The meeting noted that the draft working document on 'Good Commonwealth Electoral Practice' which was discussed should be further refined and circulated for discussion by Commonwealth electoral officers. The original document was drawn up by me. The Oxford workshop also recommended that a steering group should be set up to examine ways and means of routine networking amongst Commonwealth electoral officers.

In the mid-90s, I was instrumental in organizing a series of capacity-building workshops for senior Commonwealth African election officers, hosted in Windhoek, Namibia; Gaborone, Botswana (twice); Harare, Zimbabwe; and Mauritius. The purpose of these workshops was to refresh and orientate senior election officers with respect to best practices in organizing major election processes and to view election issues from different perspectives. A notable feature of those workshops was the invitation to specialists resource persons from other parts of the Commonwealth, namely Australia, Canada, India, Malaysia, UK and the Caribbean.

The series of regional workshops which ran parallel to the Commonwealth Chief Elections Officers (described above) were designed to fit the regional needs of Commonwealth African countries. I, as the only recognized in-house election expert in the Commonwealth Secretariat at the time, assumed the responsibility for all technical aspects of the planning and execution of each of those workshops, while George Owusu of the Management & Training Services Division of Commonwealth Secretariat was responsible for the administrative arrangements for the workshops. The first of the regional workshops was held in Windhoek, Namibia, from 6-15 June 1995. The nature and impact of that workshop may be summed up as was contained in a statement issued by the participants. It indicated that they were highly appreciative of the steps taken by the Commonwealth Secretariat to organize specialized training in electoral organization. The statement went on to recommend, among other things, the following:

- That election management personnel should be encouraged to observe elections in one another's countries and share the experiences gained; to facilitate the achievement of that goal;
- It was further suggested that regional cooperation and networking in election matters should be established;

- Electoral officials should receive intensive training in conflict management and mediation skills;
- Electoral bodies should operate independent of government control;
- There should be a level playing field to enable all political parties to participate freely in the electoral process, including the media and state resources; and
- The older Commonwealth democracies, through the Commonwealth Secretariat, should intensify their assistance to emerging multiparty democracies in fostering a democratic culture and strengthening democratic institutions.

While the Windhoek workshop was designed to take stock of election organization and conduct in Commonwealth African countries, the second workshop which was held in Gaborone, Botswana, 18-26 March 1996 focused on specific election themes. Sixteen of the nineteen Commonwealth African countries were represented at the workshop which had fifty-one (17 females) participants, including resource persons from non-African countries, namely, Australia, Canada and India.

A draft working document on 'Good Commonwealth Electoral Practice' was circulated to participants of the workshop. The themes discussed at the second workshop were: election management bodies; voter registration; costing and funding of elections; voter education programmes; election logistics management; management of technology in elections; training of election officials; role of the media in elections; pre-polling and polling day events; enforcing election offences; and election observations.

In their post-workshop statement, the participants expressed a high degree of satisfaction with the programme which they said provided an invaluable opportunity to share rich and diverse experiences among Commonwealth countries.

The third workshop in the series was also held in Gaborone, Botswana, 2-13 June 1997. It was attended by participants of fourteen countries. There were fifty-one (11 females) participants, including resource persons from non-African countries, namely, Australia and India. That workshop discussed a mixture of general issues relating to democracy in Africa, as well as a number of specific topics dealing with the election processes. A few issues such as election offences and election observations which were discussed at the second workshop were revisited but from a different viewpoint. Some issues were new such as delimitation of constituencies, opinion polls and the role of the judiciary.

At the end of the workshop, the participants placed on record their suggestions and comments on the way forward. The main issues raised in their statement were:

- That the programme afforded election managers a training opportunity which was not commonly offered elsewhere and allowed for the sharing of information on electoral process as practised by the participating countries, while at the same time gaining an insight into the wider Commonwealth practices;
- Areas of concern about the programme were the need to rotate participants as well as the host countries, and that more time should be given to each country to outline their electoral process;
- There was need for in-country training schemes which could include police personnel, journalists, political party functionaries, and accredited NGOs;
- They expressed support for the Botswana Democratic Research Project (BDRP); and
- Networking of electoral bodies should be encouraged within Africa.

The fourth workshop was held in Harare, Zimbabwe, 2-13 November 1998. It was attended by sixty-nine (including 22 females) participants. Participants came from nineteen Commonwealth African countries. The thrust of this workshop was to examine the legal and administrative rules governing the various election processes during preparation for and conduct of elections in each country. The workshop was designed so as to enable each presenter to outline briefly the election process in their country. There was opportunity for a few presenters to deal with specific topics such as the cost-effectiveness of the use of technology in elections, processing voter registration data, and the evaluation of the main elements of an election budget.

This was the best attended workshop of the series with the highest proportion of females. It considered the topics discussed, namely: the legal framework of elections; transparency of the electoral process; election management and administration; voter education programmes; voter registration; political campaign and funding of political parties; the role of the media in elections; use of technology in elections; costing elections at cost-effective levels; observation of elections; and preservation of the integrity of the electoral system; and issued a lengthy statement of recommendations.

The salient points of the statement of recommendations were as follows:

- Inconsistencies between constitutions and electoral laws should be rectified;
- Relevant stakeholders should be involved at all stages of the electoral process;
- Electoral commissions should be empowered to appoint their staff and control their finances;
- Voter education programmes should be comprehensive and well funded;
- Voter registration process should be user-friendly and the voters' roll should be permanent and computerised; the process should be continuous and subject to updating; and
- The programme was very educative and should continue.

The fifth and final workshop in the series of Commonwealth African election management workshops organized by me in conjunction with the Management and Training Division of the Commonwealth Secretariat was held in Mauritius from 2-12 May 2000. There were sixty participants, fifteen of whom were females, drawn from all nineteen Commonwealth African members like the previous workshop. Included in the sixty participants were invited resource persons to enrich the dialogue. The non-African resource persons were drawn from Australia, India, Jamaica and the United Kingdom as well as International IDEA. There was a single theme for this workshop and it was 'electoral reform in Commonwealth African countries'. It was a broad theme which enabled each country's representatives to present whatever reforms had or were about to take place with respect to the electoral process.

The reforms discussed at this workshop included: electoral systems; geographic information systems and electoral districts demarcation; human rights and elections; gender and elections (with focus on women); technology and electoral reform; improving the accuracy of voters' registers; secrecy of the ballot; time-frames in elections preparation; the role of the courts; special voting—voting abroad, postal and proxy voting; disadvantaged voters-disabled, blind, illiterate, sick, prisoners, detainees and demented persons; and electoral reform of local government.

The statement issued by the participants after the workshop noted that the presentations made were very informative and contributed to the broad goal of providing opportunities for building regional capacity. The statement also pointed out that numerous significant issues were discussed and debated and that six main themes emerged, namely, improving the accuracy of the voters' register; women and elections; election costs and accountability; need for electoral reforms; secrecy of the ballot; and need for voter education.

Total Training and Capacity Building

In 2006, I was offered a consultancy by UNDP in Liberia to design a capacity programme for the National Elections Commission (NEC) that entailed comprehensive training of employees in their respective tasks. Not since my experience as chief executive of the Jamaican EMB in the late 1970s and early 1980s did I encounter the realization of such a wide ranging need by an EMB. The fact is that most EMBs are not aware that there is a compelling need for the entire workforce in an election institution to be trained not only in their election tasks but also in the culture of fairness and non-partisanship in every aspect of elections. The concept of total training of the workforce of EMBs is one that should be embraced by all EMBs. Normally, thorough training is reserved for those election workers who are actively involved in election processes, but the nature of elections and the role of each employee and their place in the election institution should be part of the overall capacity building programme.

Where there is an ongoing total capacity building programme for an EMB, it will be developed in an almost imperceptive manner in the day to day training programme. If, however, the concept of total capacity building in EMBs is introduced and superimposed on other incomplete training programmes, it requires considerable adjustment in order to ensure that normal work routine of the persons exposed to the comprehensive programme is not unduly disruptive. Such a programme which embraces all facets, administrative support staff, technology, financial, and operational (including field staff) staff in a medium-sized EMB, may last for some 40 weeks consecutively. Professionally-oriented training programmes such as Building Resources in Democracy, Governance and Elections (BRIDGE) may not necessarily coincide with the requirements of total capacity needs.

The DEAU and Capacity Building

The African Union's Democracy and Electoral Assistance Unit's (DEAU's) (to which I was adviser) work plan was not directly focussed on the dimension of capacity building, but many aspects of its election activities had implications for EMBs' capacity building. The continental meeting of EMBs was not aimed at building capacity of EMBs, but to the extent that representatives of EMBs of the different regions of the AU articulated their problems and the solutions of some of those difficulties, there were explicit elements of capacity building involved. Meetings like the continental meeting of EMBs do facilitate the quest for technical assistance, including with respect to capacity building.

The DEAU had a joint action programme, which included the BRIDGE training course with AU EMBs and which was organized with many EMBs, individually or sometimes jointly. This programme was set to run over a period of five years from 2009. There was no doubt that this joint action programme had the potential to make a difference in the electoral capacity building area of AU Member States, but how great a difference it will be eventually was left to evaluation of the programme at its end.

The training of African Union (AU) election observers was a part of the AU Election Support Program, funded by USAID, and of which the International Foundation for Electoral Systems (IFES), with partners, the Carter Center, and the Electoral Institute of Southern Africa, (EISA), was the executing agency. I was the Chief of Party of the IFES for this program.

The aim of this program was to raise the standard of AU election observation and accord greater credibility to AU observation mission reports continental wide and internationally. The content and methodology of the orientation courses[64] for AU election observers were developed for the DEAU, under my coordination, by Carter Center and the Electoral Institute of Southern Africa (EISA). The contents of the training materials consisted of 8 modules covering background information on the principles of democratic elections and the best practices of election observation. The orientation course covered the AU's Code of Conduct for Election Observers and Monitors. Each orientation course was designed to last three days, although the first course which was held in Nairobi, Kenya, was held over two days. The course is designed for about 50 participants from a particular region, being one of the five regions of the African Union. At the end of each course, each participant was awarded a certificate of participation by the Department of

---

[64] The phrase 'orientation course' was used instead of 'training' out of deference to the station and sensibilities of some categories of the participants.

Political Affairs of the African Union Commission (AUC). This had been a modest start as I believe that the AU should have about 1,000 trained observers in its election database—at the time of writing it had about 915 entries in its database section of election observers of which less than 100 had been certified trained AU observers.

CHAPTER XIII
My Publications

I enjoy writing about election issues. My first serious election work was called **'Organizing Free and Fair Elections at Cost-Effective Levels'** which was published by the Commonwealth Secretariat in 1993. The aim of that work was to identify the activities in each election process that could attract cost-saving measures. As the Preface to that work stated, 'it attempts to provide some insights into the possibility of delivering good quality election services at low-cost levels in emerging multi-party democracies.' The work looked at situations where a significant amount of electoral reform had taken place then and instanced case studies of Jamaica (1979-80), Malta (1990-91) and Guyana (1990-92). It then examined situations where particular factors had influenced the transition from one-party to multi-party regimes and presented case studies of electoral developments in Zambia (1990-91) and Kenya (1991-92).

This election book was written at a time when there was scarce literature on the hands-on aspects of election organization in emerging democracies and the problems that had to be overcome. It took the form of a kind of election manual focussing on highlights in chapters on themes such as constitutional framework; electoral laws; the courts; election administration; costing elections; compiling of the voters' register; and polling. The case studies were included to illustrate the needed electoral reform that was taking place in emerging democracies in different parts of the world.

Dimensions of Free and Fair Elections, which was published in 1994 by the Commonwealth Secretariat, consisted of five essays highlighting some of the pillars of democratic elections. Perhaps the most interesting of these essays was the one dealing with the attributes of free and fair elections with special reference to small States. This essay threw some light on the perception of Aristotle of some of the difficulties of small States in operating the democratic system.[65] Aristotle expanded his views on the issue of small States thus:

> *For in great states it is possible, and indeed necessary, that every office should have a special function; where the citizens are numerous, many may hold office ... But in small states it is necessary to combine many offices in a few hands, since the small number of citizens does not admit of many holding office: for who will there be to succeed them? And yet small states at times require the same offices and laws as large ones: the difference that the one want them often, the others only after long intervals.[66]*

The point that the essay was making here was that Aristotle's observation was true today in respect of small States' democracy as it was more than 2000 years ago. The essay, 'attributes of free and fair elections' also examined the role of constitutions in a democratic state and cites respective relevant utterances from Aristotle and Hobbes thus:

> *The laws are, and ought to be, relative to the constitution, and not the constitution to the laws. A constitution is the organization of offices of a state, and determines what is the governing body, and what is the end of each community. But laws are not to be confounded with the principle of the constitution; they are the rules according to which*

---

[65]   Aristotle, 384-322 B.C.

[66]   Aristotle, Politics Book IV, Chapter 15, Great Books of the Western World, Vol. 9 Aristotle II,p.500. M. Hutchens, ed. Encyclopaedia Britannica, Inc.

the magistrates should administer the states and proceed against offenders.[67]

Hobbs, in writing about the fundamental law of a State put it rather picturesquely, thus:

For a fundamental law in every Commonwealth is that which, being taken away, the Commonwealth faileth and is utterly destroyed. And therefore a fundamental law is that by which subjects are bound to uphold whatsoever power is given to the sovereign, whether a monarchy or a sovereign assembly, without which the Commonwealth cannot stand; such is the power of war and peace, of the judicature, of election of officers, and of doing whatsoever he shall think necessary for the public good.[68]

The essay looked at the relationship of the constitution and early elections and noted that Aristotle and Plutarch gave examples of constitutional provisions which dealt with the holding of democratic elections in Greek city states. Aristotle states that Draco's constitution conferred the franchise on those who could furnish themselves with military equipment and that a small council consisting of four hundred and one members was elected by lot from among those who possessed the franchise.[69] Aristotle also tells us that Solon's constitution for Athens provided for elections by lot to various offices.[70] Aristotle stated that during his time, the Athenian constitution contained provisions with respect to the franchise and the register of those who were properly registered.

---

[67] Aristotle, politics Book IV, Chap. 1, Great Books of the Western World, Vol. 9 Aristotle II P.488.

[68] See Thomas Hobbs, Leviathan, or Matter, Form, and Power of a Commonwealth Ecclesiastical and Civil, Part II, Chap. 6, p. 138, Vol.23, Great Books of the Western World, W. Benton, Publisher Encyclopaedia Britannica, Inc.

[69] Aristotle, The Athenian Constitution, Chap. 4, Great Books of the Western World, Vol. 9, p.554, Hitchens ed. Encyclopaedia Britannia, Inc.

[70] Ibid., p.556

There was a Council of five hundred members who were elected by lot.[71]

Plutarch noted that, Lycurgus,[72] the lawgiver of Sparta, laid down a unique procedure for the election of senators, which was as follows:

> *The people assembled and some were selected and locked away in a room near to the place of election, so contrived that they neither see nor be seen, but could only hear the noise of the assembly without; for they decided this, as most other affairs of the moment, by the shouts of the people. This done, the competitors were not brought in and presented all together, but one after another by lot, and passed in order through the assembly without speaking a word. Those who were locked up had writing-tables with them, in which they recorded and marked each shout by its loudness, without knowing in favour of which candidate each of them was made, but merely that they came first, second, third and so forth. He who was found to have the most and loudest acclamations was declared senator duly elected.[73]*

The essay looked at the issue of entitlement to vote down the ages and made certain comparisons with the situation today. It noted that the question of the voting franchise had occupied the minds of democrats since time immemorial. It cited the ancient literature which indicated that Plato favoured conferring the vote to elect the magistrates of Athens on those who were horse and foot-soldiers, or had seen military service. He would support a council of 360 members divided into four tribes in which the counsellors of each class would be elected by all the members of that class, although in some classes, Plato envisaged compulsory voting which would not

---

[71]   Ibid. p.572.

[72]   Lycurgus, legendary 9th Century B.C. Lawgiver.

[73]   See Plutarch's Lycurgus, Great Books of the Western World, Vol. 14 p. 45, W. Benton, Publisher Encyclopaedia Britannica, Inc.

be extended to other classes.[74] Under the constitution of Draco, the franchise in Athens was given to all who could furnish themselves with military equipment,[75] while the constitution of Solon[76] based the franchise on property qualifications in each of the four tribes into which Athens was divided. The property qualification was blunted some what by the fact that the final selection of candidates was done by lot and the person on whom the lot fell held office even though he might have been poor. During the time of Aristotle, the franchise, as required by the constitution of Athens, was open to all who were citizens by virtue of being born of parents who were citizens. They had to attain the age of eighteen before being able to enrol as a voter. Only persons who were born free could be enrolled.[77]

This essay was largely about the attributes of current credible democratic elections and merely sought to relate modern democratic practices to the origins and evolution of small Greek city-states democratic development.

The **Compendium of Election Laws Practices and Cases of Selected Commonwealth Countries** was a major individual undertaking by me. It encompassed four volumes-two of the volumes hold the constitutional provisions relating elections and the electoral laws of thirty-seven Commonwealth countries, and two volumes consisted of randomly selected election cases from Commonwealth countries. The compilations took four years commencing in 1994 through to 1998 when the final volume was published through the auspices of the Commonwealth Secretariat.

The motivation for launching out on the compilation of the compendium of Commonwealth election laws was the need to

---

[74] Plato, Laws VI, Great Books of the Western World, Vol. 7, p. 698, Hutchins, ed. Encyclopaedia Britannica

[75] Aristotle, The Athenian Constitution, Chap. 4, Great Books of the Western World, Vol. 9, p. 554.

[76] 594 B.C.

[77] See Aristotle, The Athenian Constitution Chaps. 58-63 , p 580-81

provide member States of the association with materials that would facilitate quick means of comparative analysis. It was also aimed to capture the emerging electoral reform in Commonwealth Africa and elsewhere. Thus the electoral laws of several countries, for example, Guyana, Malawi, South Africa, and to an extent, Mozambique's, were transitional legislation which would be largely modified or replaced within a stipulated period. The compendium was also designed to assist the Commonwealth Secretariat to offer improved advice to governments and EMBs on electoral reform, particularly election legislative schemes and formulae for the management structure of EMBs. The compendium was made available to every EMB in the Commonwealth to use as a tool in comparing the treatment of electoral issues. It found its way to the libraries of universities and CSOs involved in electoral matters.

As was to be expected, the task of collecting the materials for the compendium was an enormous one, since it was done by me alone when on observation or technical assistance missions in Commonwealth countries. In some cases EMBs were written to directly requesting the required documents which included the annotated constitution and electoral laws. Some EMBs, like Pakistan's and Malaysia's, were able to provide complete annotated copies of the electoral law, while others like Singapore's was decidedly reluctant to provide an up-to-date copy of the constitution and electoral law, although those were supposed to be public documents. The access to annotated constitutions and electoral laws was made more difficult as very few of those documents were available on-line then, and even today, as a cursory search of the African Union Member States will show, most electoral laws are not found on-line. Hard on the trail of the publication of my compendium, several election experts from India and elsewhere wrote me in congratulatory terms and indicated their desire and commitment to producing a similar work, but no such comprehensive work has so far emerged to date. Unless concerted efforts are made to collect up-to-date annotated constitutions and electoral laws, the end product is unlikely to be very useful.

The presentation of each constitutional provision relating to elections and each country's electoral laws was paraphrased in coherent and simplified prose to facilitate user-friendly application without altering the legal import of the provisions. It was this aspect of the compilation that took much time and effort. The volumes of election cases were more straightforward, as less paraphrasing was necessary or appropriate. The cases were collected from EMBs and many were included in the compendium before they were formally reported on in the local law reports, or in some instances before the appellate procedures were exhausted. However, each case included in the compendium illustrated an important point of electoral law and the role of the courts in election organization and conduct.

The constraints included lack of resources to undertake more extensive research, and yet, as my attempt to undertake a similar exercise in the African Union showed, the Commonwealth enabled me to avoid language issue, as I worked exclusively in English which was not possible in the African Union. Another constraint was that at the time of compiling the compendium, electoral reform was rather fashionable-one-party regimes were giving way to democratic multi-party systems and the apartheid system of South Africa had just ceased to exist, and electoral legislative schemes were being changed often, leading to constant changes to the manuscripts.

Election Management Bodies: Constitutive Instruments—was published by the Commonwealth Secretariat in 1999. I compiled this small work for the purposes of providing easy access to comparative instruments, including constitutional provisions dealing with elections, when setting up EMBs. Many of the instruments contained therein have now been upgraded.

The Commonwealth African Workshops for Election Managers—I edited selected papers from four of the five workshops which I conducted for election managers from Commonwealth African countries between 1995 and 2000. These selected papers were published through the Commonwealth Secretariat following each workshop commencing in 1997. They were entitled as follows: ***Let's Talk About Elections***-*The Themes: Legal Framework; Management Bodies; Voters' Registers; Relevance of Technology; The Media; Managing the Logistics; Affordable Elections?; Training Officials; Managing Polling Day; and Assessing the Process;* ***Discussion of Elections Issues in Commonwealth Africa; Rules of Elections in Commonwealth Africa; and Electoral Reform in Commonwealth African Countries.*** The purpose of editing and publishing those papers was to preserve and publicise the valuable contribution that participants in those training courses made to election organization in Commonwealth African countries. A further aim of those publications was to ensure that members of EMBs who were not able to attend the workshops also had the benefit of accessing the presentations made at the workshops. This was particularly relevant with respect to the discussions of the final workshop of 2000 which dealt with *Electoral Reform in Commonwealth African Countries.*

Improving the Organization of Elections—A 2006 Perspective—This work was published in 2006 by Ian Randle Publishers of Jamaica. It was aimed at updating many important election processes by injecting best practices consideration in planning election organization. It looked at the content of 'electoral modernization', although some EMBs encountered in the course of writing the book, for example Guyana's, preferred the use of the term 'electoral reform'.

This book tackled some of the issues that always seemed to lurk in the background whenever credible or free and fair elections are discussed, for example, review of electoral systems, constructing fair constituency boundaries, and modernization of election management operation.

The book examined developments with respect to several topics which form the foundation of democratic elections and discuss them in the light of developments internationally. These topics included electoral legislative schemes, voters' registers, registration of political parties, nomination of candidates, and the polling preparation and conduct.

The book contains what it styled as forward thinking discourses. There are five such discourses, namely, electoral norms, privatisation of elections, transparency in election organization, managing the disappointment of election losers, and failed EMBs.

Observing Elections the Commonwealth's Way—The Early Years: This work was published by Ian Randle Publishers of Jamaica in 2007. It describes the growth of the Commonwealth's election observation efforts through the Commonwealth Secretariat which was established in 1965. Election observation efforts prior to 1965 like observation of the 1964 Guyana election was not covered in this work.

The purpose of this short work was to describe how a particular organization developed its election observation rules and practice and its impact on the rapidly growing methodology of pronouncement on credible or free and fair elections. It gave insights into the way Commonwealth observer groups (COGs) arrive at decisions as to whether or not an electorate voted freely in a credible election. This issue was important as each member of COGs formed their own judgment as to the freeness and fairness of the election process which he/she observed and then weigh the experience of fellow members of the COG to see if consensus could be reached even though the balance of the evidence as a whole might be different from what happened in the area of his/her deployment.

The work also throws light on some of the problems which the leadership of COGs had to deal from time to time, such as unfit observers who could not be deployed in certain areas of the host country, or running off to have a good time at the expense of the observation task, or not abiding by the code of conduct. It also throws light on the COGs' handling of election irregularities which its members observed during their deployment.

Contributions to other publications:—*Electoral Management Design: The International IDEA Handbook*

This work was one in a series published by the International Institute for Democracy and Electoral Assistance (International IDEA) (SE-103 34 Stockholm, Sweden) in 2006 and aimed at presenting comparative analysis, information and insights on a range of democratic institutions and processes. It dealt with all aspects of electoral management bodies (EMBs) and was designed to facilitate policy-makers, politicians, civil society organizations and election practitioners.

I was a lead writer of the text of this handbook.

International Electoral Standards: Guidelines for Reviewing the Legal Framework of Elections-

This concise work was published by International IDEA in 2002. It was aimed at facilitating improved techniques in reviewing electoral legislative frameworks. It offered guidelines to anyone wishing to initiate or amend electoral legislation in accordance with international standards. It followed regional guidelines which were applicable to the Organization for Security and Co-operation in Europe (OSCE) region, jointly developed by International IDEA and the Office for Democratic Institution and Human Rights (ODIHR) of the OSCE in Warsaw, which was published in 2001.

The Guidelines looked at the many issues which may be in need of treatment in a given electoral legislative scheme, including internationally recognized standards; structure of the legal framework; the electoral system; boundary delimitation of electoral units; EMBs; voter registration; political parties and candidates; democratic electoral campaigns; media access; campaign finance; balloting; counting and tabulating votes; representatives of political parties and candidates; election observers; and compliance with and enforcement of electoral law.

I was a member of a group of election experts who reviewed the draft Guidelines before their publication.

Funding of Political Parties and Election Campaigns-

This work was another in the Handbook Series published by International IDEA in 2003. It dealt with various aspects of political party funding as well as the funding of election campaigns.

My contribution to this publication was limited to background studies and information.

Books in the Process of Writing: *The Lag of 21ˢᵗ Century Democratic Elections In the African Union Member States*—This is a substantial work which looks at origins and growth of democratic elections in the African Union in the first decade of the 21ˢᵗ Century. It examines a number of regional economic community instruments and structures to see the extent, if any, they contributed to the development of democratic elections during the period, or if they have the potential to do so. It looks at the impact on democratic elections of related mechanisms and institutions under the umbrella of the AU, such as African Peer Review Mechanisms (APRM) and the Pan-African Parliament.

This work addresses many issues that relate indirectly to the fostering of democracy and democratic elections in the AU, such as the reasons for the high levels of democratic deficits in the Union and how they could be redressed. It contains several election case studies and APRM case studies, as well as a discourse on CSOs' compacts.

Close Elections and Political Succession in the African Union
This is a more concise work than *Democratic Elections . . . .'* mentioned above and it examines the twin issues of close elections and political succession in the AU. It took its cue from the Kenyan elections of 2007 and its bloody aftermath and the Zimbabwean elections of March and June 2008, and made comparisons with close elections in Ghana in 2008.

Unpublished books:
The **Ballot Box** was written to record my Jamaican experience as the technical legal adviser to the Joint Select Committee of the House of Representatives and the Senate and as the first Director

of Elections in Jamaica during the period of 1979-80. It examined the agonizing experience of a political party and a small emerging democracy facing a change of government through the ballot box. It re-counted the hazards of directing a general election of a mere million or so electorate in which more than eight hundred people lost their lives through political violence. It recorded some favourite election anecdotes of mine, as well as party functionaries' clever attempts at rigging elections.

This work was not attractive to publishers. Perhaps the commercial component of an essentially technical work on elections in an obscure small country was rather low. In the early 1980s there was limited international interest in free and fair elections in small emerging democracies like Jamaica's.

Stealing Elections—
Part one of this work was a reflection on almost fifteen years of observing elections and offering technical assistance in electoral matters. It probed the secrets behind and the methodology of stealing elections by stealth. It looked at the gerrymandering of constituency boundaries, at the compilation of flawed voters' registers, at electoral systems that produced outlandishly distorted distribution of seats to votes cast, at unfair or poorly administered procedures relating to the registration (nomination) of candidates and/or parties to contest an election, at election campaigns that lacked a level playing field, and flawed polling, counting and tallying procedures.

Part two was a collection of election cases, including Zanzibar (1995 & 2000), Zimbabwe (2002); Guyana (1997 & 2001) and USA Florida presidential election 2000. It caught the eye of a publisher and although a signed contract ensued, the work was never published. Although the work was aimed at exposing the way stealing elections by stealth and offering suggestions how to identify and remedy such practices, it might have been feared that coincidentally at the same time the book gave ideas to those who might wish to practice election rigging.

Election Anecdotes and Snippets-

The work is a mere collection of my favourite election anecdotes and snippets drawn from personal experiences and election reports from all over the world. It is meant for light reading and to reveal the funny side of election planning and conduct. It also records unusual election practices and procedures many of which entered into election legislative schemes. It has not yet been put forward for publication.

CHAPTER XIV
Important Electoral Meetings

Commonwealth CEO meetings
Meeting 1985 in Halifax, sponsored by CPA?
GEO Network meeting 1999 (Canada)
International seminar on EDR in China 2004
Africa EMBs continental meeting 2009
AU Election Observers' Orientation Courses

Introduction
Since 1979 when I became Director of Elections in Jamaica, I have attended many electoral conferences, seminars and workshops and presented numerous papers on electoral matters. I have dealt at some length above with the six Commonwealth Chief Election Officers' meetings and the five Commonwealth African countries' election managers' workshops and so I will not deal with those meetings here. Instead, I will relate my encounter and role in some other equally interesting election gatherings.

Study Group Meeting on Electoral Law and Practice 1985
The first such meeting that I will discuss is the study group of the Commonwealth Parliament Association on "Electoral Law and Practice" which met in Halifax, Nova Scotia, Canada, in September 5-28 1985. I was special guest to the Study Group meeting representing the Commonwealth Secretariat and another special guest was Mr. B.R. Nugent, Australian Electoral Officer for New South Wales. The Group's report described the contribution of the special guests to the discussions as most competent.

The Study Group was comprised of Members from seven Branches of the Commonwealth Parliamentary Association, one from each of the seven regions of the Association. The representatives present were: Chairman-Mr. Patrick Boyer, MP (Canada); Members—Hon. C. J. Butale, MP (Botswana); Shri Somnath Rath, MP (India); Mr. Kenneth Shirley, MP (New Zealand); Hon. W. St. Clair-Daniel, CBE, CStJ, JP, MP (Saint Lucia); Dr Lau Teik Soon, MP (Singapore); and Mr. Michael Colvin, MP (United Kingdom).

The reporter of the meeting was Mr Jean-Marc Hamel, then the Chief Electoral Officer of Canada.

The Study Group identified seven topics for discussion, namely, electoral systems; electoral constituencies; electoral procedure; voting rights; candidates; electoral campaign; and election results.

Although some members of the Study Group might have found the two first topics—electoral systems and electoral constituencies, most engaging, the treatment of each topic in the report followed a similar format, that is to say, a summary introduction of the topic, an abstract of the paper presented and highlights of the discussion. The discussion of these issues and the excellent report of the Group's work contributed much to the roots of democratic elections at a time when one-party and apartheid regimes appeared to be firmly set in Africa, including in some Commonwealth countries.

The Report of the CPA Study Group on Electoral Law and Practice was widely acclaimed by delegates participating in the third plenary session the 31st Commonwealth Parliamentary Conference which opened on 9 October 1985.

The Global Electoral Organization (GEO) Network Conference 1999

The Global Electoral Organization (GEO) Network Conference which was held in Ottawa, Canada, from April 11-14 1999 was the first worldwide meeting of regional associations of election officers. The participants were representatives of various associations of election authorities, including Association of African Election Authorities (AAEA); Association of Asian Election Authorities (AAEA); Association of Caribbean Electoral Organizations (ACEO); Association of Central and East European Election

Officials (ACEEEO); Council for Government Ethics Laws (COGEL); Inter-American Union of Electoral Organizations (UNIORE); International Association of Clerks, Recorders, Election Officials, and Treasurers (IACREOT); International Institute for Municipal Clerks (IIMC); Pacific Islands, Australia and New Zealand Electoral Administrators (PIANZEA); Protocol of Tikal; Protocol of Quito; and Southern Africa Election Administrators (SAEA).

Institutional representatives invited to this conference included Australian Election Commission (AEC); Canadian International Development Agency (CIDA); Caribbean Community (CARICOM); Center for Electoral Assistance and Development (CAPEL); Commonwealth Secretariat; Federal Electoral Institute of Mexico (IFE); Organization of American States (OAS); OSCE Office for Democratic Institutions and Human Rights (ODIHR); United Nations Development Programme (UNDP); and United States Agency for International Development (USAID).

I, along with Mr. Hanif Vally, represented the Commonwealth Secretariat at the conference.

The GEO Conference had four objectives, namely:

- To provide an opportunity for associations of election officials to communicate with each other in a global professional network. The conference took the first steps in establishing such a network;
- To offer organizational and programmatic models for collaboration and cooperative ventures among association members, between associations, or with the supporters of electoral governance projects.
- To serve as a forum to identify areas of need in electoral governance, and the programs which can be developed to respond to these needs; and
- To identify a common agenda for all election management bodies around the world.

In terms of its perspectives, the conference program addressed electoral history lessons, techniques for organizing, project opportunities, and policy issues. It was projected that conference delegates from the regional associations, their associate memberships, could benefit from programming in four potential areas, namely, programs to benefit the membership; programs to improve electoral governance; bilateral and multilateral initiatives; and the common agenda, those elements of electoral governance common to all delegates. With respect to representatives of international organizations and bilateral development agencies, the conference offered a forum in which they expressed their priorities and exchanged programming ideas with practitioners.

The conference laid the foundation for further international meetings of this kind.

International Conference on Sustaining Africa's Democratic Momentum

In 2007, I represented the International Foundation for Electoral Systems (IFES) at an International Conference on Sustaining Africa's Democratic Momentum held in Johannesburg, South Africa, during the week of 5th March. I was also a resource person at the conference. The Conference was attended by election officials and academicians from all over the continent, with senior electoral managers from Latin America and South Asia as special invitees. It was well organised and the papers presented were informative and forward looking.

The sponsors were the African Union, the Independent Electoral Commission of South Africa (IEC) and the International Institute for Democracy and Electoral Assistance (IDEA).

The purpose of the Conference was to analyse the difficulties facing the Continent with respect to democracy, development and electoral organisation and propose solutions.

The topics discussed at the conference included the following:

- Politics, Representation, and Participation: The Political Dimensions of Electoral System Design in Democratic Building
- Enhancing the Capacity of Political Parties as Agents of Democratisation: Towards Creating Political Parties that are Democratic, Representative, and Trusted by Voters
- Re-engineering Constitution Frameworks for Peace. Democracy, and Development
- Supporting Democracy and Elections across the Globe: Unilateralism vs. Multilateralism
- The Nexus between Democracy and Development
- Enhancing the Legitimacy and Capacity of Electoral Management Bodies (EMBs): EMB Independence and Financing of Elections
- Panel on Latin America: Elections and Democracy; and the
- Panel Discussions on Asia: Managing Representation in Pluralistic and Diverse Societies.

Among the participants were: EMBs' Commissioners Cameroon, Democratic Republic of Congo, Ivory Coast, Liberia, Kenya, Tanzania and Zanzibar, Mauritius, Malawi, Namibia, Nigeria, Seychelles, Sierra Leone, South Africa and Zambia. I had discussions with many of the Commissioners who gave me a brief account of recent and pending developments on the activities of their respective EMBs. Cameroon expects to have a new EMB in a few months' time. In Sierra Leone, Dr Christiana Thorpe, the Chairperson and Chief Electoral Commissioner, indicated that her EMB was preparing for national elections which was then due in July 2007. The Hon. James Fromayan, Chairman of the Liberian EMB, brought me up-to-date on the post-election review and expected reform of the structure and election processes in that country. Prof. Iwu, Chairman of the Nigerian EMB, who made a brief appearance at the Conference, indicated to me that preparations for the pending election were well on course. Justice Makame of the Tanzanian EMB (Mainland) exchanged views on the electoral scene which was quiet at the time in mainland Tanzania, while Justice Augustino Ramadani, Vice Chairman of the Zanzibar EMB, expressed the view that the electoral landscape in Zanzibar was improving. Justice Msosa, Chairman of the Malawian EMB, briefed me on developments in her EMB. Mr Gappy of the Seychelles EMB told me of the improvements which had been made to electoral register. I had several brief exchanges about the Conference with Dr. Brigalia Bam, Chairperson of the Electoral Commission of South Africa, (IEC) and Ms Thoko Mpumlwana, Vice-Chairman.

Dr. Bam extended recognition to those persons, of whom I was one, attending the Conference who had assisted in the 1994 South African elections. I was one of the few participants of the Conference who received a memento in the form of a small artwork.

The Conference was designed to have three 'breakout' sessions and I served as facilitator for one of them. Judged by the attendance and the quality of the presentations in the Plenary Session, the Conference was a major success.

International Seminar on Election Disputes Resolution in 2004 in China

This seminar was sponsored by the Chinese village election authorities with a view to share the experiences of election disputes resolution in other parts of the world. The seminar was held in Beijing, China. I made a presentation on the international practice of settling election disputes in a democratic environment. The exchanges were frank and the Chinese lawyers and academicians articulated the fundamental weaknesses in the Chinese election dispute settlement procedures.

According to a paper circulated by the Chinese participants, the relief for the villagers' right to democratic elections should observe the following five principles. One is the principle that rights and obligations are inseparable. The right that cannot receive relief is merely a scrap of paper. If the villagers cannot receive relief for their right to democratic elections, that will inevitably impede the advance of the grass-roots democratic politics in the rural areas and harm the other rights of the peasants, thus affecting social stability in China's rural areas. Two, is the principle that relief is offered in a timely manner according to law. That means that the encroachments upon the democratic rights of villagers should be handled in a timely manner, on the spot and according to law. The institutions and individuals who have been found to have truly violated laws and disciplines as complained about should be dealt with promptly. Three, is the principle that internal relief comes first. The subject of internal relief is the village committee or the village electoral committee, whose relief only covers some minor cases within the self-government unit, such as voter eligibility and minor encroachment upon the voting by villagers. Internal relief is more operable, simple, efficient and cost-effective. Four, is the principle that external relief, such as relief by Party and government and power relief, comes second. Of all forms of external relief, relief by Party and government should be a preference, followed by the relief by power organs and then by social relief. Five, is the principle that judicial relief is the final resort. Judicial relief is the last shield fo r other forms of relief and only preferred when all other forms of relief do not work, or go wrong.[78]

The African Union's EMBs' Continental Meeting 2009

In chapter X above, I discussed the EMBs' continental meeting from the point of view of the DEAU's public relations strategy. Here I am addressing that meeting broadly as an important electoral meeting. As the election consultant to the African Union's Democracy and Electoral Assistance Unit (DEAU), I was instrumental in the convening of a continental meeting of electoral management bodies (EMBs) in December 2009 in Accra Ghana. The meeting was attended by twenty-nine representatives from twenty-three EMBs. The main purpose of the meeting was to bring representatives of as many EMBs as possible in order to get them to know each other and create the groundwork for a practical networking of exchange of information and ideas with respect to improving the organization of credible national elections. Selected representatives of EMBs from each of the five regions of the African Union gave reports on their current position with election organization. Perhaps the most interesting account came from the Head of the Provisional Electoral Commission of Kenya who outlined the electoral developments

---

[78]   A study report on relief mechanisms for villagers' right to democratic elections.

surrounding the appointment of Commissioners to the revamped Electoral Commission after the previous Commission was dissolved post the 2007 post-election conflicts.

A number of general issues of concern to AU EMBs were discussed. For example, the problems which EMBs were experiencing in delivering credible elections; the funding of EMBs; the relationship between EMBs and stakeholders; and the need to introduce continuous voter education.

Certain issues, such as the creation of a mechanism for the operation of a network of EMBs and the establishment of a set of procedures to regulate the prioritization of requests for technical assistance from the DEAU, were raised but were not fully discussed, as they were not formally on the agenda of the meeting.

Recommendations
The meeting recommended, *iter alia* that:

DEAU promote the idea of creating an interactive mechanism through which experiences can be shared and support between EMBs can be strengthened;

Pursuant to its mandate the Unit should endeavour to build the capacities of electoral commissions through the provision of training, material and financial resources;

AU put into place key mechanisms that would enable interactive debate on electoral processes;

The cost of running elections should be examined and more effective ways of organizing and conducting less expensive elections be explored;

AU should conduct a study to assess the effectiveness of electoral commissions work and to take stock of electoral commissions successes and failures;

The possibility of ensuring continuous voter education should be examined as part of citizen education campaigns, especially in schools;

Promote exchange of experiences between EMBs by organizing annual meetings; and
That DEAU prepare a best practice handbook based on the information to be gathered through questionnaire.

Orientation Courses for AU Election Observers
In chapter XIII above I discussed my contribution to electoral capacity building generally. Here the focus is on the capacity building with respect to African Union's election observation. In my capacity as the Chief of Party of the IFES-USAID Program of Election Support to the African Union and consultant to the DEAU, as well as the co-ordinator of the contribution of IFES' partners, the Carter Center and the Electoral Institute of Southern Africa (EISA), I was instrumental in organizing the two first orientation courses to provide refresher training for African Union election observers. The broad objective of these orientation courses was to ensure that AU election observers in observing elections across the continent apply common standards of observation. With respect to individual AU election observers, the aim of the orientation courses was to better equip them with the latest nuances of election observation and reporting thereon.

The training materials, which consisted of eight major teaching modules, was supported by a toolkit, and were prepared by the Carter Center and EISA, and coordinated by the DEAU and myself. The modules covered the general nature of democratic elections in the African Union and the historical background to the current election observation efforts. They also took account of the election cycle and the preparatory election processes which long-term observers might have to contend with in given cases. In addition to international instruments and practice which the modules took account of, the courses encompassed presentation of relevant instruments and procedures developed by the AU and its predecessor organization, the OAU. In this regard, of particular interest were the AU's *principles governing election observation and monitoring.*

The first orientation course was held in Nairobi, Kenya, in September 2009. It was designed to draw participants from the East Africa Region, one of the five officially designated regions of the African Union. There were thirty-six participants drawn from various institutions in that Region, namely, EMBs, CSOs, parliamentarians from the Pan-African Parliament (PAP), academia, and politicians in the Region.

Presentations at the course were made by representatives of the Carter Center, EISA, and me in a somewhat dual capacity, as the CoP of IFES, one of the sponsors of the course, and as the consultant to the DEAU. The organization of the meeting was done jointly by DEAU and IFES and partners. Similarly, the costs of the course were met jointly by DEAU and the Election Support Program which was funded by USAID. At the end of the two-day refresher orientation course, each participant was presented with a Certificate of Attendance issued by the Political Affairs Department (PAD) of the African Union Commission.

The **second orientation course** was a three-day affair and was held in Dakar, Senegal, from 1-3 March 2010. It was designed to serve the West Africa Region. There were thirty-three participants, drawn from institutions and bodies similar to those in the East Africa Region from which the participants of the Nairobi course had come. The second course was arranged in a different format from the first in that there were 'breakout sessions' in three groups in which special topics were discussed and the recommendations reported back to plenary session. This approach was not as productive as it might have been, because there were no translation facilities to serve the breakout groups.

The arrangement also featured a 'mock' episode of voting at a polling station with observers and voters drawn from the participants. This exercise provoked lively participation from the 'voters' as well as the 'observers'.

The presenters were the same as at the Nairobi course and the subject matter and materials were the same as at the first course. The administration arrangements were largely undertaken by IFES Offices Ethiopia and Washington D.C. The cost of the course was met jointly by DEAU and IFES. At the end of the three-day course, the participants were each issued with a Certificate of Participation from the PAD.

CHAPTER XV

Personalities that I have Inter-acted with in my Election World-Females/Males

FEMALES
Ms. Frances Johnson Morris (Liberia)
Dr Christina Thorpe (Sierra Leone)
Dr. B. Bam (South Africa
Dr. Pires Helena (Cape Verde)
Justice Msosa (Malawi)
Ms. Mokhothu Limakatso (Chairperson) (Lesotho)
Mrs. Tembo M. Kalwa (Commissioner) (Zambia)
Ms Shumbana Karume (AU)
Ms. J. Lucas (T&T)

MALES
Mr. N. Lee (Jamaica)
Mr. Danville Walker (Jamaica)
Dato Harun Din, Chairman Electoral Commission, Malaysia
Jean-Marc Hamel, Chief Electoral Officer, Canada.
Jean-Piere Kingsley, Chief Electoral Officer, Canada
Dr. Stephen Surujbally, Chairman, GECOM Guyana.
Justice Ephraim Akpata election 1998-99-died January 2000 (Nigeria)
Prof. Abel Guobadia conducted 2003 elections, violence & irregularities (Nigeria)
Prof. Maurice Iwu, Chairman INEC 2005 (election 2007 below international standards (Nigeria)
Dr. Afari-Gyan (Ghana)
Mr. Samuel Kivuitu (Kenya)
Mr. Abdool Rahman (Mauritius 1998)

Mr. Bill Gray, Electoral Commissioner, Australia, 1995-
Justice Lewis Makame, Chairman EMB, Tanzania
Justice A.S.L. Ramadhani, former Vice Chairman of EMB, Tanzania

Introduction
During my thirty years of close association with the development
of democratic elections in Jamaica, the Commonwealth, the
African Union and elsewhere, I have worked or come in contact
with personalities who have made or are making an outstanding
contribution to democratic election development. These dedicated
personalities consisted of both females and males. I will discuss my
impressions of some of these people who were mainly at the head
of the EMBs concerned, but there were numerous other officers of
both sexes who gave unstinting support to their respective heads
and who have not been singled out for praise. These personalities
impressed me in varying degrees, but the bottom line is that they
strove to organize credible elections.

Ms. Frances Johnson-Morris, former Chairperson of the
Independent Elections Commission of Liberia (IEC), (also a former
Chief Justice of that country) during 2004-05 who presided over the
elections that restored multi-party democracy to that country. As
the sole election consultant of the European Commission in Liberia
during 2004-05, I was also legal and technical adviser to the IEC.
The EC was an important partner of the IEC having contributed the
equivalent of more than US$4 million to the election organization.

Ms. Johnson-Morris was a good partner to work with who was
always willing to listen and consider new ideas and different ways
to solve problems. She was not afraid to let the United Nations
and other partners know that the ownership of the elections
belonged to the Liberians. She was also no push over as was seen
once when the Representative of a certain partner engage her in a
verbal eruption for several minutes, Ms. Johnson—Morris did not
hold back and let him have her tongue in no uncertain manner. She
handled the grumpy political parties with firmness, yet politely.
With the assistance of the UN and other partners, she succeeded in
delivering credible democratic elections in 2005.

Dr Brigalia Bam, Chairperson of the Electoral Commission of South Africa. Dr. Bam is a competent electoral manager with a cheerful personality. I first met her when she was a member of the Commission under the chairmanship of Judge Kreigler from whom she later took over the chair of the Commission. Under the leadership of Dr. Bam, the South African Electoral Commission has delivered three credible national elections (up to the time of writing). She was active in organizing and participating in regional as well as continental elections activities.

Justice A. Msosa, Chairperson (twice) of the Electoral Commission of Malawi-
I met Justice Msosa in 1994 when she became Chairperson of the newly revamped electoral commission which I had assisted in shaping legally. As soon as the Commission was established in 1994, I was on the scene to offer technical assistance on behalf of the Commonwealth Secretariat and so throughout the preparatory stages for the 1994 elections, I worked closely with Justice Msosa. She is of a quiet disposition and understands the culture of fairness of democratic elections. After the credible elections of 1994 and a new government were installed, the Electoral Commission soon came into conflict the new Government due to attempted interference and non-cooperation with the Commission. I participated in a problem-solving workshop convened by the Commission with UN participation aimed at smoothing out stand-off relations between the government and the Commission. Eventually, Mrs. Msosa and the members of the Commission were relieved of their mandate, perhaps somewhat unconstitutionally.

Justice Msosa was restored to the position of Chairperson of the Electoral Commission in 2006, and delivered credible elections in 2009 despite strong tension between the two major parties.

Dr. Christina Thorpe—was the Chairperson of the Electoral Commission of Sierra Leone. She took over in the wake of post-conflict Sierra Leone and up to the time of writing, had delivered a credible general election, as well as local elections, under her watch. I met Dr. Thorpe on several occasions from 2007 through to 2009 and had discussions with her. My impression was positive; she was committed to delivering transparent and credible democratic elections for the electorate of Sierra Leone.

Ms Joycelyn Lucas—is a former Chief Electoral Officer of Trinidad and Tobago and a well-known election personality in the Caribbean and the Commonwealth. Ms. Lucas conducted training of electoral officers in South Africa and Malawi in 1994, as well as assisted in the preparation of training materials in those two countries. She was also closely associated in preparing and or reviewing voter education materials in both South Africa and Malawi in 1994. She was involved in orientation retreats for election commissioners in South Africa, Malawi, Botswana and Nigeria. Ms. Lucas served as election observer on many Commonwealth observer groups. She also served as an expert election adviser to International IDEA.

Ms. Mokhothu Limakatso (Chairperson) (Lesotho), she was head of an EMB that had been making steady progress in organizing credible democratic elections. I have known her since she joined the Commission in the early part of the past decade. She was one of the earliest EMBs' head to complete the DEAU's Questionnaire on EMBs. She was an active participant in the AU's continental meeting of EMBs in Accra, Ghana, in 2009.

Dr. Pires Helena, Commissioner, (Cape Verde) a regular participant in electoral meetings in the West African Region. Dr. Pires Helena was an active participant in the AU's continental meeting of EMBs in Accra, Ghana, in December 2009.

Mrs. Tembo M. Kalwa (Commissioner) (Zambia). Mrs. Kalwa attended the AU's continental meeting of EMBs in Accra, Ghana, in 2009. She was an ardent advocate of continuous voter education in Zambia and elsewhere in the Union.

Ms. Shumbana Karume, Head of the Democracy and Electoral Assistance Unit (DEAU) of the African Union. Ms. Karume was instrumental in implementing the programme of the DEAU, including mobilization of resources for the election activities of the DEAU.

Males—

The list of male election personalities that caught my eyes may be longer than that of females, but only because there are far more males at the head of EMBs than females and not necessarily that males are more outstanding performers than females. I have formed the impression that the males under-mentioned, like the females above-mentioned, have made or are making an outstanding contribution to the development of democratic elections in their respective countries.

Mr. Noel Lee was a former Director of Elections in Jamaica. He was my successor as Director. He made considerable contribution in moving the electorate on a path from indulging in idle rumours about the influence of the Electoral Office on election campaigns to focussing on the issues. I was instrumental in recruiting Mr. Lee who was efficient and, while he served with me, was non-partisan. I regarded him as a good elections officer and an honourable individual.

Mr. Danville Walker, also a former Director of Elections in Jamaica—Mr. Walker completed the goal of Mr. Lee and me which was always to remove the Electoral Office out of the way of the whipping post of politicians whenever they failed to win power or a seat. Walker, no doubt with the invaluable help of the Electoral Advisory Committee and later the Commission, had instilled confidence in the stakeholders of elections in Jamaica that I and others had always dreamt of and that has made a great deal of difference to the integrity of the process in Jamaica. I met Mr. Walker on the election circuit in Guyana and I invited him as a special guest at my final Commonwealth African workshop in Mauritius in 2000 to make a presentation on electoral reform in Jamaica under his watch.

Dato Hurun Din, was Chairman of the Electoral Commission of Malaysia during the 1990s. He took over just about a week before the general election of 1990. Dato Harun was of quiet disposition and was committed to organizing credible democratic elections. He believed in transparent election processes. He became a prominent member of many Commonwealth observer groups, including in the COG that observed the 1993 Pakistani general elections.

Mr. **Jean-Marc Hamel,** former Chief Electoral Officer, Canada, in the 1980s. I met him while he was reporter for the Commonwealth Parliamentary Association Study Group on Electoral Law and Practice in September 1985 in Halifax, Nova Scotia, Canada. Mr. Hamel and his team produced a good report on the Group's work.

Mr. **Jean-Pierre Kingsley,** former Chief Electoral Officer of Canada and former President of IFES. I first met Jean-Pierre in July 1993 at the Oxford workshop for Commonwealth Election Officers, and subsequently at Commonwealth Chief Election Officers meetings as well as at meetings in Canada. Jean-Pierre became President of IFES while I was doing a stint with that institution as Chief of Party for their Election Support Program to the African Union.

Justice Ephraim Akpata was a former Chairman of the Independent National Electoral Commission (INEC) of Nigeria who conducted the elections 1998-99 that restored civilian rule to Nigeria. The late Justice Akpata handled a difficult task well and with equanimity. The series of elections, that is to say local elections, followed by State and Gubernatorial, followed by Federal and presidential elections, over which he presided, were not perfect, but, under the circumstances, were successful. I was a close adviser of the Chairman who was good at paying attention to advice. Sadly Justice Akpata passed away in January 2000.

Prof. Abel Guobadia succeeded Justice Akpata as the Chairman of INEC and conducted the 2003 elections. Although I was not as close to INEC as I was in 1998-99, I did work closely with that Commission as a United Nations consultant and also as a consultant to the Department for International Development (DfID) on voter education. I met Prof. Guobadia many times. He was a jovial personality, but he did not win the trust of many election stakeholders who felt that he was under the influence of the ruling party and government. The election of 2003 was widely believed to be not credible democratic elections and judged to be far below international standard. There was widespread violence and irregularities.

Prof. Maurice Iwu, succeeded Prof. Guobadia as Chairman of INEC in 2005. I knew Prof. Iwu when he was a member of INEC before he became the Chairman. He was a pleasant person to meet and have a discussion with, but he believed that the INEC should have full ownership of the election process. He was always open to advice, but he was always selective in the advice he accepted and sadly he often ignored the hard choices that would really make a difference. Thus, like his predecessor, Prof. Guobadia, Prof. Iwu presided over elections in 2007 which were again considered to be below international standards. He resigned from the office of Chairmanship of INEC in 2010.

Mr. Rudy Collins, former Chairman of Guyana Elections Commission, was a former distinguished civil servant and diplomat with little experience in electoral matters. However, Mr. Collins was a distinguished Guyanese of integrity and accepted as such by most stakeholders. He strived to give of his best efforts in terms of transparency and non-partisanship, but the 'Carter formula' whereby the members of the Elections Commission were nominated in equal numbers by the ruling and opposition parties and with the Chairman being the only one on the Commission independent of the political parties, the Commission did not perform well. (The 'Carter formula' was brokered by former President Carter of the United States—and it is fair to point out that at the time due to the fierce competitive nature of the parties, it was the Carter formula that paved the way for the establishment of the GECOM then.) Mr. Collins' watch was important as he was presiding over the first genuine multiparty democratic elections since that country gained its independence from the United Kingdom in 1966. Although the elections were beset by problems with the voters' register and polling experienced riots during which the Electoral Headquarters were badly damaged, the elections were declared credible by international observers, including the Commonwealth Observer Group.

I was leader of the Commonwealth Secretariat Support Team to the Commonwealth observers. I knew Rudy Collins when he was the Permanent Secretary in the Guyana Ministry of Foreign Affairs and I was Legal Counsel of CARICOM which was headquartered in Georgetown, Guyana.

Mr. Doodnauth Singh, SC, former Chairman of GECOM, presided over the second democratic elections in Guyana in 1997. I met Mr. Singh many times in the period leading up to the elections. I was, like at the first democratic multiparty elections in 1992, again the leader of the Commonwealth Secretariat Support Team to the Commonwealth election observation group to these elections. The ill-fated 'Carter formula' was still in effect and was as divisive as during the previous general election. Chairman Singh was less adept in managing the partisan members of the GECOM than Rudy Collins and the confidence of the stakeholders in the electoral process waned. The Chairman's premature announcement of victory of the incumbent political party and swearing in of the incumbent President before the tallying of the votes was completed, although the Chairman's calculation and reasoning might have been mathematically correct, gave the impression that the Chairman was partisan. There was considerable post-election conflict which resulted in substantial regional and international intervention to ease tension between the two main political parties.

Dr. Stephen Surujbally, Chairman, GECOM, at the time of writing. Dr. Steve Surujbally presided over a credible but disputed general election in 2006. The election went infavour of the ruling party by a significant margin of victory and hence challenges were less vocal. However, the 'Carter formula' was still in use and there was not much improvement in the relationship between the political nominees of the ruling party and the opposition parties on the GECOM. I knew Chairman Surujbally. Prior to the 2006 elections I was retained as a consultant to the RTI under a USAID funded programme to undertake a reform of the election laws, including a revision of the 'Carter formula' for appointing the members of the GECOM. I did discuss my draft proposals with the Chairman and his Commissioners, but the matter was deferred as such extensive amendments, some with constitutional implications could not be undertaken before the pending elections.

Dr. Afari-Gyan, Chairman of the Electoral Commission of Ghana—He has presided over several credible democratic multi-party elections in Ghana. Dr. Afari-Gyan is well known throughout the African Union and the Commonwealth as a reliable advocate of credible democratic elections. He has personally undertaken assignments in electoral technical assistance matters in many African and Commonwealth countries, including Lesotho, Liberia, Guyana, and Tanzania. He has participated as leader and some times as member of many African Union and Commonwealth election observation missions.

I have known Dr. Afari-Gyan since the early 1990s. We have been on election projects in Mozambique in 1994, in 1995 in Tanzania, in Liberia 2004 and Guyana in 2006, to name only a few. Our latest contributions were to the AU's continental meeting of EMBs in Accra, Ghana, in December 2009.

Justice Lewis Makame, Chairman of the Tanzanian (Mainland) Electoral Commission. He was also a past Chairman of the SADC Forum of Electoral Commissions. He has made a sterling contribution to the development of democratic elections in Mainland Tanzania. I have known Justice Makame since 1995. I led the Commonwealth Secretariat Support Team to the Commonwealth Observer Group to the Tanzanian elections of 1995. I noted that there was a breakdown in the management of the election logistics in the capital city of Dar es Salaam to the extent that elections in the seven constituencies had to be repeated. On behalf of the Commonwealth Secretariat, I offered technical assistance to the Tanzanian Electoral Commission through its Chairman, Justice Makame and he accepted. Dr. Afari-Gyan of Ghana was despatched to Tanzania for six weeks to redesign the Tanzanian logistics management model. In 1998, we led a joint team from the Commonwealth and from SADC to conduct an orientation retreat for newly appointed Commissioners in Botswana. We met at many election conferences, including the International Conference on Sustaining the Election Momentum in Africa which was held in Johannesburg, South Africa in March 2007 and the continental meeting of EMBs held in Ghana in December 2009.

Justice A.S.L. Ramadhani, former Vice Chairman of EMB, Tanzania. Justice Ramadhani was the Chief Justice of Tanzania at the time of writing and was a well-known election personality in Mainland Tanzania as well as in his native Zanzibar. He had shown a keen interest in election meetings in the SADC Region and attended the International Conference on Sustaining Africa's Democratic Momentum in South Africa in March 2007. I first met Justice Ramadhani in 1995 when he was Vice Chairman of the Tanzania (Mainland) Electoral Commission and have met many times since.

Mr. Leshele Thoahlane was a former Chairman of the Electoral Commission of Lesotho, from April 2000 to April 2008, and Barrister-at-Law by profession. As Chairman of the Independent Electoral Commission (IEC), Mr. Thoahlane contributed to the vision of the I.E.C. which made a public commitment to deliver acceptable, free, fair, transparent and accessible elections. He was also responsible for organizing an effective consultative mechanism between the Commission and stakeholders. That strategy increased the ownership of the process by stakeholders, which in turn engendered confidence and mutual trust amongst the various stakeholders. That approach culminated in the successful running of the Lesotho National Assembly Elections 2002 and 2007 which won many accolades both locally and internationally as having been well organized, transparent, free and fair.

I met Mr. Thoahlane in 2001 during the fist of several technical assistance consultancies to the Electoral Commission while he was Chairman. I was mainly concerned with election rules and regulations, as well as with the general management of the electoral affairs. Thus on two separate assignments, I was involved in smoothing out administrative difficulties with staffing and funding of the Commission, and steam-lining of the management operations. Mr. Thoahlane had a keen interest in the efficient working of his Commission.

Hon. James Fromayan, Chairman of the Independent Elections Commission of Liberia. Mr. Fromayan was Vice Chairman of the newly constituted Commission in 2004 and succeeded to the position of Chairmanship after the 2005 elections when Chairperson Frances Johnson-Morris demitted office. Mr. Fromayan has successfully presided over the conduct of several bye-elections since the 2005 general elections, but his real challenge (at the time of writing) will be the pending general elections of 2011.

I worked closely with Mr. Fromayan during the years 2004-05 when I was election consultant to the European Commission in Liberia. Under Mr. Fromayan's watch as Chairman of the Commission, I was contracted as consultant to the Commission (funded by UNDP) to undertake a comprehensive review, including concerning the Constitution as it related to elections, and capacity building, of the operations of the Commission and its needs to meet the challenges of the 2011 general elections.

Mr. Fromayan is a passionate believer in the delivery of credible democratic multi-party elections. He attended continental meetings on elections, for example, the International Conference on Sustaining Africa's Democratic Momentum in South Africa in March 2007 and the African Union's continental EMBs meeting in Accra, Ghana, in December 2009, as well as regional meetings on electoral matters.

Chapter XVI

Reflections on My Contributions

30 years of contribution
Positive developments
Weak responses
Disappointments
Where do I go from here?
Thirty Years of Contribution

Introduction
I have had thirty years of experience in the world of elections. During that time, I have contributed to all facets of the electoral process in many countries. As my professional discipline is legal, my way into the election world was through the route of the election law, including constitutional provisions relating to elections. In other words, my initial attraction had more to do with the reform of the electoral legislative scheme, that is, not only the law proper, but also the election regulations and rules. My appreciation of the public perception of the weaknesses in the electoral process was placed largely on flaws in the electoral legislative schemes.

Advising the Joint Select Committee
In advising the Joint Select Committee of both Houses of Parliament in Jamaica in 1979, I soon realized that there were other key elements in election organization and conduct in addition to the legislative framework. For example, the nature of the management structure laid down in the legislative scheme was very important, but equally so were the personnel selected to manage the entire operations. So, perhaps the first major lesson learnt was that in the matter of organizing general elections, one of the keys to success is

the quality and training of the election personnel at headquarters and particularly the field officers.

Director of Elections

When I moved from the legal role as the technical legal adviser to the Joint Select Committee of Parliament in 1979 to the post of Director of Elections which was a creature of the reform, I tested my fledgling theory that the key to organizing credible democratic elections largely rested on the quality and training of the personnel of the EMB. I had relieved all the senior field officers of their post, although they could re-apply for employment, if they so wished. I interviewed all applicants, including persons who had held the post previously, for the 60 posts of returning officers, and graded each of them. I wrote the training manuals and conducted training of the returning officers as the trainers of lower-level field officers. In a small electorate of just about a million then, the approach yielded measurable success, although it was complemented by large scale reform to the voter registration system in particular. Yet those steps were not sufficient to restore confidence to the electoral process, as many stakeholders still believed that vote rigging had taken place in the 1980 general election and that notwithstanding the 'experiment' with recruitment and training of election personnel, a few officers exhibited partisan tendencies. Perceptions, even if divorced from reality, held sway in elections in Jamaica in 1980, and that taught me another lesson in election organization and conduct—that perceptions about non-credible democratic elections can only be overcome gradually and by demonstrably transparent conduct.

My election world started with me grappling with the overcoming of negative perceptions about credible elections and spent the last three years towards my thirtieth year in elections striving to overcome negative perceptions about the credibility of the African Union's election observation missions' reports. There are no easy answers to overcoming this issue, but it is believed that periodic outside independent and impartial peer professional reviews will gradually replace negative with positive stakeholders' perceptions. The Electoral Commission of Botswana has instituted a procedure of election audit of each general election since 1999. These audits are carried out by independent election experts who are allowed to meet stakeholders and are mandated to examine the performance of all aspects of the legal framework and management structure. This is a good example to follow.

Perceptions about the voters' register

It is understandable why there is a strong perception in many new and emerging democracies that the voters' register is below internationally acceptable standard. This belief is encountered amongst stakeholders in countries as far a part as Côte d'Ivoire, Guyana, Kenya, Malaysia, and Pakistan, just to name a few countries by way of examples. More often than not, the perception is founded on elements of facts, though not infrequently highly exaggerated. It should be admitted that in many countries ruling parties and governments, with the connivance or due to incompetence of the EMBs concerned, aid and abet the compilation of corrupt voters' register. In some cases, low voter registration may be due to the voluntary and democratic nature of the registration procedure where eligible persons choose not to register. There are situations where, like in certain areas of Pakistan, religious and cultural traditions militate against women registering to vote—they may not be able to go out without being accompanied by a male, or they may not wish their photograph to be taken for identity purposes.

These time-honoured perceptions are being mitigated by the introduction of the use of new election technologies, such as the capture of bio-metric features of each prospective voter for the purposes of voter identification. There is a cost factor which will prevent some EMBs from acquiring bio-metric technology for some time yet and so steps need to be taken to improve traditional voter identification procedures.

The inability of some countries, like Nigeria, to conduct reliable population census does not generate much confidence in voters' register, and the lack of up-to-date delimitation of electoral districts' or constituencies' boundaries added to the perception that the register of voters in electoral units cannot accurately be assessed.

Many continental countries where ethnic groups straddle the border, particularly in times of conflict, the issuance of national identity (ID) cards is one way of ensuring that nationals of a particular State are properly identified for the purposes of registration and voting. However, experience has shown that often times issuance of national ID cards is manipulated, because the possession of a national ID card is a condition precedent to voter registration. There has been a longstanding perception in countries such as Côte d'Ivoire, Kenya, Liberia, Malaysia, Namibia, Pakistan, Sierra Leone and Lesotho, that the potential for non-nationals to infiltrate the voter registration process was considerable and indeed often took place.

Perceptions regarding Polling and Counting

Many of the false perceptions about polling and counting can be dispelled by transparency of the procedures applied by the electoral officers. The notion of 'false bottoms' in ballot boxes, or ballot stuffing before the commencement of polling can be overcome by showing the empty ballot boxes before use to all those present in the polling station at the time. The stationing of trained party or candidates' agents and or independent election observers at polling stations can prevent ballot stuffing as reputed to have occurred at every national election in Nigeria since 1998-99. The perception of buying and selling votes in the countries of south-east Asia, in particular, Thailand, Cambodia and Indonesia, has become a well-rehearsed art form according to stakeholders. The tallying of votes has been attracting perceptions of being avenues of cheating without detection due to lack of transparency and the vulnerability of the procedures at this point. An early attempt at fiddling the election results in South Africa in 1994 was quickly detected and corrected. Attempts at fiddling the tallying process had greater success in Zanzibar in 1995 and limited success in Guyana in 1997.

Perspectives-new election technologies; refugees; IDPs; fragile states, failed states, cost-effective elections

The future of technologies in election organization and conduct is bright. Already, in all but those EMBs lagging far behind, computerization plays an important role in many election processes, including delimitation of electoral districts' boundaries, voter registration, and polling and counting of votes in some jurisdictions. A number of countries have successfully introduced electronic voting and counting of votes. These include India, Brazil, Venezuela and some States in the USA. Other countries in which some form of electronic voting or internet voting takes place include Australia, Belgium, Canada, Estonia, France, Germany, Ireland, Italy, the Netherlands, Norway, Romania, Switzerland and the United Kingdom.

Internet voting is gaining ground, although some view it as risky at this stage of the technology available. Criticism of internet voting encompasses lack of safeguard from coercion and vote buying and selling. There is also exposure to service attacks and the possibility that the vote may be cast by the wrong person. Software virus could also interfere with the internet vote. Notwithstanding these problems, it is believed that with the improvement in the technologies available, the prospect for the use of electronic voting and counting are very positive. Indeed, the possibility of voting by mobile phone may revolutionize voting in emerging democracies by ensuring voting from remote location and at one's convenience. These developments promise not only greater voter turnout, but also significant reduction of vote rigging.

Large developing democracies, like Brazil and India, which committed to using electronic voting and counting for their national elections can only be positive examples in favour of setting the pace and blazing the trail for other large developing countries like Egypt, Ethiopia, Nigeria, Mexico and South Africa.

The cost-effectiveness of electronic voting has not yet been clearly established at least as far as the not-so-well-off emerging democracies are concerned, but it is known that the initial capital outlay to acquire the voting machines and related equipment is relatively high and beyond the means of many EMBs at the present time. It is hope that as the use of electronic voting systems increases the cost of units of electronic voting machines will be reduced to affordable levels.

The foregoing positive prognostication assumed that the electronic voting machines with end-to-end auditable voting capabilities will be available at affordable cost in developing countries.

Refugees and Internally Displaced Persons

The issues of internally displaced persons and refugees pose serious challenges for electoral administrators in conflict areas. There are no easy solutions, but examples abound in Africa and elsewhere and so there are lots of experiences in the electoral sector in tackling the challenge

Internally displaced persons come about as a result of people fleeing conflict zones to safer areas in a particular jurisdiction. The electorate becomes dislocated and lose their place of registration. This situation may be so severe that some voting districts may become wholly depopulated. The circumstances became so pronounced in Sierra Leone that the electoral system had to be temporarily changed from first past the post to proportional representation. In Liberia, the consequence of conflict resulted in temporary electoral districts had to be constructed. In those circumstances, the whole electoral process was affected in some measure, but perhaps none so much as the compilation of the register.

Refugees are those citizens who fled outside the borders of their countries in times of conflict. This situation may render it even more difficult for these citizens to register to vote in their national elections. This may be because their country lacks the resources to mount registration exercise outside of its territory, or by policy as the government and the EMB concerned may not wish to do so, or their country may fail to secure the agreement of its neighbouring countries to conduct registration of voters on their soil, as happened in Liberia in 2005.

These challenges can be overcome by proper planning and by seeking expert advice on a timely basis. International attention has been drawn to these issues and many non-governmental organisations have formulated strategies to tackle them with a view to finding solutions to meet the circumstances.

Nomadic Peoples

There are several cases of nomadic people who regularly, and some seasonally, cross national borders. The issue that often arises is how to ensure that these people are properly registered to vote. One challenge is to establish the nationality of the nomads and the typical method is to issue to each nomad a national identity card which can be produced at the time of registration by qualified persons (and if required, at polling). It is important for the electoral franchise of nomadic peoples to be recognized and facilitated. In terms of electoral justice, accommodating nomads in the electoral process is consistent the principle of equal respect for nomadic voters.

Electoral justice principles

The concept of electoral justice principles conjures the need for dialogue on the nature and application of these principles. It is clear that a process which is as complex as the elections is founded on principles. The application of these principles may give rise to best practices or bad practices. The final chapter below explores the scope of electoral justice principles in which concept I do have an interest.

CHAPTER XVII

Women in Election Administration

-As election managers
-As election executives
-As election consultants
-As election administrators

Introduction
Women have been performing key roles in election administration for a very long time. However, during this long period there have not been as many women involved at all levels of election administration as was desirable and their contribution was not highlighted at most national levels as it should have been. A closer examination of the electoral landscape in the new and emerging democracies of Africa and elsewhere does reveal that a growing number of EMBs are headed by women and many of the commissioners are also women. Further, in many EMBs senior departments, such as the legal department and the mapping section are managed by women. In a similar vein, women have held the position of chief executive in some EMBs.

In the lower tiers of election administration, such as returning officers and presiding officers who manage polling stations and count and tallying centres, women have often played important roles. While my own experience in interviewing and grading candidates for returning officer posts in Jamaica some thirty years ago led me to believe that there was no discernible difference between the performance of males and females returning officers, I am not aware of any recognized research findings in this area. It is not known, for instance, if female election officers are less prone to behave in a partisanship manner than their male counterparts, or whether female heads of EMBs generally would respond differently to attempts to influence the decisions of their commissions from the way males do.

The Current Position

Today, it is considered good practice to start off with the approach of gender equality in every electoral activity. Sometimes gender neutrality is preferred to gender equality, but too often the former slips silently from the conscious awareness and the male preponderance again takes over. Electoral management bodies need to recognize and implement as best practice the policy that at all levels women should be included in the election administration. This approach will quickly facilitate gender equality, while also ensuring that women's perspectives are taken into account in the decisions dealing with the training and development of women in election administration. Some EMBs have development training programmes to assist women to qualify for positions as election administrators. An increasing number of EMBs are developing policies to enhance women's participation in election administration and some have gone even further in setting up mechanisms by way of focal points or committees in their respective jurisdictions to consider how decisions or pending decisions will affect women, as well as men.

Women at the TOP in My Time[79]

I have met and dealt with many outstanding women of EMBs which performed well in delivering free and fair democratic elections to the satisfaction of all stakeholders. Ms. Joycelyn Lucas, a former Chief Elections Officer of Trinidad & Tobago, was one such distinguished electoral official. Ms. Lucas not only served with distinction in the electoral field in her native Trinidad and Tobago, but she was internationally recognized as an election expert in many areas of election organization. She served on many Commonwealth

---

[79] Some of these women were discussed above in chapter XV under prominent election personalities, but at the risk of repetitiveness, I find it necessary to refer to them again in this unique situation with emphasis more on their professional ability rather than on their persoality.

election observer group missions to Commonwealth countries' elections. She also offered technical assistance in the fields of training of election officers and worked as a specialist in preparing and reviewing materials training courses of election officers in South Africa and Malawi in 1994. Ms. Lucas was also well known as a specialist in the preparation of voter education programmes and worked as a Commonwealth consultant in that area in Malawi in 1994 and South Africa in 1995. She also served as an expert on EMBs in an International IDEA project.

I worked with Ms. Lucas in South Africa in 1994-5, in Malawi in 1994, and on the EMB International IDEA project.

Dr. Brigalia Hlophe Bam

Dr. Bam has been the Chairperson of the Independent Electoral Commission of South Africa since 1999 and has successfully seen off three general elections. Under Dr. Bam's stewardship, IEC has developed a reputation for the delivery of free and fair elections in South Africa. Indeed, the IEC of South Africa has been admired as one of the successful EMBs of the African Union.

I first met Dr. Bam when she became a member of the IEC when I was offering technical electoral assistance to the South African authorities on behalf of the Commonwealth Secretariat. After she succeeded former Chairman Judge Kiregler as Chairman, I have met Dr. Bam at several election conferences at which she has become a familiar performer.

Justice Frances Johnson-Morris, former Chairperson of the Independent Elections Commission of Liberia, (also a former Chief Justice of that country) during 2004-05 who presided over the elections that restored multi-party democracy to that country. In her capacity as Chairperson of the Liberian Independent Elections Commission, Justice Johnson-Morris displayed a strong determination to take ownership of the elections which were being funded and managed largely by the United Nations and other partners, including the European Commission. Justice Johnson-Morris was a good electoral manager who listened to the several advisers from many partners and sometimes inexperienced advisers gave conflicting advice which the Chairperson had to sort out. She was at ease with the core principles of EMBs' operation, including transparency and practices consistent with good internal democracy in the conduct of the affairs of the Commission. Chairperson Justice Johnson-Morris welded a nationalistic bond with her fellow Commissioners and with their own contributions they repaired or build a couple of outstation electoral offices which had been damaged or destroyed during the conflict.

As the sole election consultant of the European Commission in Liberia during 2004-05, I was also legal and technical adviser to the IEC. The EC was an important partner of the IEC having contributed more than US$4 million to the election organization.

Ms. Johnson-Morris was a good partner to work with who was always willing to listen and consider new ideas and different ways to solve problems. She was not afraid to let the United Nations and other partners that the ownership of the elections belonged to the Liberians. She was also no push over as was seen once when the Representative of a certain partner engage her in a verbal eruption for several minutes, Ms. Johnson—Morris did not hold back and let him have her tongue in no uncertain manner. She handled the grumpy political parties with firmness, yet politely. With the assistance of the UN and other partners, she succeeded in delivering credible democratic elections in 2005.

Justice A. Msosa, Chairperson (twice) of the Electoral Commission of Malawi-

I met Justice Msosa in 1994 when she became Chairperson of the newly revamped electoral commission which I had assisted in shaping legally. As soon as the Commission was established in 1994, I was on the scene to offer technical assistance on behalf of the Commonwealth Secretariat and so throughout the preparatory stages for the 1994 elections, I worked closely with Justice Msosa. She is of a quiet disposition and understands the culture of fairness of democratic elections. After the credible elections of 1994 and a new government were installed, the Electoral Commission soon came into conflict with attempted interference and non-cooperation with the Commission. I participated in a problem-solving workshop convened by the Commission with UN participation aimed at smoothing out stand-off relations between the government and the Commission. Eventually, Mrs. Msosa and the members of the Commission were relieved of their mandate, perhaps somewhat unconstitutionally.

Justice Msosa was restored to the position of Chairperson of the Electoral Commission in 2006, and delivered credible elections in 2009 despite strong tension between the two major parties. The record of Justice Msosa in the electoral field in Malawi speaks for itself. She displayed a well-developed sense of a level playing field for the contestants during the 1994 election campaign in Malawi. An example of this was seen when a political party organized an advertisement just before the closing deadline for the election campaign so that advertisement was published after the deadline. Other parties drew the breach of the campaign rules to the attention of the Commission and the Chairperson permitted the complainant parties to advertise a response in the prohibited period in order to level the playing field.

In the electoral field, Justice Msosa led Commonwealth observer missions, and in 1995 Justice Msosa was accepted by the Electoral Commission of Tanzania (Mainland) as a liaison peer with observer groups and other stakeholders as a form of technical support provided by the Commonwealth.

The 2009 pre-election environment could not have been more confused or competitive, as two of the main parties contesting the elections could not agree on most things. In the midst of the confused atmosphere, the Commission had to rule on whether a former President of Malawi, Mr. Muluzi, could be nominated for a third term, as there was an intervening presidential term since the second term of the former President occupied that position. The Electoral Commission ruled against the former President's eligibility for nomination for a third term. The case subsequently went to the highest court of Malawi and the ruling of the Commission was upheld by the court.

The tension between the former President's political party and supporters and the incumbent President's party and supporters was so high that the African Union (AU) had to dispatch two high-level missions to Malawi a few weeks prior to the election in 2009. First, the AU sent a mission led jointly by the former presidents of Mozambique, Mr. Chissano, and Mr. Kufour of Ghana. The joint former presidents' mission made several recommendations designed to ease tension and improve the electoral environment. Then a couple weeks before the election, the Chairman of the African Union Commission, H.E. Mr. Ping, led a delegation to ascertain how well the stakeholders had abided by, or implemented the recommendations of the joint former presidents' mission which took place a few weeks earlier.

With the help of the AU's missions, and despite the confused electoral environment, under the guidance of Justice Msosa credible election was conducted which met international standards.

Dr. Christina Thorpe—was the Chairperson of the Electoral Commission of Sierra Leone. She took over in the wake of post-conflict Sierra Leone and up to the time of writing, had a credible general election as well as local elections delivered under her watch. I met Dr. Thorpe on several occasions from 2007 through to 2009 and had discussions with her. My impression was positive; she was committed to delivering transparent and credible democratic elections for the electorate of Sierra Leone.

Dr. Thorpe has displayed an interest in many aspects of the development of democratic elections. She was present at the meeting on electoral justice principles held at Cambridge University in July 2010. At that meeting, the concept of electoral justice and the formulation of the principles that flow from the concept were discussed. I was the lead drafter of the electoral justice principles along with a strategic paper which were presented at the Cambridge meeting.

Female Returning Officers & Presiding Officers

Ever since I re-wrote the training manuals and personally participated in the cascade-type training for returning officers in the electoral reform procedures in Jamaica during 1979-80, I have kept a keen interest in the role of returning officers in the delivery of democratic elections. More specifically, I have paid particular interest in number of female returning officers and their performance on the job on polling day. Stretching as far back as the 1980 elections in Jamaica when fewer than one-sixth of the returning officers were women, their performance was just as good as that of the male ROs. I have observed elections where 'all female' polling stations run by women only were properly managed, for example in Pakistan. Throughout the 1990s, there was gradual increase in the number of female returning officers, especially in States of Southern Africa, Malawi, Namibia and South Africa, as well as certain other African States like Tanzania.

Although the emphasis is on female returning officers in this section, the male returning officers were given equal treatment in training and supervision where necessary. The performance requirement goals were the same for all returning officers regardless of gender. The deployment of returning officers was governed by different considerations sometimes often by local circumstances, for example, intimidation and violence, custom, religion or traditional practices which may restrict the deployment of females in certain locations.

More established democracies such as United Kingdom and India set strict performance standards to guide returning officers in executing their election tasks. These standards are basically in line with good electoral practices. With the increasing use of electronic voting machine (EVM) in substitution for the paper ballots, as is seen in India, returning officers are faced with new procedures for voting and counting of votes, as well as educating the voters in the use of the EVM.

Nevertheless, whatever the voting procedures, a returning officer, of whatever gender, has to be trained to meet certain minimum performance standard in conducting democratic elections. A returning officer should be familiar with electoral legislation and the rules and instructions made there under, so that any errors in the guidance materials could be detected early. He/she should have a clear understanding of the major processes and procedures of the election in order to be able to review the planning and approve the quality of the entire election process. He/she is tasked with the responsibility of overseeing the planning, operations management and risk analysis aspects of the election organization. He/she provides support to the administrative staff and is required to provide adequate oversight of their work, receive feedback and give direction to them. He/she should ensure that full financial accountability is achieved on a timely basis.

The role of the returning officer includes preparation of plans for an election, including national elections, in his\her district. The issues that should be contained in the ROs' election plan include—the objectives to be achieved; the constraints; recruitment and training of staff; selection of access premises for polling and counting of votes; the roles of polling and counting officers. Where appropriate, conclusion of outsourcing contracts (and adequate backup measures, should any outsourcing contracts fail). In some jurisdictions, the outsourcing contracts are handled at the electoral central office. Before the RO finalizes his/her election plan, he/she should discuss it with the principal stakeholders in his/her district, including candidates and political parties (where appropriate). The RO may find it necessary to make adjustments to the plan before finalizes it.

To achieve acceptable standards of performance at every level in the field of electoral activities thorough training is required. In many jurisdictions, the ROs are responsible for ensuring that temporary field staffs on a continuous basis are trained not only in polling station polling procedures but also in ancillary matters such as disability awareness and related access issues. Training activities should be subject to evaluation of the training materials and the activities.

The RO is responsible for the security and the integrity of the electoral process in his/her district. In order to discharge these effectively, the RO needs to develop a plan which contains links with the local police to detect malpractices and apprehend the miscreants in a timely manner. The plan should also deal with public order and safety matters during the campaign and polling and the immediate post-polling period.

The RO is required to prepare an appropriate voter education programme for his district—in most cases where there is a central EMB, that body would prepare a comprehensive awareness programme and the RO would be expected to see to its proper implementation in his/her district. The RO would be expected to contribute to any evaluation exercise involving the methodology of the effectiveness of the awareness programmes.

ROs should pay particular attention to awareness programmes designed to educate candidates and agents. Their education should be in addition to the normal voter education programmes. Matters such as filing nomination papers and adherence of party supporters to codes of conduct should be included in their special briefings. There should be evaluation of the effectiveness of these briefings.

The foregoing brief outline of what is expected of each RO regardless of gender applies with respect to performance standards generally. This applies whether paper ballots or EVMs are being used. However, where EVMs are in use the following changes in instructions would be encountered regarding the use of the EVMs. Beside the obvious exchange of the ballot books for the electronic voting machines, the EVMs require checks by engineers to certify that they are in good working order before polling commences. The RO ensures that working copies of the electoral roll are authentic. The RO ensures that the availability of EVMs is assessed. Then there is a 'first level checking' of every EVM by authorized engineers provided by an authorized company. The checking of each EVM continues with all the switches in the presence of a representative of the district election officer (DEO). Further all EVMs are tested with dummy votes for each candidate and at each location at least 1% of EVMs are tested with 50 dummy votes. The engineer and the DEO representative who witnessed the checking sign off on a sticker which is pasted on each of the units of the EVM. The defective EVMs are put aside for repairs. The DEOs ensure that all EVMs that passed the checking are equipped with new batteries. The preparation of the EVMs is done by the RO in the presence of observer and candidates or their agents. During the preparatory stage of the EVM a mock poll with result verification is done to ensure that the EVMs are functioning and at least 10% of EVMs are tested by the RO and Assistant RO.

Not unlike the procedure when dealing with paper ballots, the transportation of EVMs to polling centres is done under armed security and the company of observers and candidates or their representatives. Presiding officers are advised to compare the machine number and the adhesive sticker and also verify the PS number indicated on the sticker compared with the PS number mentioned in the address tag.

The post-poll safety measures to protect polled EVM are no less than those needed in some jurisdictions to protect the ballot box. The Indian approach is to provide two-tier security for strong rooms where EVMs are stored. Fire fighting equipment is placed around strong rooms. Candidates, election agents or authorized persons are permitted to affix their seals on the doors and windows of the storage place and they or their agents are allowed to keep watch from a considerable distance. The security measures are enhanced by the use of 'videography' at all stages of the checking, backed by properly kept records. This short description of the use of electronic voting machines is based on the Indian model. Variations of these procedures may be found in Brazil and Venezuela.

This cursory account of ROs' role does not do justice to the importance of ROs in the delivery of acceptable elections in his/her district. As will be seen below, the performance of the presiding officers (PrO) depends to a large extent on the training by the RO and his/her supervision during polling and counting exercises. Together, the RO and the PrO form the pillars of the election process.

Presiding Officers (PrO)

Usually there are almost as many PrOs as polling stations. It inevitably means that many females will be involved. (Although in some jurisdictions language or other academic qualifications may be required and that requirement may work to the disadvantage of females due to custom and tradition where women may be less exposed to education than men.) Subject to the caveat about education qualification, in general in most jurisdictions, the standard of performance would be stipulated for all PrOs male and females.

The Pr. O. is usually the head of the polling station team which is responsible for smooth polling, good order and the delivery of high quality election services at the polling station. The Pr. O. and his/her team should ensure that polling begins on time as stipulated by the electoral law. They should be at the polling station at least forty-five minutes before the appointed time of opening of the poll. The role of polling-station staff, led by the Pr. O. is to enable voters to cast their vote in secret and without the unauthorized interference. The Pr. O. is responsible for the conduct of the balloting in the polling station and should be knowledgeable about the voting procedures.

A Pr. O. should comply with any instructions from the RO and take charge of the polling station to which he/she is assigned. Care should be taken to ensure that all electors are treated with respect and impartially. The Pr. O. must make sure that the secrecy of the vote is protected and supervise the poll clerks at the polling station. The Pr. O. may be required to attend training and briefing sessions. He/she may have to make sure that the access to buildings is secured and in the case of multiple polling stations, establish contact with other Pr Os. The Pr. O. may need to work with the Poll Clerk to ensure that travel arrangements to and from the polling station are satisfactory. The Pr. O. should collect the ballot box and polling materials before the poll opens and ensure their safety.

The big day for a Pr. O. is polling day. He/she is required to be at the station about one hour before the opening of the polls to oversee the setting up of the station. He/she will transport the ballot box and its contents to the polling station. Before the opening of the polls, the Pr. O. oversees the erection of the required polling booths in the station, organise the layout of the station and where necessary ensure that there is safe access for disabled people. The Pr. O. should ensure that the polling station opens on time. He/she should ensure that all signs and instructions are posted up in place where they are clearly visible to voters. The Pr. O. is responsible for the peace and good order of the station and for the safety and health of all staff and visitors there to. He/she is expected to keep the station clean and tidy.

The normal tasks of a PR. O. during polling may include giving guidance to the poll clerk; keep an accurate account of the ballot papers issued and unissued and ensure that voters' names are marked off and their numbers in the register of voters and on the corresponding numbers lists where appropriate. The Pr. O. ensures that ballot papers are issued to voters and that upon receiving the ballot paper the voters cast their votes in secret and then place the ballots in the correct ballot box. The Pr. O. may be called upon to offer assistance to voters who need help in the polling station and to ensure that those who have the right to enter the station, for example, candidates, agents, Commissioners and observers, are received courteously and do not interfere with the voting process. The Pr. O. should make sure that the polling station closes on time. In some jurisdictions, the Pr. O. is required to carry out the function of counting officer and counts the votes immediately after the close of the polls. In other cases, the Pr. O. merely undertakes the completion of the ballot paper account and related paperwork and delivers the ballot box and related paperwork to the count location as designated by the RO.

Where there are multiple polling stations in a centre, the RO may appoint a single supervising Pr. O. to oversee all staff in the stations.

The foregoing description of the tasks of a typical presiding officer at a paper ballot polling station bear much in common with the tasks of a presiding officer at an electronic voting machine polling station, except that the EVM replaces paper ballots and the EVM also records the vote and the count. Procedurally, the Pr. O. has to become fully familiar with the operation of the voting machine through hands-on training. The Indian instructions for Pr. O. using the EVM provide detailed guidelines for the setting up and use of the EVM at the polling station, as well as measure to protect the machine after polling. The instruction to the polling party to collect their polling materials for use at the polling station follow a similar line to that of paper ballots, but the EVM requires particular attention, for example, that the control unit and the balloting unit given to each Pr. O. pertain to his/her station and the machine number inscribed on the metal label and the adhesive sticker and also verify the polling station number indicated on the sticker and compare it with the polling station number mentioned in the address tag before accepting the EVM.. The Pr. O. who is the leader of the polling party has to ensure that all necessary polling materials, including indelible ink and a copy of the list of candidates, are collected and transported to the station along with the EVM.

The Pr. O. should reach the polling station on the day stipulated by the RO and prepare the station according to the specification laid down by the RO., but the voting machine and the polling materials in the custody of the PR. O. should remain so until the poll is completed and the voting machine and materials are handed over by the Pr. O. An interesting difference between the Pr. O.'s pre-polling preparations at the EV polling station is the requirement for the Pr. O. to conduct mock polling half an hour before the time fixed for the start of poll in the presence of polling agents. After the mock poll, the Pr. O. clears the data from the voting machine before sealing the control unit. At the completion of polling, the Pr. O. close and seal the voting machine and switch off the battery of the control unit before sealing the EVM. The number of females who voted is ascertained.

Capacity Building Papers by Female Officers
In the mid-nineteen nineties until the year 2000, I was instrumental in conducting a series of training courses on behalf

of the Commonwealth Secretariat for senior election officers from the Commonwealth African electoral management bodies (EMBs). There were five such training workshops—held in Windhoek, Namibia, June 1995; Gaborone, Botswana, in March 1996; Gaborone, Botswana, in June 1997; Harare, Zimbabwe, in November 1998; and in Mauritius in May 2000. In broad terms, these training courses were designed to enhance capacity building in election organisation by EMBs in Commonwealth Africa.

The essence of this discussion is to highlight and assess the contribution of African female participants to the courses. Each course lasted for approximately 15 days and the participants from each EMB (country) were assigned themes to consider and make written presentation to the plenary session. The presentations gave a picture of how well or otherwise an EMB was grappling with a particular theme. The themes were allocated to EMBs randomly with no special reference to gender, except where they expressly refer to gender.

The discussion below is based on random selection of female contributors from different EMBs and addressing themes identified randomly:

Ms. A. J. Koll, Namibia, at the 1996 course presented a paper on *'The pros and cons of the use of advanced technology available in election management'.*[80] Addressing the use of up-to-date technology in elections in many African States, using Namibia as an example, Ms. Koll identified some of the challenges to be overcome as the lack of trained personnel and the unavailability of access to computers. She explained that in an attempt to deal with that twin problem of shortage of computers and the lack of computer expertise, the Namibian Government set up a central department, the Public Service Information Technology Management (PSITM) which was responsible for all computer systems used in the Public Service

---

[80] See 'Let's Talk about Elections- The Themes etc.' ed. Carl W. Dundas, p. 71, Commonwealth Secretariat 1997.

in Namibia. The PSITM was not very effective due to inadequate staffing.

Despite the existence of the PSITM, the Electoral Directorate during the preparations for the 1994 presidential and National Assembly elections had to employ a private firm to assist with the installation, support and maintenance of computers throughout Namibia.

Ms. Koll gave an example of the use of computers in election preparation going badly wrong. During the preparation for the 1994 presidential and National Assembly elections, computer equipment was allocated to each region. An administrator and data-processing personnel was appointed for each region and was given two-week's training in Windhoek and one-day's training in their respective region. Each region was responsible for data-entry and verification process. The diskettes were then sent to Windhoek for verification. During validation it was found that too many mistakes were made and thus the products were not fit for purpose. The PSITM withdrew the field computers and had the data entry and verification done in Windhoek under supervision of trained personnel. It was clear that two-weeks training for the field staff was inadequate and that there should have been evaluation of the training and quality control of the data inputs before the diskettes were returned to Windhoek.

Ms. Koll concluded that due to lack of skilled manpower and shortage of financial resources, Namibia would have to continue to process electoral data manually combined with the use of computers for the time being.

Ms. Shirley Smith, Administrator of Independent Electoral Commission, South Africa, presented a paper entitled 'voter education: materials and objectives, public awareness programmes and the gender dimension' at a training course in Gaborone, Botswana, in June 1997.[81]

---

[81] See paper in: *Discussion of Elections Issues in Commonwealth Africa,* p. 88, ed. by Carl W. Dundas, Commonwealth Secretariat, 1998.

Ms. Smith described the unusual circumstances under which the 1994 national elections in South Africa were held with respect to voter information. She made the point that up to that time the vast majority of South Africans had no experience in voting and that a high percentage of those people was rustic and illiterate. Further, many of those persons had not been exposed to mass communication media. In order to deal effectively with these challenges, the Independent Electoral Commission (IEC) designed a strategy which, among other things, required that:

- The educational materials developed should be as close as possible to the real thing, for example, the ballot papers and ballot boxes should be exactly like those to be used on polling day;
- Practical voting exercises should be undertaken;
- The use and design of materials should take account of illiterate voters;
- Both visual and audio materials should be used;
- Programmes should be carried out in all South African languages; and
- Pamphlets should be provided for people to take home.

The IEC recognized the role of non-governmental organizations in voter education in South Africa and adopted a set of criteria and guidelines for the accreditation of a voter education programme as follows:

- Voter education programme should be non-partisan;
- It should support democratic principles and values;
- It should have a measurable delivery capacity;
- It should have clear objectives; and
- It should be easy to comprehend.

Other dimensions of the voter education programme included targeting faith-based institutions (churches), schools whose students were of voting age, and women for whom a special desk was established in the IEC to encourage the active participation of women in the election process.

A particular feature of note was the activity called 'Operation Access' which was aimed at opening up 'no-go' areas to candidates of all political parties. Those areas were characterized by violence and intimidation. The programmes under Operation Access used a fleet of minibuses equipped with loudspeakers, and the parties were afforded equal time to address gatherings which were arranged, publicised and chaired by the IEC. After the party representatives had addressed the meeting, the IEC would then hold voter education sessions.

Ms. Stella M. Katinda of the National Electoral Commission of Tanzania gave her impressions of the EMB's training programmes at the training course in Gaborone, Botswana, in June 1997 in a paper entitled, 'evaluation of election management training programmes in Tanzania'.[82]

Ms. Katinda, in this paper outlined the electoral training environment that prevailed in Mainland Tanzania in the lead up to the 1995 general election which was the first national election since the re-introduction of multi-party elections. The National Electoral Commission (NEC), being responsible for holding and supervising elections, conducted training programmes for national leaders in government and political parties. With respect to the 1995 elections, the focus of training was on the electoral process and in particular registration of voters, nomination of candidates, objection to disqualification of candidates, appeals and voting.

The paper lists the training materials used and sets out the target groups as follows:

- Regional election co-ordinators;
- Returning officers;
- Registration assistants;
- Presiding officers;
- Security personnel;

---

[82]   Ibid. p.122.

- Polling agents;
- Voters; and
- Government and parties' leaders at regional and national level.

The highlights of the training programmes were emphasised in the paper with respect to voters and political parties respectively as follows: qualifications and disqualifications criteria to register as a voter; and remedial measures open to aggrieved persons with the registration, nomination or voting processes. With respect to political parties and candidates, emphasis was placed on their respective roles in the electoral process, including mobilization of qualified persons for registration to vote, as well as on dispute resolution mechanism, and the conduct of the election campaign.

The NEC's training programme extended to voter education for which it supplied Khangas (brightly coloured cotton fabric with NEC's logo for women) and T-shirts with messages such as: *A right to vote is a basic right;* and *Multi-parties are not antagonism.*

The paper pointed out that the effect of the training programme was positive and resulted in a total of 8,929,969 voters were registered out of 11, 017,429 eligible voters and 76.75% of the registered voters turned out to vote. The number of spoilt or rejected ballots was few, indicating that the training was effective. Complaints against the process were minimal, suggesting that stakeholders were satisfied with the electoral process.

The paper pointed out however that there was a high percentage of staff turn over both in the field and at the Commission Secretariat due to the fact that those staffs were drawn either from local government authorities or the civil service respectively. It meant that the NEC has to undertake training continuously.

Ms. Clara Olsen, an African media consultant of the Botswana firm of News Company (Botswana) Pty Ltd, presented a paper captioned 'fair access to the media by political parties'.[83]

Ms. Olsen pointed out that the long distances to cover and the poor infrastructure in many African countries made it necessary for political parties and candidates to rely on the media to convey their message to voters. This made fair access to the media especially important in election campaigns. The paper advocated a strong central authority, such as the EMB, to act as the arbiter in settling disputes arising over access to the media. It proposed that there should be legal sanctions available to support the role of the arbiter.

The paper advocated a media code, preferably drawn up voluntarily. It cited examples of South Africa and Namibia where political parties were treated equitably in terms of allocation of media access. The paper made a distinction between the status and role of publicly owned media and the privately owned media. It noted that because most political parties perceived the publicly owned media as public resources, they demand fair access. The paper advocated that there should be guidelines regulating the use of the public media by parties during an election.

The paper dealt with the vexed issue of incumbent government members abusing their position, particularly with respect to the use of public resources and especially access to the media. It pointed out that when parliament was dissolved in preparation for an election, the executive (cabinet) remained in place until the election was held. The out-going government was thus in a position to influence the election preparation and use public resources for campaign purposes. The political parties' code of conduct should seek to regulate the incumbent party's behaviour during election campaign, as was done in countries like India and Bangladesh.

---

[83]   Ibid. p.138.

Ms. Lucie Kasanga, Commissioner, Zambia, presented a paper entitled 'the count and the result of the election in Zambia' at the training course in Gaborone, Botswana, in June 1997.[84]

Commissioner Kasanga stated that the Zambian electoral system was based on the British system which enshrined the freedom to vote. The paper indicated that a constitutional amendment in 1996 in Zambia made changes to the status of the Electoral Commission which became a full-time autonomous body charged with responsibility of managing and supervising elections. In that year, the procedure with respect to the counting of votes and the location were changed, so that the count was no longer done in a central place, but at every polling station and the results were consolidated at a central place in each constituency by the returning officer.

The count at each polling station was done by the presiding officer assisted by counting assistants. The valid ballots were counted and recorded. Rejected ballots were those ballots which had the following characteristics:

- Did not bear the official mark, unless the presiding officer was satisfied that such an omission was a bona fide error;
- Contains more than one vote;
- Contain any mark or writing by which the voter can be identified; and
- Is unmarked or invalid for uncertainty.

Where a ballot was rejected by the presiding officer, a notation of "Proposed Rejected Ballot Paper" on the ballot paper was made by the presiding officer. The presiding officer then sent the proposed rejected ballot paper to the returning officer who, if he concurred, wrote "rejected" on the ballot paper and added "rejection objected to" if any objection was made to the returning officer's decision by a candidate, his/her election agent or polling agent present at the count. The returning officer prepared a statement showing the

---

[84]   Ibid. p.152.

number of ballot papers rejected under the several heads, namely, absence of official mark; more than one vote; writing or mark by the voter could be identified; and unmarked or invalid for uncertainty. The returning officer received the results from the presiding officer and aggregated the results from all polling stations in the constituency and the person who received the highest number of votes was declared elected. The returning officer then declared the winner publicly.

Where there is an equality of votes between two candidates after a recount, the electoral law stipulated that the returning officer was to cause a decision to be made by lot between the two candidates. Detailed procedure for the conduct of the lot was set out in the law.

Mrs. Fati Mu'azu, Commissioner, Independent National Electoral Commission, Nigeria, presented a paper entitled 'the electoral process in Nigeria' at the training course in Harare, Zimbabwe, in November 1998.[85]

Commissioner Mu'azu in her paper described the Nigerian political system as strikingly chequered with three aborted republics and five 'successful' military interventions. In her excellent paper Commissioner Mu'azu recounted the political and electoral environment since Nigeria's independence in 1960 and advanced some reasons for the poor electoral record. The paper gave three causes for Nigeria's political and electoral difficulties, namely, the orientation of the Nigerian political elite who sees politics as an avenue for making money and the gateway to wealth; the irrational group fear that if the party which the group supports loses, the loss would mean disaster for the group; and the weak political party system that had always existed in Nigeria. The paper argues that the fore-going factors account for the systematic rigging of elections, the intimidation and violence that surrounded electoral

---

[85] In *Rules of Elections in Commonwealth Africa*, p. 55, ed. by Carl W. Dundas Commonwealth Secretariat 2000.

processes and the failure of losers to accept election results at all levels in Nigeria.

Turning to the electoral system then in place at the time (November 1998, the new INEC was only set up in August of that year), Commissioner Mu'azu, a member of the INEC, stated in her paper that despite Nigeria's failed attempts at democratization, it had an electoral system that could match any in the world. The paper dealt with three aspects of the Nigerian electoral system, namely, political parties; electoral constituencies; and the voting system.

Of political parties, the paper pointed out that the Nigerian Constitution required anyone seeking an elective office should be a member of a political party. In other words, independent candidates were not allowed. The paper gave a background of political parties that contested previous elections and indicated that up to that time nine new political parties were provisionally recognized by INEC. It concluded that multiparty politics was the foundation of the electoral system in Nigeria.

With respect to electoral constituencies, the paper outlined the structure of the three tiers of government in Nigeria, thus: 774 local government councils, each with a chairman; 990 state constituencies, each of which returns a member to the State House Assembly. There were 36 states each of which elected a Governor as the State Chief Executive. At the federal level, there were 360 federal constituencies each of which returned a member to the House of Representatives (lower arm), and 109 senatorial districts each of which returned one member to the Senate (the upper arm) of the National Assembly.

The President of the Republic is elected by the constituency of the whole country.

Concerning the voting system, the paper explained that Nigeria had used four voting 'systems', namely:
- The secret ballot 'system'—under this system a voter presented himself/herself to the presiding officer at a polling

station and after undergoing all the formalities, was given a ballot paper. He/she entered a cubicle (voting booth) where a ballot box is placed. He/she administered the thumbprint and then puts the ballot paper in the ballot box in secret. At the end of the voting, the ballot box was brought out and opened and its contents poured out. Counting the ballots was done on the spot in the presence of candidates or their agents and the number of votes recorded in words and in figures on a prescribed form. That was the procedure used during the first and second republics.

- The open ballot 'system'—under this procedure prospective voters report at a polling station and are accredited within a specified period of time. After accreditation voters were required to queue behind the candidate of their choice or in front of their posters. Counting was done on the spot and the score of each candidate recorded in words and figures on a prescribed form. This method was used during the aborted third republic.

- Modified open secret ballot 'system'—a modification of the open ballot system. In this system, which was used in the later stages of the third republic, a prospective voter attends at a polling station and was accredited within the specified period. After accreditation the voter was given a ballot paper with which he/she entered a cubicle to thumbprint. He/she then came out to put his/her ballot in the ballot box placed in the full view of all present. At the end of the voting the ballot box was emptied on the spot and its contents counted. The votes were then recorded in words and in figures on a prescribed form. This system was adopted by INEC for all election during the transitional period.

- Open secret ballot 'system'-the voter presents himself/ herself to a polling station and collects a ballot paper after satisfying all the formalities. He/she entered a cubicle to thumbprint his/her choice of candidate and came out to put his/her ballot in a ballot box placed outside in the full view of all present. At the end of the voting, the ballot box was emptied of its contents and counted on the spot in the presence of the candidates or their agents. The number of votes was recorded in words and figures on a prescribed form. This system was used in the fourth republic.

Turning to the situation that developed after the death of the Head of State, General Sani Abacha on June 8th 1998, the paper stated that the successor to Abacha, General Adulsalami Abubakar, set about reintroducing multiparty democracy. A new independent electoral management body, the INEC was created with wide powers to organize and conduct free and fair democratic elections in Nigeria. Importantly, the paper under scored the status of the INEC as an entity with full independence from government control and directives in the performance of its duties.

New guidelines were set for the registration of political parties which the paper noted resulted up to that time in nine parties being provisionally registered. The new Commission conducted voter registration in October 1998. The election calendar for the series of planned elections was as follows: 5th December 1998, Local Government Councils elections; 9th January 1999, Governorship and State Assembly elections; 20th and 27th February 1999 respectively, National Assembly and presidential elections.

Ms. Rachel N. Mzera, Commissioner, Electoral Commission of Kenya, presented a paper, entitled *'reforms undertaken/taking place in the Electoral Commission of Kenya'*, at the training course in Mauritius in May 2000.[86]

This paper briefly traced the evolution of election management in Kenya prior to independence in 1963 and there after until in 1991 when multiparty elections were restored in Kenya. Consistent with the Kenyan Constitution, which was amended in 1991 to facilitate the creation of multiple political parties and to give broad powers to the nine-member Electoral Commission, the old position of Supervisor of Elections became redundant. The number of Commissioners was soon increased to 11 in 1992 and to 12 in

---

[86]   See *Electoral Reform in Commonwealth African Countries*, p.23, ed. by Carl W. Dundas, Commonwealth Secretariat 2001.

1993. The Commissioners were appointed by the President and in 1997, at the instance of the Inter Party Parliamentary Group (IPPG), the opposition proposed an additional 10 Commissioners and the President appointed them.

Not only was the number of Commissioners greatly extended in 1997, but the competence of the Commission was significantly expanded by section 42A in that year, particularly with respect to constituencies' boundary delimitation, registration of voters, voter education. In fact, it was not so much an extension of the competence of the Commission as the clarification and improvement of certain procedures in the areas stipulated.

Similar streamlining and improvement of the electoral management structure took place with respect to the establishment of the Commission's Secretariat, which was mainly staffed by civil servants.

The mainstream of proposed electoral reforms listed in the paper included the following areas:

- Registration of voters—the introduction of continuous registration was well on its way with a Bill being before Parliament to facilitate that procedure;
- Assisted voters—a voter may choose a person to assist him/her and not as in the past rely on the presiding officer for assistance;
- Voting—any mark to indicate a person's choice would be sufficient and not a cross only, as previously;
- Counting votes—the count would in future take place at the polling stations and not at counting centres as previously;
- Method of counting—multiple counting tables would be introduced to speed up the count;
- Overseas voters—this proposal was for limited overseas voting by Kenyans working in Kenyan embassies abroad;
- Funding of the Electoral Commission—the paper explained that the Commission proposed that its funding should be charged directly on the Consolidated Fund (although it

does not clarify whether all election expenses should be included);
- Commission's staff—should be completely under the control of the Commission; and
- Electoral system—a study of proportional representation and its application was contemplated.

Ms. Jovita Byamugisha, Uganda Electoral Commission, presented a paper entitled 'electoral reform undertaken in electoral system in Uganda' at the training course in Mauritius in 2000.[87]

The paper briefly recounted the constitutional development in Uganda prior to independence in 1962. It stated that between 1962 and 1980 no national elections were held and that the electorate had not developed confidence in the electoral process as a result of the flawed organization of elections in 1958, 1961 and 1962. The paper argued that the 1980 national elections were also flawed and soon triggered conflict which led to electoral reform. In 1988 a Constitutional Commission was established and its mandate included a study of the electoral system.

The findings and recommendations relating to the electoral system were, among other things, that elections should be conducted in a free and fair manner; that electoral constituencies should be constructed in a fair manner; that the term for which a government was elected should not be extended; that elections should be held regularly; that any system of indirect elections was not recommended; that the election management body (EMB) should be free from control or influence of the incumbent government; unprincipled, or unethical and unfair practices in election campaigns should not be allowed; a number of changes were proposed to the voting procedures; and certain changes were proposed to the structure of local government.

---

[87] In *Electoral Reform in Commonwealth African Countries*, p. 55 ed. by Carl W. Dundas, Commonwealth Secretariat 2001.

The National Resistance Movement (NRM), which came to power in 1986, continued its policy of electoral reform when in 1994 a Constituent Assembly was set up to debate and promulgate the new Constitution. Consequently, the changes were embodied in three enactments, namely, the Local Government Act 1997; the Parliamentary Elections (Interim Provision) Statue No. 4 of 1996 and the Electoral Commission Act 1997.

The Constitution confers independent status on the Electoral Commission which has the competence to construct constituencies. A stipulated amount of seats were reserved for women under the Local Government Act.

The paper discusses the law relating to candidates and election campaigns. It pointed out that no candidate could organize, hold or address his or her own individual candidate's meeting. All candidates in an electoral area had to meet collectively and address and answer questions from voters. The returning officer, in consultation with all the candidates prepared and conducted a candidates' meeting in each parish where applicable in an electoral area. All candidates were allowed equal treatment. Candidates were not allowed to use or publish defamatory words, or words that were insulting, or incited public disorder, or hatred, or insurrection, violence or threatened war, during election campaigns. During the campaign period, no person was allowed to use or attempt to use any political party colour or symbol, or tribal or religious affiliations as a basis for his or her candidature for election, or in support of his or her campaign.

In voting, there was no polling booth, voting was done in the open without compromising the secrecy of the ballot. There was one ballot box for all the candidates.

Ms. Julie Ballington, Electoral Institute of Southern Africa (EISA), presented a paper entitled 'electoral systems, electoral processes and gender equality' at the training course in Mauritius in 2000.[88]

---

[88]   Ibid. p. 193.

The paper looks briefly at the history of the enfranchisement of women which began in New Zealand in 1897 and lamented the slow evolution of women representation in parliaments internationally. It gave a broad picture by regions of the world of women's representation in parliaments. It also recorded in tabular form women's representation in parliaments in Commonwealth Africa. The paper noted that the Nordic countries averaged 38.8% women's representation was the highest in the world and was largely attributable to the proportional representation electoral system based on party lists. The paper posited that the experience of Commonwealth countries supported the thesis that proportional representation (PR) electoral systems were the most favourable for electing women to parliaments.

The paper carefully pointed out that it was not the PR electoral system alone that worked so well for the Nordic region, as other regions such as Central and South America also use the List PR and yet those regions averaged 12.1% women's representation in parliaments. The paper ascribed the success of the Nordic region to the willingness of the political parties in the countries of that region to place women on the lists. It cited examples outside the Nordic region of political parties, namely, Frelimo in Mozambique and the African National Congress (ANC) adopting internal gender quotas and where women were placed in 'electable' position on the party's list. An example of the ANC was instanced where women were placed in every third position on the national list for the 1999 elections and resulted in 110 of the 266 seats won by the ANC were held by women. The paper took the view that open lists system was potentially less beneficial for women's representation than closed list system, as voters may select male candidates over female candidates.

Citing as examples the local government level in South Africa in 1995 where the representation of women stood at 19% of whom 26% were elected on party lists and 11% on a constituency basis and the New Zealand elections of 1999 where, under the mixed PR and constituency system more women were elected on the PR party list system than under the constituency system, the paper concluded that those were further evidence of PR List system was more beneficial to women's success in elections than the constituency system.

The paper stated that an electoral quota system for women may provide them with a 'critical mass' in representation to influence policies and legislation. However, it noted that electoral quota for women may relieve the pressure off political parties to increase the number of women within their party ranks.

The paper argues strongly for more women to be included in senior positions in election administration so that they can fully inform on electoral policies from the point of view of gender.

CHAPTER XVIII

My Interest in Electoral Justice Principles

Introduction
Electoral justice principles have not received nearly enough attention by electoral practitioners, scholars in political science or electoral commentators. Elections are an essential feature of genuine democracy. The prevailing perception is that elections can exist without democracy, but democracy is unlikely to flourish without elections. The true foundations of democratic elections have not been popularly articulated in terms of their underlying principles. These principles need to be identified and examined in such a manner as to enable them to be pivotal in assessing the quality or standard of elections, particularly in new and emerging democracies.

What is electoral justice? What is its scope? Does it include contestable issues, or only clear departure from existing election laws and rules? Does electoral justice encompass individuals as well as electoral institutions?

The notion of justice often connotes fair play or balanced treatment. In electoral terms, these connotations in respect of the application of the law and rules with respect to all stakeholders hold good. The application of electoral justice may be discerned from a few simple examples as where rules are broken through the omission of qualified persons wishing to register are excluded from the registration exercise, or where ballot boxes are stuffed with ballot papers unlawfully. These practices would offend against electoral justice in most democratic jurisdictions. Electoral justice goes much further than obvious irregularities. It touches controversial issues such as campaign financing, exit polls, racial redistricting (well known in the United States of America), and the choice of electoral systems.

Some research efforts on electoral justice have focussed on electoral disputes resolution as the centrepiece of electoral justice. While dispute resolution is an important issue in any electoral legislative environment, it would be doing injustice to the nature and scope of electoral justice to confine it to the resolution of disputes. The embarkation on the journey to identify the principles underlying electoral justice makes it necessary to look much further than electoral disputes. The contestable elements in some electoral issues may present themselves long before any legal dispute arises.

Electoral justice has much to do with institutions and individuals. Election management bodies (EMBs), even if multi-dimensional, often are the custodian of the electoral process and are charged with safeguarding its integrity. EMBs are often well placed to administer the electoral process to avoid conflicts or the deal with complaints before they develop into formal disputes.

Conflicts within and between principles.
Electoral justice principles are underpinned by values in a democratic society. Sometimes these values are closely intertwined and even conflict with one another. This may happen in the case of values relating to equality and participation. In framing campaign finance rules, it may be necessary in some jurisdictions, like that of the United States of America, to take account of candidates who can largely fund their campaign from personal funds and those who depend on contributions and or public funding. The issue of allowing a person the freedom to fund his/her election campaign has to be balanced against the need to moderate the influence of money on campaigns, thereby restricting rich candidates' undue advantage over less wealthy candidates. Similarly, the equality of treatment of voters may need to be diluted to ensure fairer representation either through political redistricting (delimitation of electoral districts), as in the USA to cater for increased minority representation in Congress, or through reserved seats in Parliament

for women and minorities (disadvantaged castes) on the Indian subcontinent.

Identification of principles

The identification and selection of electoral justice principles is based on the core values that underlie democratic elections, including the electoral process, institutions and the electoral environment. In mounting a search for the identification and selection of electoral principles, the basic precept followed was to regard citizens as free and equal persons. This assumption readily points to values of equality and liberty with respect to citizens and the electoral process. The issue of who should decide the rules that govern elections throws up the answer that points to the voice of the people or popular sovereignty.

Scope of electoral justice principles

The principles of electoral justice are inclusive and touch all matters that may have an impact on the outcome of an election. Simple routine electoral procedural rules when departed from or improperly administered may affect the outcome of an election, as the Florida presidential election 2000 showed when confusion crept into the counting of ballots with respect to the treatment of 'chads' that were not cleanly punched through.[89]

In more general terms, electoral justice principles cover clear electoral irregularities, such as ballot box stuffing, or tampering with the statement of the count in an election, as well as contestable issues such as the timing of release of exit polls or the limits of election campaign expenditures. Electoral justice principles should not be confined to electoral disputes, since good electoral practice may impact positively on election organization as to result in an irreducible minimum of electoral disputes, while the principles are being followed.

Application

Electoral justice principles serve as a barometer of the application of good electoral practice. Election administration and organization

---

[89]   See **Bush v. Gore** 531 U.S. 98 (2000) ·

should be carried out in accordance with the electoral law and rules. The electoral law should reflect the values that underpin the electoral justice principles which embody the electoral procedures consistent with free and fair democratic elections. The electoral law should ensure that the frameworks of institutions like electoral management bodies (EMBs) are able to operate on principles such as independence, impartiality, professionalism and transparency, consistent with democratic values.

Electoral Justice Principles Project

In the summer of 2010, I was associated rather briefly with a small non-governmental outfit, Tiri, to be 'lead drafter' of electoral justice principles in a project designed to promote dialogue and better understanding of those principles.[90] The project afforded me the opportunity to focus on the issue of electoral justice principles and to collect my thoughts on the concept of electoral justice principles. I sketch below my approach to electoral justice principles which, I hope, will attract further discourses:

1. Underpinning Value: *Popular Sovereignty*

Principle: Popular sovereignty sums up the popular notions of democracy from the times of the ancient Greek city states. At present, the concept of popular democracy is manifested in different forms and remains a pillar of modern democratic values.

The application of popular sovereignty may produce diverse effects depending on the constitutional make up of the particular State concerned. For example, in a federal State like the United States of America, which uses the first past the post electoral system, decisions are taken by majority at the Centre (Congress). However decisions relating to elections and particularly electoral procedures are taken at the level of the States. Thus, with respect to

---

[90] Tiri is an independent, international non-governmental organisation, registered as a charity in the United Kingdom. It was founded on the conviction that integrity offers the single largest opportunity for improvements in sustainable and equitable development worldwide. 'Tiri' is a Maori word, whose meanings include the protection of society by the removal of taboos and lifting of prohibitions.

the application of the principle of popular sovereignty, the majority in the Legislature of the particular State of the USA is what comes into play. This situation existed for many decades and worked to the disadvantage of minorities, particularly African Americans. [91]

In discussing the concept of popular sovereignty in the context of the federal system in the USA, Dennis F. Thompson, in his work *Just Elections* looked at the behaviour of majority in individual State Legislatures, as well as citizens' initiatives and creation of commissions.[92] The research showed that the application of popular sovereignty, at least in Federal America does not function smoothly.

Judicial decisions

The following judicial decisions and case study touch upon the application of the popular sovereignty principle of electoral justice:

Wesbury v. Sanders 376 U.S. 1 (1964)—The issue in this case was re-districting (delimitation of constituency boundary). The Supreme Court held that one person's vote in a congressional election should be worth as much as another's, thus creating the standard of "one person, one vote".

U.S. Term Limits, Inc. v. Hill 316 (1994) and U.S. Term Limits, Inc. v. Thornton 514 U.S. (1995) The Supreme Court did not support ban on congressional term limits.

In the case of Meyer v. Grant 486 U.S. 414 (1988), the Supreme Court struck down laws that prohibited payments to petition circulators.

In the case of Buckley v. American Constitutional Law Foundation, 525 U.S. (1999) the Supreme Court ruled against the badge

---

[91]   See for example work: *'The Tyranny of the Majority'* by Lani Guinier, Free Press, 1994, pp.1-20.

[92]   Dennis F. Thompson, *Just Elections p. 123* University of Chicago Press 2002.

requirement for circulators of petitions as being contrary to free political speech.

For a relevant case study touching popular sovereignty and concerning getting people to register as voters in the 2005 registration exercise, the apt slogan of 'making every vote count' was used in New Zealand.[93]

2. Underlying value: Lawfulness
Principle: Every electoral justice act should be founded in lawfulness.

It is a basic proposition that every electoral act and the activities triggered by such act must be lawfully done in accordance with the governing electoral laws. This issue raises the nature and content of the governing electoral legislative framework. The legal framework should be objective, clear, transparent and accessible. It should cover the fundamental suffrage rights such as the right to register as a voter, to vote, and to contest electable office. The legal framework should ensure that all rules and instructions are consistent with the electoral legislative scheme and capable of delivering free and fair democratic elections.[94]

A judicial decision which sought to deal with many procedural strands may be seen in the American case of Bush v. Gore 531 U.S. 98 (2000), although the lawfulness of the Supreme Court decision itself was questioned by some legal commentators.

3. Underlying Value: Integrity
Principle: The integrity of the electoral process forms the core of electoral justice.

The electoral integrity value system closely resembles legitimacy or just outcome, but true electoral integrity may not necessarily

---

[93] See: http://www.elections.org.nz

[94] See *International Electoral Standards-Guidelines for reviewing the legal framework of elections* Chapter 2, International IDEA, 2002

produce either outcome. Legitimacy depends largely on the acceptance of an election outcome by the majority of the stakeholders. A just outcome may be quite a different matter as the influence of the electoral system in place may yield seats to a political party exceeding the proportion of votes gained compared to other parties.

The case of Bush v. Gore (mentioned above) demonstrated that a legitimate election may be unjust, although it may be questioned whether the Florida presidential elections of 2000 could lay claim to full integrity of the electoral process in that State.

4. Underpinning Democratic Value: Honesty
Principle: Propriety and honesty are essential qualities which electoral administrators should demonstrate in the execution of their election tasks.

The Kenyan case of Jaramogi Odinga v. The Electoral Commission illustrated the slight of hand by the Attorney General and the Chairman of Kenyan Electoral Commission (KEC). In this case, the Attorney General issued a Legal Notice on 23rd of October 1992 purporting to rectify Section 13(3) (b) (1) of the National Assembly and Presidential Election Act. The Legal Notice was issued in exercise of the powers conferred on the Attorney General by Section 13 of the Revision of the Laws Act. The amendment had a substantial effect on the meaning of section 13(3) (b) (1) since potentially it reduced to zero the number of days which a political party had to nominate a candidate after the publication of a notice pursuant to the Section. The effect of the Attorney General's revision was to change the word "less" to "more" in the following passage:

"The day or days upon which each political party shall nominate candidates to contest parliamentary elections in accordance with its constitution or rules which shall not be less than twenty-one days after the date of publication of such notice."

The amendment of the law by the Attorney General was challenged by the leader of one of the political parties, Mr. Jaramogi Odinga.

The High Court held that the amendment of the law by the Attorney General was null and void and of no effect.

In making the ruling the Court said that "(B)y using the formal amending provisions of the Revision of the Law Act to effect a change or alteration in substantive registration so that it operates to the prejudice of one or more political parties by not affording them adequate time to arrange for the nomination of candidates, the Attorney General's action can only be construed to have been a misuse, if not abuse, of the powers conferred upon his office."[95]

5. Underpinning Democratic Value: Fairness
Principle: Fairness, impartiality or non-partisanship is a fundamental norm that underpins every democratic electoral activity.

Although principle of fairness runs throughout the range of activities that span the organization of elections, it is often highlighted in election campaigns with respect to the creation of a level playing field as well as with respect to construction of new electoral districts. However, as the Australian case of McGinty v. Western Australia showed the concept of equal weight to every vote is not always attainable.[96]

6. Underpinning Democratic Value: Professionalism
Principle: Professionalism of electoral administrators generates confidence in the electoral process by political parties and other stakeholders.

---

[95] High Court of Kenya Civil Case No. 5936 of 1992; see also Compendium of Election Laws, Practices and Cases of Selected Commonwealth Countries, Vol.2 Part 1 p.65, ed. by Carl W. Dundas, Commonwealth Secretariat 1998.
[96] [1995] HCA 46 (1996) 186 CLR 140.

Professionalism embodies all the qualities on which the integrity of the electoral process and conduct of an electoral management body (EMB) rely. Thus professionalism in election management means that an EMB and its staff must be competent, non-partisan, efficient, and be service oriented. They should ensure a high standard of conduct, including code of conduct for commissioners and staff, if any, at all times.

7. Underpinning Democratic Value: Independence.
Principle: The body responsible for organizing elections should be free from the pressures and influence of the incumbent political party and government, as well as from the influence of any other entity. Likewise, judicial independence is an indispensable quality that should ensure a fair trial in electoral disputes and generally.

For a judicial decision to illustrate the lack of independence of an EMB, see Jaramogi Odinga v. The Electoral Commission of Kenya (1992)[97] Also see case studies which illustrate EMBs' independence or otherwise:

Jeannette Bolenga's study of Vanuatu;[98] case study on India "The Embodiment of EMB Independence, by Vijay Patidar and Ajay Jha;[99] and Bosnia and Herzegovina: "A Success Story for the Independent Model"[100]

---

[97] See Note 89 above. The Report of the Commonwealth Observer Group on the Presidential, Parliamentary and Civic Elections in Kenya 1992 stated that "the fact the Electoral Commission, headed by a former experienced Justice of Appeal, had accepted this obviously invalid exercise of the amending power of the Attorney General as proper and had allowed the short period to be fixed, confirmed the opposition's suspicions that the Commission was acting in collaboration with the authorities", p.15.

[98] Electoral Management Design: The International IDEA Handbook, p. 247.

[99] Ibid., p. 192

[100] Ibid. p. 196.

8. Underpinning Democratic Value: Transparency
Principle: Transparency injects confidence of stakeholders in the electoral process and thus plays a key role in the acceptance of the election results and legitimisation of an in-coming administration.

Openness at all stages of election organization, access to relevant information on a timely basis, readiness to provide justification for decisions and prompt and frank admission of mistakes or oversights can have a positive effect on the perception of transparency. There may be justifiable limits to transparency, for example, protecting information with respect to ballot paper secret water marks and other security measures designed to prevent election fraud.

9. Underpinning Democratic Value: Timeliness
Principle: Timeliness is a key factor in achieving electoral justice at various stages of the electoral process.

Timeliness enhances transparency and creates an air of public confidence in the electoral process. An election calendar plays an important role in assisting election administrators to improve planning and preparation in order to comply with statutory and administrative deadlines.

Although not often occurred, sometimes the un-timeliness of election campaign events can trigger court action to resolve electoral dispute, as happened in the case of Houston et al v. British Broadcasting Corporation (BBC) in 1995. In that case, the Scottish Court granted an injunction against the BBC, restraining it from conducting an extended interview with the British Prime Minister three days before local elections.[101]

10. Underpinning Democratic Value: Equality
Principle: Voters should be treated with equal respect, unless there is a respectful reason to depart from this norm.

---

[101]   1995, Times Report 9/5/95.

This principle extends to all phases of election organization, particularly drawing electoral districts, voting and counting of votes in the jurisdiction of the USA. The judicial decisions below touch on the application of this principle of equal respect for voters.

In Harper v. Virginia Bd. of Elections the U.S. Supreme Court banned poll tax in State elections. The Court held that the Equal Protection Clause in the Fourteenth Amendment, which prohibits States from placing any restriction on the franchise, unless they can be justified by a compelling State interest, applied.[102]

The Supreme Court ruled against the 'write-ins' of candidates in Burdick v. Takushi.[103] With respect to equal representation in districts demonstrating the equal respect principle, there are several judicial decisions, for example, Baker v. Carr;[104] Gray v. Sanders;[105] Wesbury v. Sanders;[106] Reynolds v. Sims which established the 'one person, one vote' rule.[107]

11. Underpinning Democratic Value: Free Choice

Principle: Free choice touches how voters decide, whether with respect to candidates under a single or multi-member constituency electoral system, or a party-list system.

Free choice may be demonstrated in the procedure for selecting candidates to contest elections. It may also be demonstrated in the manner and means by which voters are informed about candidates and their programmmes. The principle of free choice may also impact on the nature and degree of control finance regulations might have on election campaigns.

---

[102] Harper v. Virginia Bd. of Elections 383 U.S. 663 (1966).

[103] Burdick v. Takushi 504 U.S. 428 (1992)

[104] Baker v. Carr 369 U.S. 186 (1962).

[105] Gray v. Sanders 372 U.S. 386 (1963).

[106] Wesbury v. Sanders 376 U. S. 1 (1964).

[107] Reynolds v. Sims 533 U. S. 1964.

The under-mentioned judicial decisions might assist in illustrating how the principle of free choice is applied in a jurisdiction such as the United States of America:

In the case of California v. Jones, the U.S. Supreme Court ruled against blanket primary elections whereby any voter can vote in a Primary in the State.[108] In Cook v. Gralike, the Supreme Court struck down a notation law in Missouri on the ground that State law should not seek to regulate that aspect of congressional elections.[109] In 1976, the Supreme Court of the United States ruled that, concerning campaign finance, contribution limits were permissible, but expenditure limits were not.[110]

---

[108] California Democratic Party v. Jones 530 U.S. 567 (2000).

[109] Cook v. Gralike 531 U.S. 510 (2001)

[110] Buckley v. Valeo 424 U.S. 1 (1976).

SCHEDULE

List of Countries Visited on Election Missions

REGION OF WORLD	COUNTRY/ PROVINCE	NATURE OF WORK	NUMBER OF VISITS/DURATION
Caribbean	Cayman Islands	Boundary delimitation	Chairman of Electoral Boundary Commission, 2003 & 2010.
	Antigua & Barbuda	Advice on Electoral reform	16 Weeks, 2001
	Jamaica	Director of Elections	1979-80
	St. Lucia	Electoral workshop	One week
	Trinidad & Tobago	Election Observation	Two weeks, 2000
South America	Guyana	Election observation & Technical assistance	Several weeks-1992, 1997, 2005, 2006.
South Asia	Bangladesh	Special assignment & workshop	3 days, 1996 & one week 1997
	Indonesia, (Aceh)	Technical Assistance	6 weeks, 2006
	Pakistan	Observation & Planning and Assessment missions	Several weeks, 1993 & 2000.
Africa	African Union	Technical Assistance	3 years & 3 months

Central Africa	Cameroon	Special election mission (twice)	A few days each time
		A.U constitutional meeting	One week
East Africa	Ethiopia	Working at African Union	3 years 3 months
	Kenya	Assessment mission, technical assistance & election observation	Several weeks, 1992 & many visits thereafter 2008; 2009
	Mauritius	Election workshop	Two weeks, 2000
	Tanzania (&Zanzibar)	Planning mission, election observation & technical assistance	Several weeks, 1995, 1999, 2000, 2004
Southern Africa	Botswana	Regional election workshop, orientation course for Commissioners	Three weeks, 1998
	Lesotho	Technical assistance	Several weeks, 2001, 2002 & 2003
	Malawi	Technical assistance, Planning mission & election observation	Several months, 1994—1996
	Mozambique	Technical assistance, orientation course for Commissioners & election observation	Several weeks 1993-94
	Namibia	Technical assistance, election workshop & election observation	Several months, 1989, 1995, 1998.
	South Africa	Technical assistance, election observation & election workshops	1994-5; 1997, 1998 and 2007

	Zambia	Election observation & technical assistance	Three weeks 1991, 1993
	Zimbabwe	Election workshop	Two weeks, 1998
West Africa	Ghana	Election workshop	One week
	Guinea	Election meeting (ECOWAS) & IFES retreat	Two weeks, 2008, 2009
	Liberia	Technical assistance	18 months 2004, 2005, 2006
	Nigeria	Technical assistance & election observation	Many months, 1998-9; 2002-03; 2004.
	Senegal	Orientation course for A.U. observers	One week 2010
	Sierra Leone	Assessment mission & technical assistance	Two visits of a week each.